1,001 Gardening Secrets

The Experts Never Tell You

Publisher's Note

The editors of FC&A have taken careful measures to ensure the accuracy and usefulness of the information in this book. While every attempt has been made to assure accuracy, errors may occur. We advise readers to carefully review and understand the ideas and tips presented and to seek the advice of a qualified professional before attempting to use them. The publisher and editors disclaim all liability (including any injuries, damages, or losses) resulting from the use of the information in this book.

The health information in this book is for information only and is not intended to be a medical guide for self-treatment. It does not constitute medical advice and should not be construed as such or used in place of your doctor's medical advice.

"And we know that the Son of God has come, and has given us understanding so that we may know Him who is true; and we are in Him who is true, in His Son Jesus Christ. This is the true God and eternal life."

1 John 5:20

FC&A Publishing
103 Clover Green
Peachtree City, GA 30269

Produced by the staff of FC&A

Distributed to the trade by National Book Network

Table of Contents

Super-charge your soil

To till or not to till. If you feel like tilling a new bed, wait until fall. In the spring, the ground is too wet to dig, and you will just compact it even more. Tilling in the fall will save you work. The freezing and thawing of winter will work any large clumps loose, leaving you with soft, fluffy earth in the spring.

Quick test for hard soil. There's an easy way to check if your soil is compacted. After a drenching rain, use a red surveyor flag. If you can easily push it into the ground at least 12 inches, your soil is fine. If it gets stuck and won't budge just a few inches below the surface, you might want to add organic matter to your beds.

Be patient with wet soil. If you till or work your garden beds before they have a chance to dry out, you'll compact the soil, leaving air and water no place to go. As if that's not enough, when the soil dries out, you'll end up with big chunks of dirt as hard as bricks. Take your time and wait until spring is well underway before digging. To quickly test your soil, make a ball out of dirt and throw it in the air. If it sticks together until it hits the ground, put your shovel away and wait for drier days.

Rule out lawn rolling. Resist the urge to "roll" your lawn in the spring. Instead of evening out the turf, or pushing newly scattered seed into the ground, it will simply compact the soil beneath the lawn — and make it harder for water to get to the roots.

Give your dirt some air. To supply your lawn roots with oxygen, stick the tines of a pitchfork into the ground and wiggle it around slightly. Remove the fork without lifting out any soil and move on to the next spot. This will compact the earth around the tines a little, so make sure you don't aerate in the same holes twice.

Effortless way to aerate your lawn. Playing golf on your lawn could damage it, but a pair of old golf shoes, the kind with metal spikes, can actually improve it. When you make holes in the soil with your spikes, you'll provide new ways for water and fertilizer to reach grass roots and keep root-strangling thatch from forming. Wear your golf shoes whenever you mow. Your game might not improve, but your lawn will thank you for it.

Put on your dancing shoes. You may have seen them in the garden shop — hard, plastic soles with long, pointy spikes on the bottom. Strap into a pair of these aerating sandals and dance on your lawn in the morning hours. Not only will you add some air to the roots of your plants, you'll kill Japanese beetle grubs at the same time.

Tread lightly on prepared soil. Before you dig up your garden in the fall, have some stepping stones handy. As you turn over the soil, install a walking path through the bed so you don't compact the ground by walking on it. Lay the stones an easy step distance away from each other. As soon as you're finished digging, cover the bed with a thick layer of organic matter, like dried leaves or compost.

For peat's sake, keep it moist. What is so light it can be blown about by the wind, but so absorbent it holds up to 20 times its weight in water? It's peat moss — the popular mulch mined from the petrified remains of bogs in northern climates. It's ideal for loosening heavy soil and helping it retain moisture. The same mechanism that helps it retain water will make it repel water when the peat moss is dry. That's why it's important to dampen it thoroughly before you add it to your soil. The peat moss should feel like a wrung out sponge.

Autumn's gift to your garden. The best soil conditioner is right under your feet — in the fall, that is. Put dried leaves in an old garbage can, about half full. Shred them with a weed eater, then lay them in your garden. They'll soon turn into humus, the rich, earthy stuff gardeners dream of.

Add zest to your dirt with lime. Lime is famous for "sweetening" acid soil, but it also provides much needed calcium and magnesium. Used in large quantities, it can change the quality of your soil — allowing air and water to move through it more easily. To determine if lime can improve your soil, have it tested. If the pH is below 6.0, sprinkle 5 pounds of dolomitic lime for every 100 square feet of ground. Add it to your soil and wait a couple of months. Spare the areas around acid-loving plants, like azaleas and gardenias.

Winterize your garden. Lime your garden as you tuck it in for its winter nap. This will give the soil plenty of time to soak up the lime and activate it before your new plants take root in the "sweetened" soil.

Take advantage of free compost. If you live near a mushroom farm, you're in luck. Make friends with the owner, and he may let you cart away the spent compost from his mushroom flats. This sterile soil is perfect for making your slightly acidic soil more alkaline.

Discover your soil type. Here's an easy way to find out what type of soil you have. In a glass jar, mix a generous handful of dirt with two-thirds of a quart of sterile water and a teaspoon of dishwashing soap. Shake it up and let it

settle. Heavy sand will drift to the bottom quickly. But leave your jar undisturbed overnight so medium-grade silt and the lightest clay can settle more slowly. You should see clear lines dividing the soil types. Dirt that is about 40 percent sand, 40 percent silt, and 20 percent clay is ideal, and it's called loam.

Develop a sense of humus. Loam, humus, chocolate cake — whatever you call it, dark, rich, crumbly earth is the Holy Grail of every gardener. If your soil is yellow-gray and sandy, water will run through it too quickly, and your plants will die for lack of water and food. Don't dig it up and add better soil. Instead, lay down a thick carpet of dried leaves, wood chips, or garden clippings. Mix the mulch with the top 4 to 6 inches of soil. The organic matter will trap moisture and break down to feed your plants and build humus.

Sand or clay? You be the judge. Here's a simple test to see if your soil is sand or clay. Grab a small clump of dirt and roll it between your hands to form a cylinder. Now study your soil. Heavy clay is sticky and will form a neat worm, even conforming to your finger marks. Clay loam will hold together relatively well, but come apart in crumbly clumps when pressed. Sandy loam will feel gritty and hold together only loosely. Sandy soil is gritty and won't even form a cylinder. The best soil will hold its shape but crumble easily when pressed.

Weeds reveal soil's secrets. Does chicory grow in your garden without any encouragement? Or do you frequently see buttercups, sorrel, or thistles? If so, your garden is probably mostly clay. Yards with abundant natural hawkweed are dry, and those with cattails are wet and boggy. Ground ivy is a good sign since it hints at wet, well-drained soil, but pretty clover signifies only compacted, poor soil.

Grow where you're planted. If your heart is set on azaleas and blueberries, but your garden is too alkaline, you can spend most of your summer fighting your soil type — or you can relax and enjoy a low-care rock garden full of plants that thrive in "sweet" soil.

Improve your soil with plaster. If your soil is hard as a rock, try powdered stone to change the texture. Horticultural gypsum, commonly used in wallboard and plaster of Paris, loosens it up and improves drainage. Gypsum is safe, cheap, and easy to find at garden centers, builder's supply stores, and even craft stores. Azaleas and rhododendrons are especially fond of it because it gives them a jolt of calcium without changing the acidic soil they love.

Save drywall scraps. To add calcium and improve the composition of your soil, shred regular, clean drywall in your wood chipper and work it into your soil. Take the time to rinse the machine every few minutes to keep the dust from damaging the engine. Don't worry about the paper covering. It will decompose harmlessly in the soil. Fire-retardant and moisture-resistant drywall are the exceptions. Chemicals in the paper can harm your soil.

> ! Lime and manure are a bad combination. Don't add them to your soil at the same time. Together they produce ammonia, which can destroy your plants.

Latest advice for improving soil. Unless you have hardpan, don't strain your back digging a bed very deeply. Garden experts stopped recommending this because it destroys the complex webs of tiny organisms that keep your soil spongy and light. Instead, lay down a thick layer of compost and mulch every season, and you will build up a rich topsoil.

Lazy way to perfect topsoil. Here's a simple way to get great dirt. Don't worry about tilling up a bed. Instead, lay cardboard or a thick layer of newspapers where you want your bed to be. Water it down, then add a layer of manure. Top with a thick layer of dry mulch. Water your layered bed until it is completely wet, and let it sit for a whole season. Dirt that was rock hard will soften, and the weeds under the cardboard will rot. By spring, you'll have a thick layer of rich topsoil, ready for planting.

Smell dirt before importing. If you are bringing in topsoil mixed with compost for your new raised beds, smell it. It should smell clean and fresh, like the ground after a rain. If it smells like ripe manure or has a sour smell, the added fertilizer is still too fresh and will burn the roots of your plants.

Leave dirt undisturbed. When you dig a hole to plant something, don't replace the soil you just removed with topsoil. Although your plant will love topsoil, the roots will never leave this pocket of rich soil and will eventually strangle the plant. Instead, carefully dig out the dirt in layers, anchor the plant, and back fill the hole in the same order of layers — poor dirt on the bottom, richer earth on top. A plant grown in its natural environment from the start will send out strong roots and flourish.

Simple math helps uncover fertilizer mystery. If you have trouble figuring out how much nitrogen is in your fertilizer, you are not alone. This vital information is hidden in the NPK formula. Each of the numbers separated by dashes tells you what percentage of the bag is pure mineral. N stands for Nitrogen, P for phosphorus, and K for potassium. To figure out how much nitrogen is in a bag, multiply the weight of the bag by the percentage of nitrogen. If a 50-pound bag has an NPK of 10-4-4, multiply 50 by .10 — you have 5 pounds of nitrogen in your 50-pound bag.

Watch for signs of overdose. Be careful not to add too much of a good thing to your soil. Overdose on nitrogen and your plant will produce nothing but green leaves. Too much phosphorus, and your plant will have a strong root system, but little greenery on top. Your plant will have trouble taking in other nutrients if you give it too much potassium.

Detox overfed dirt. Don't overfeed your plants. They could get salt burn and die. If you applied too much fertilizer to your soil, water it deeply for a long period of time. This gentle flush will carry the salts out of the soil. If you overfeed a potted plant, set a low-pressure hose in the soil for 15 minutes to wash the salt away.

> ! Whenever you mix up your own potting soil, be especially careful with vermiculite. It contains small particles of asbestos. To avoid inhaling the dust, keep the vermiculite damp and add it outside or in a well-ventilated area.

Keep plant food pet safe. Your plants are not the only ones that will thank you for a ready supply of blood meal. If you keep this nitrogen-rich soil amendment around your shed, the dry, flaky blood, leftover from meat processing, will be irresistible to your pets, especially dogs, leaving them with constipation or diarrhea. Keep the bags well-sealed and out of their reach.

Age sawdust before using. On a quest for the perfect soil amendment? Steer clear of an unlimited supply of sawdust or wood chips. These materials will fluff up your soil but deplete it of nitrogen as they break down. Throw them in the compost pile to mellow for a year before using them. But don't use sawdust from chemically treated wood.

Horse feed makes cheap plant food. Need a quick and easy organic fertilizer? Run out and buy some pelletized horse or cattle feed from a local farm supply store. The combination of crushed grains and molasses will give your plants all the NPK (nitrogen, phosphorus, and potassium) they need. Put some pellets in your planting holes or lightly sprinkle them over the soil.

Sterilize soil in your oven. If you concoct your own potting soil for containers or houseplants, make sure you sterilize it first to kill pests and weed seeds. Here's how. Spread the mix in a metal pan and stick half of a potato near the edge of the pan. Cover it tightly with aluminum foil. Heat the oven to 160 degrees and "bake" the dirt for about an hour. Check the potato for doneness. When the potato is cooked, the dirt is sterile. Sterilize your dirt when you can leave the windows open to spring breezes. Soil cooking in an oven doesn't smell very appetizing.

Make the best dirt. Mix your own custom garden soil in a portable cement mixer. Throw in equal parts sand, moist peat moss, and finished compost. For especially poor beds, add a pound of limestone and a handful of iron sulfate. Once your soil mix is well-blended, spread it in your garden to lighten and enrich your soil. Bag some once it's dry to add to your planting holes to give transplants a head start.

Grow your own compost. If you have a few seasons to prepare your soil before you plant a new bed, sow a cover crop. Alfalfa, clover, rye grass, or vetch all have deep roots that loosen the soil and add nutrients. Till them in or cut them down just before they reach maturity and start producing seed. Let them compost directly on the ground. Two weeks later, you will be ready to plant your bed. The rich, loamy earth will be a pleasant start.

Plant legumes to loosen soil. Don't waste your precious gardening time trying to break up hard soil. Sprinkle lupine, bean, or alfalfa seeds in your beds and let them do the work for you. These deep-rooted crops grow quickly in poor, hard soil, and their strong root systems crumble compacted earth and add nitrogen and air to it. Pull up these hard workers by the roots before they seed, and your soil should be ready for planting.

Replenish your soil with birdseed. A cover crop, like oats or rye grass, can keep your soil in tiptop condition until you are ready to plant again. The cheapest source for seeds is birdseed or deer plot mix. Sprinkle the seeds thickly in a recently plowed or cleared plot, and let them grow for a few weeks. Just before the flowers mature, plow them under or cut them down. The rotting greens will quickly enrich your soil with nutrients.

Make peace with stones and rocks. If your garden resembles a stony gulch more closely than a well-tended bed, don't fight it, plant it. Instead of investing backbreaking hours sifting out the rocks, make sure the drainage on your slope is good and cover it with alpines and succulents. These hardy plant families thrive in harsh environments. They include many easy-care plants with exotic names, like hen-and-chicks and living rocks. Far from being boring or desolate, your wildly original bed may soon become the focal point of the neighborhood.

Keep soil loose with narrow beds. If you can't reach it, you can't pick it. Keep your garden beds narrow — no more than twice your arm's length. Bounding into the garden to remove a pesky weed can damage your plants and compact the soil. If you want a wide bed, leave a sodded path between the mid-size plants and the tall background plants to reach both sides easily. If existing beds are too wide, strategically place decorative stepping stones throughout so you can safely get to problem areas.

! Don't use rock salt to de-ice a patio or sidewalk near your garden. The salt will leach into the soil and poison it. Use cat litter or granular fertilizer instead.

Protect native soil during construction. As you finalize the details on a building contract for your new home, make sure you discuss a "building envelope" with your contractor. Explain to him that you would like the topsoil around the work site left undisturbed, and only the topsoil from the actual spot the house occupies hauled away. It might drive the cost of the project up a little, but it will ensure that your garden sits on native topsoil instead of arid backfill.

Tip-offs to poor drainage. Poor water drainage can leave a plant bedraggled, while its roots rot. Look for these common signs of water retention — a green, slimy residue on the soil; moss, mint, and willow trees that thrive, while regular plants don't; and trees that flourish as saplings but die young because of shallow root systems. Finally, if your spring growth is slow to grow, the tender plants may have wet feet. Standing water keeps the soil cold and blocks oxygen from reaching plant roots.

Diagnose drainage woes. Dig a hole, about a foot square, in the lowest spot in your garden. Fill the hole with water and time how quickly it drains. If it takes only a few minutes, your soil is light and won't hold water well. If the water is still there a day later, your soil has too much clay and won't drain properly. But if it drains in two to six hours — congratulations, you have great soil.

> If you plan to putter in your garden, you need to be up to date on your immunizations. You never know when you will cut, scratch, or puncture your skin. It's better to be prepared before you have a problem.

Uncover the mystery of poor drainage. Water will move toward the center of the earth until it hits a rock or a hard place. If you have drainage problems, dig a hole, one-and-a-half feet deep, to see what's the holdup. If you hit a dirt version of concrete about 6 to 8 inches below your topsoil, you have hardpan. Dig the bed deeply to get rid of this layer of compacted earth. If your spade hits rock, plant a rock garden and water it sparingly. A bedrock battle is not worth fighting.

Block the sand castle effect. In some gardens, you might dig a hole to plant a tree only to watch it fill with water. A high water table, or water running too close to the surface, can kill plants and keep roots from growing deeply. If your soil is mostly clay, add gypsum to soak up some of the water. Otherwise, plant your garden in raised beds to keep the plants' roots from rotting.

> Keep a small cut clean and dry by slipping a latex glove over the bandage. If you miss the feel of dirt, cut off the tips of the glove's fingers.

Keep soil dry under wraps. Want to start working a patch of ground early in the spring? Cover it with dark plastic for two weeks. The ground will stay dry, and the weeds will suffocate. Soon enough, you'll be the first person to plant in the warm, spring soil.

Rescue your soil from salty residue. Crust is great on bread, but not so good on your soil. A powdery, white crust could mean your plants are getting too much salt. They will soon show their displeasure by turning a little brown. Switch to a salt-free fertilizer and water your garden well with rain water. If water tends to sit in the beds instead of draining, deal with that problem before flooding your yard. You don't want to create a mini Dead Sea in your backyard.

Cheap way to protect hands from irritation. Just a little garden lime can leave you with alligator skin. Wear gloves and rinse your hands in vinegar after puttering in your garden. It will neutralize the lime and help keep your hands soft and smooth.

Soap up before you head out. Before you go out to play in the dirt, rub your fingernails over a bar of soap. There will be no place for dirt to lodge under your nails, and washing your hands when you're done will be a snap.

Be safe when gardening. Make sure you wear gloves when you play in the dirt. Chemicals and sharp objects left in the soil can damage your skin. On top of that, the larvae of some parasites often infects the soil. If you live for the feel of dirt in your hands, buy a box of surgical latex gloves at the pharmacy. They will protect you when you do light gardening. Finally, wash your hands carefully when you've finished gardening, and apply olive oil to keep them moist and soft.

Marble chips change soil pH. Don't use crushed limestone or marble chips as mulch unless you want to increase the alkalinity of your soil. These rocks will neutralize the soil's acidity.

Lay mulch after the first frost. Before you pile on the winter mulch, let the ground go through one small frost. If you lay the warm bedding down too soon, insects and rodents may find a safe haven for the winter and be waiting for your plants come springtime.

Best time to mulch. Timing your mulch can be tricky — too early and you smother tender shoots, too late and you have a full-blown weed problem. As a rule of thumb, mulch early in the spring around well-established plants, like shrubs and trees, and later around perennials and seedlings. Early mulching may slow plant growth a little because the ground takes longer to warm up. Mulch vegetable and annual gardens after they are well-established. This will keep the plant roots cool during the summer and prevent water from evaporating.

Spy on sprouts often. If you spread a thick layer of mulch in the fall, peak under your carpet regularly in the spring to check for emerging plants. A thick layer of mulch will smother not only weeds, but bulbs and perennials making their return appearance. If you see bulb tips pushing through, remove the mulch so they can grow. Do the same around your perennials. If you staked your plants before you cleaned your garden bed last summer, it will be easy to find your hidden sprouts.

> ! Getting free, spent coffee grounds from the local java hut can be a bonanza for any gardener. Just make sure you wear sturdy gloves while handling it. Sometimes glass shards and other sharp objects make it into the recycle bin with the aromatic leftovers.

Trap water beneath mulch. Water the ground deeply before you lay down mulch. Then water it again once you lay the mulch down to compact it and keep it from blowing around.

Calculate your ground cover. Once you choose your mulch, it's easy to figure out how much you need. Measure your garden in feet and multiply the width by the length. Now multiply your number by the thickness of mulch you need (in inches). Count on 2 to 3 inches for heavier mulches, like wood chips and gravel, but at least 4 to 6 inches of lighter fluff, like pine needles, straw, and paper. Divide this number by 324 to find out how many cubic yards of mulch to order.

Clean the curb for fall mulch. Mulch is easy to come by in the fall. Make your neighbors an offer they can't refuse — do curbside pickup of their discarded leaf bags or piles. You can also contact your local waste management company. They often collect limbs and leaves and shred them, offering the free mulch to the community. Just be aware that recycled mulch may have weed seeds or garbage in it.

Make mulch with your lawn mower. A bed of autumn leaves can take a while to decompose. Before you use them as mulch, shred them. Run your lawn mower over recently raked piles of leaves and spread the mulch in your garden. In spring, these shredded leaves can simply be turned under to become rich, organic matter in the soil.

Depend on nitrogen before mulching. Before you mulch, add a source of nitrogen, like grass clippings or commercial fertilizer, to the soil. Many mulches leach out nitrogen as they decompose. Good sources of nitrogen include sawdust, wood ashes, corn husks, and shredded bark.

! Don't use the leaves of black walnut, eucalyptus, or laurel trees to mulch your garden. They have a compound that stops new growth in the soil around them.

Dry clippings before mulching. If you have the good fortune of using grass clippings as mulch, make sure you lay them down in thin layers. Too much, and the grass will think its in the compost bin and turn black and slimy as it rots. While this will eventually feed the garden, it will starve existing plants of oxygen.

Keep the chaff, throw out the seeds. Straw, especially straw that's been ruined by rain, is very cheap and easy to find in rural areas. Horses might turn their nose up at it, but it's perfect to till into the earth in the early fall. Straw breaks down readily and will enrich your soil. Make sure the straw is free of weed seeds, then lay it at least 6 inches thick around your plants. Lightly dig it in and let nature run its course. It will soon crumble into rich earth.

Cypress mulch lasts a lifetime. Though this may justify the cost, remember to carefully move it before digging a planting hole. If you accidentally mix the cypress chips into the soil, you could develop a drainage problem. When you're finished planting, move the mulch back again. By keeping the cypress chips on top, the plants below will benefit for a long, long time.

Get tough with termites. Keep organic mulch, like wood chips and pine straw, at least 12 inches away from the foundation of your house. Too close and termites might move in. Instead, put down some light-colored stone mulch. It will keep weeds away and prevent dirt from splashing on your house when it rains.

Brew an attractive mulch. Aromatic coffee grounds work as hard on top of the ground as they do in it. Make an attractive mulch using a thin layer of coffee grounds — don't use very much, or they will form a waterproof crust. This works best around acid loving plants in small beds that aren't frequented by your pets. Dogs, especially, can get caffeine poisoning from sampling the mulch.

Go nuts for mulch. Peanut shells make excellent mulch. Many restaurants offer unshelled peanuts as an appetizer. Next time you frequent one of these restaurants, ask a friendly manager if you can dispose of their empty shells for them. Layer the shells thickly around your plants for a decorative and biodegradable mulch. Just remember to warn guests before you take them out into your garden. If they are allergic to peanuts, even the dust of this mulch can provoke an allergy attack.

Recycle newspaper as mulch. Keep your garden updated on current events, but use only black newsprint with soy-based ink. Lay the newspaper down flat, several sheets deep, poking holes in it where plants will come up. Or mulch with shredded paper to a depth of about 6 inches. Water it and cover the rotting paper with some dirt or a thin layer of wood chips to disguise its humble origins.

Stop weeds with cork. Find a new home for a wine cork collection gone crazy. Put those stoppers to good use in the garden — stopping the spread of weeds. Wine corks are specially treated to break down slowly, so they make great mulch. They are also natural enough to eventually turn into compost.

Recycle castoffs as ground cover. Bet you never thought you would thank the local mill for their waste products, but they're great in the yard. Ask agricultural processing plants in your area for valuable organic castoffs you can use as cheap mulch. Their trashed treasures might include peanut, coconut, cocoa bean, and buckwheat shells; oat husks; rice hulls; ground oyster shells; corn husks and ground cobs; bark chunks; shredded wood; and — if you're willing to compost it first — sawdust and grain chaff.

Happy hour for mulched plants. Live next to a brewery? Ask the owner if you can haul away the used hops. They make wonderful mulch.

Enrich your soil with sea plants. Seaweed makes a wonderful mulch. It will keep your topsoil in place and feed your soil as it breaks down. If you live near the ocean, keep an eye out for piles of washed up eelgrass or other seaweed. Bring it home and hose it down in your driveway to wash out the salt. Spread it about 2-inches thick around your plants, being careful not to touch their stems.

Carpet your garden with fronds. Palms blowing in the wind are beautiful to watch — until the fronds start turning brown. These large, prickly leaf shafts are hard to dispose of, but they make great mulch. Put them through a sturdy wood chipper or industrial shredder and use the attractive brown pellets in your garden. As you may already know from your experience with the compost pile, they last a long time.

Watch out for trunk rot. When you mulch too close to your trees, you run the risk of trunk rot. Keep mulch 3 to 6 inches away from the trunk of a young tree and increase that space to 8 to 12 inches as the tree matures. This should give the trunk plenty of room, yet still control weeds.

Mulch like a pro. Trees love mulch, but don't make the mistake of heaping it around their trunk — a style known as volcano mulching. This just encourages pests and mildew to destroy the base of your tree. Instead, make a large, donut-like ring under the drip line of the tree, leaving a breathing space around the trunk. When a tree is first planted, make sure the "donut" is at least 2-feet wide. Enlarge the circle as the tree grows to protect its roots.

Christmas tree makes great mulch. It's important to mulch tender plants in the winter to keep the freezing and thawing ground from spewing up their roots. The best mulches are light and fluffy, using air itself to insulate and warm. Try laying a thick carpet of evergreen boughs, straw, or hay around plants that prefer warmer weather.

Reuse old carpets as mulch. It's easy to lay a carpet in your yard. Simply trim the carpet to the size of your bed or path and lay it face down to slow water evaporation. Cut X-shaped slits in the carpet where plant stems will grow, and pull the flaps apart to plant your seedling. Wool carpets work best since they break down and become a part of the soil. Otherwise, choose Berber, which comes apart in long strings instead of tiny tufts and is easier to clean up.

Careless weeding hurts lawn. In summer, it seems the weeding is never done. When you remove the offending greenery, be careful not to leave the piles of discarded weeds on your lawn. They will eventually become compost, but before they turn to earth, they can suffocate the grass underneath. Better drop them in a compost bin, and let nature take its course away from your lawn.

Warm beds before mulching. Wait until the ground warms in late spring before putting mulch around your perennials. If you mulch them too early, they won't wake up from their winter sleep. They need the sunlight of early spring to warm the soil and get them started.

Maximize sweet berries. Mulch blueberries deeply in September, and come June, your bushes will thank you with a lush harvest. Blueberries are acid lovers with roots very near the surface of the soil. To protect them, feed them regularly, keep the weeds down, and maintain a 6-inch layer of decomposed pine bark, pine needles, or wood chips around their trunks.

Tile your paths with shingles. To cover a patch of ground with persistent weeds, recycle old asphalt shingles as mulch. Asphalt won't harm your soil. Just make sure the shingles are asphalt and not tar paper, which does break down. Shingles are particularly effective in walkways. Cover with an inch of organic mulch if you don't like the shingled look.

Select mulch carefully. Though it seems almost anything natural can be used as mulch, some materials do more harm than good. Steer clear of used tar paper and clear plastic dropcloths. Tar paper will poison the soil as it degrades, and the plastic will trap moisture and heat underneath while letting light in, the perfect weed greenhouse.

Consider synthetic mulch. Black plastic or fabric mulch can keep the soil an extra 3 to 10 degrees warmer in winter. This could make the difference between life and death for tender plants. To anchor it in place, dig two shallow trenches along the edges of the plastic. Anchor the edges in the trenches using the displaced dirt. Partially cover the plastic with wood chips or dirt to keep your garden looking natural and to avoid slipping on it when it's wet.

Choose paper over plastic. If you like the efficiency of black plastic mulch but don't care for the drain on your pocketbook, make your own sheet mulch. Buy a roll of inexpensive brown paper and cut it into long strips. Coat the paper with soybean oil and hang it up to dry. Arrange it around your plants, and it will decompose slowly while keeping the weeds at bay.

Get creative with rocks. Crushed granite, smooth river rocks, gravel, and even glass beads make a beautiful, permanent mulch that will look great around trees and shrubs in your yard. Just be sure you won't be planting anything else in those beds. These mulches are almost impossible to remove, and they can drift down into your soil over time.

> ! Lightning storms may be scary, but they are good for your garden. All that electrical activity releases nitrogen into the soil.

Beware of reflected heat. Shiny, light-colored stone mulch can brighten up your garden beds in more ways than one. Though the color may be pleasing, stone mulch reflects sunlight and can raise the temperature around your plant. Use an organic mulch in areas with a sunny exposure.

Don't throw away winter compost. Too cold to tend to a compost pile? Try this. Whenever you eat a banana, don't throw the peel away. Dry it on an old screen in your garage. Come spring, you can shred the dry peels and add this nutrient-rich compost to your garden.

Tip the pH scale in plant's favor. Add a cup of vinegar to a gallon of water and sprinkle some under your thirsty, acid-loving plants, like rhododendrons, gardenias, and azaleas. The vinegar will lower the soil's pH to a level they like and release iron in the soil for the plants to use.

Plants need a morning pick-me-up, too. Make friends with your local coffee shop. Many shops will be happy to give you their spent grounds. Take them home and sprinkle them around your trees and shrubs. Coffee grounds are rich in nitrogen and make wonderful mulch.

Make fertilizer from feathers. Here's another reason to love the hunter in your home. Collect the feathers from a plucked fowl and soak them in an empty bucket. Place a light screen over the feathers to keep them under water. After about two months, you will have a nitrogen-rich tea to boost your plant growth.

Household cleaner to the rescue. Need a quick remedy for a stunted plant? Add a tablespoon of ammonia to a gallon of water. Ammonia is an instant source of nitrogen that can jump-start the plant without sticking around to harm it.

Comfort plants with comfrey leaves. Comfrey can do wonders for your soil. Its leaves are rich in potassium, nitrogen, and trace minerals. Bury the leaves directly in your beds and let them break down naturally. Or you can make a soil-enriching brew with comfrey cuttings and a pound of blackstrap molasses. Mix the two in a 5-gallon bucket and add water. Let the tea ferment for 10 days, then serve it to your plants. Container plants really love comfrey.

Mineral "smoothie" for your soil. Dirt has minerals that keep plants happy. Sometimes too little of one or another can cause plant problems. Here's an all-purpose mineral smoothie that can keep your soil well-stocked. Dissolve one teaspoon of Epsom salt in a gallon of warm water. Add one teaspoon each of saltpeter (available at drugstores), baking soda, and ammonia. Water your plants at least once a month with this mineral cocktail to keep them energized.

Work wonders with Epsom salt. Here's a rule of thumb for feeding Epsom salt to both tomatoes and roses — add one teaspoon of salt for every foot of height. Sprinkle it in a circle around the stem and work it in. If the leaves are turning yellow and looking mineral deficient, mix the salt with some water and spray it directly on the plant. Brew up this mineral feast twice a month for great flowers and fruit.

> ! Old timers say you can taste soil to check its pH. If it tastes sweet, it's alkaline. If sour, it's acidic. Unfortunately, you risk getting a parasitic infection from dirt, so try a home pH test instead.

Feed bulbs fiery food. Let your winter fires nourish your spring garden. Keep the ashes from a wood burning stove in a metal bucket until spring. Mix in half a cup of Epsom salt and sprinkle the nutritious mixture over your garden when your bulbs start to peek through. The calcium, phosphorus, and potassium in ashes and the sulfur and magnesium in Epsom salt will help your bulbs flourish.

Treat your plants to eggshells. The next time you whip up some scrambled eggs, wash the shells and let them dry. Then crumble them up and sprinkle them at the base of heavy-feeding plants, like tomatoes. The shells will slowly add calcium to the soil, which the plants greedily take up as they produce fruit.

Unusual source of calcium. Love seafood? Don't throw away those empty crab and oyster shells. Crush them and sprinkle the powder around the plants in your garden to give them some calcium. Tomatoes are especially fond of seafood.

Find free fertilizer at the beach. Next time you're at the beach, collect fresh seaweed instead of seashells. Seaweed is a rich source of nutrients and a potent fertilizer. Be sure to wash the seaweed to get rid of the sea salt. To make a seaweed cocktail, suspend the slimy greens in a laundry bag submerged in a large pail of water. Add a cupful of molasses to get the juices flowing. Water your plants after the brew has fermented for a few days.

Check pH with litmus paper. To get a rough idea of your soil pH, mix a few samples of dirt from your garden with an equal amount of distilled water. Take some blue litmus paper strips and bury a few in the soil. After about 10 seconds, remove one strip and rinse it off. If it's pink, the soil is very acidic. If it's still blue, wait five minutes and pull a second piece out. If this strip is tinged pink, your soil is slightly acidic. If it remains blue, your soil is alkaline.

Veggie juice reveals pH. You can make your own soil pH indicator at home. Shred some red cabbage leaves. Cook them in hot water until the water turns light red. Strain out the cabbage. Collect a soil sample from your garden and put it in a white bowl. Carefully add some red cabbage juice. If the red color of the water deepens, your soil is acidic. If it remains the same, your soil is neutral. But if it takes on a blue or purple tint, the soil is alkaline.

Collect rain for soil tests. Don't throw out the water in your rain gauge once you've measured the rainfall — it will come in handy when you test your soil pH. Instead of buying bottled water, mix your dirt sample with a few inches of rain water, which is relatively clean. It should give you an accurate reading.

Test your soil with baking soda. Here's some vital information just a pinch of baking soda can reveal about your soil. Sprinkle a pinch of this kitchen staple on a tablespoon of wet garden soil. If it fizzles, your soil is acidic with a pH under 5.

Try this sweet and sour dirt test. Vinegar and baking soda are arch enemies. If you have already tested your soil for acidity with a shot of baking soda and nothing happened, repeat the experiment with vinegar. Vinegar fizzes when it comes in contact with alkaline soil. The more explosive the fizz, the higher your pH.

Get an expert opinion

To collect the best specimen for a soil test at your local extension office, mix samples from 10 to 12 different areas in your garden. Gently push aside debris and dig a hole about 6 inches deep. Remove a sliver of earth from the side of the hole without disturbing its layers and move on. Mix all your samples together and scoop out a handful for the testing bag. Remember to specify if you are an organic, or chemical-free, gardener. The report will tell you if your soil is alkaline or acidic, what nutrients it's lacking, and how to amend it to grow healthy plants.

Time soil test for speedy results. Avoid the winter and spring rush and get your soil sample results that much faster. Send in your test in mid-June or early autumn when the number of samples sent to local extension offices is at its lowest.

Lower pH with pine needles. If your soil is too alkaline, with a pH of 7 or higher, spice it up a bit with pine needle mulch. Although it's slow acting, this highly acidic mulch can drive your pH number down just enough to make your soil perfect for planting.

Recycle your fireplace ashes. Collect the ashes from your fireplace or wood stove in a bucket, and leave it outside during the winter to mellow. In the spring, sprinkle the watered down ashes around your plants to increase the pH of the soil. If you want to cover an entire bed, sprinkle about 5 to 10 pounds of ashes for every 100 square feet of ground.

Learn about soil from a hydrangea. Sometimes figuring out your soil's pH is as simple as looking out the window — if you have a hydrangea bush within sight. Blue blooms indicate acid soil, while pink blooms mean alkaline soil. Slightly purple blooms are just right, since they suggest your soil's pH is perfect for most plants.

Indicator weeds reveal soil pH. If you can't find the time to do an official acidity test, take a quick look at your pesky weeds to "guesstimate" your soil pH level. Dandelion, dock, horsetail, lady's thumb, and sorrel thrive in acidic soil, while ironweed, pennycress, peppergrass, sagebrush, and woody aster thumb their nose at anything but alkaline soil.

Read your tomatoes for clues. Not sure about the state of your soil? Set some tomato plants in the ground and watch them grow. These blushing beauties can't keep a secret. If the bottom leaves of your tomato plant turn yellow between the veins, your soil is low in iron. If they turn purplish brown, or the tomatoes have a black spot at the blossom end, you probably need to add calcium. If the fruit ripens unevenly, with blotchy skin or a shoulder left green, you may need to add potash. And if a tomato plant is just pathetic and stunted, the soil is low in nitrogen.

Correct a mineral deficiency. When your plant refuses to grow, and its bottom leaves turn yellow, it's not being contrary. It's just screaming for nitrogen. Nitrogen is one of the three most important soil minerals and encourages plant and leaf growth. Add one of these ready nitrogen sources to the soil around your plant to remedy the problem — well-aged manure, grass clippings, blood meal, hoof and horn meal, fish emulsion, cottonseed meal, or soybean meal.

Give starved plants the jiggles. If the leaves on your plant turn yellow from the tip toward the stem, it's in serious need of nitrogen. Give it a quick boost with a shot of unflavored gelatin. Dissolve an envelope of unflavored gelatin in a cup of hot water and add three cups of cold water. Then drizzle the mixture around the base of your plant before the gelatin sets. Repeat once a month, but let your plant dry out between waterings.

Too well-fed for flowers. Ever wonder how your plant can be so green and healthy, but refuse to give you flowers? You might have overfed it with nitrogen. If the plant is potted, run water through the pot for 15 minutes to leach out the nitrogen. Otherwise, wait until the rain does the job for you.

Diagnose a potassium deficiency. It's easy to identify a potassium-hungry plant — the leaves are mottled, look grayish, or the edges turn yellowish-brown and curl. Potassium is the third of the three most important plant nutrients — the K in the N-P-K formula on fertilizer bags. To add some to your soil, spray it with fish emulsion or sprinkle a light dusting of dry wood ashes around your plants.

Pump up your azaleas. Striking as they may be, pale leaves with dark veins are a sign of iron deficiency in plants. The fastest solution is to spray them with iron chelate, but some experts say lowering the soil's pH will help release bound iron in the soil. To do this, add one teaspoon of vinegar to a gallon of water and give your plants a drink.

New life for a rusty nail. Variegated leaves are very attractive on plants bred to show color, but if your green leaves are sporting yellow between their veins, your plant might need more iron. Soak some rusty nails or old steel-wool scouring pads in a tin can and use the water to quench your sick plant's thirst. The extra iron could solve your problem.

Give tired plants a new lease on life. If your plants are quick to show their age, with the oldest leaves turning sickly yellow at the slightest disturbance, they might be starving for magnesium. Dissolve two tablespoons of Epsom salt in a gallon of water and carefully water your tired plants. Just remember — too much salt can poison your soil, so don't overdo it.

Squelch weeds with moonlight. Ready to start a new bed? Dig it out by the light of the moon. Weed seeds only need a few seconds of sunlight to germinate. Even if you bury them immediately, they will find a way to the surface. Till by the moon and weeds won't have a chance to grow.

Make friends with an earthworm. Earthworms can till and aerate a whole plot of soil and fertilize it with their castings. They multiply readily and are an important ecosystem to develop. Regular gray earthworms are great in the garden since they burrow through the soil, leaving rich castings in their air-filled tunnels. But for the compost pile, encourage red worms. These wigglers are easily identified by their red and brown stripes. Encourage these little guys by providing lots of garden waste, like grass clippings, straw, and leaves, and they will produce compost that is pure gold.

Keep local worms happy. Your worm population is the most important group of tenants your garden will ever have.

Encourage them to stay by practicing organic gardening. Skip the chemical fertilizers and pesticides. Use natural sprays and remedies instead. If you keep your soil rich and your plants thick, weeds and pests will stay away, and worms will take up permanent residence.

Invite an earthworm to dinner. Want to attract earthworms? Besides adding grass clippings and dried leaves to your garden, hide fruit and vegetable peels under hay or straw. Many gardening experts say worm eggs stay viable for a long time. So even if your plot is barren from neglect, the eggs will hatch if they have food.

Count your blessings ... and worms. Don't wait until your plants are growing to check how fertile your soil is. In the spring, once the ground starts to dry, dig out a section of your garden 12-inches square by 6-inches deep. Spread out your dirt on a clean piece of plastic and sift through it. If you find 10 or more earthworms, your ground is very fertile.

Pathway to perfect planting

Simple plan for an abundant crop. Growing a successful vegetable garden is a three-season process. In season number one, stick with crops that suck nutrients out of the soil, like corn, squash, broccoli, tomatoes, and melons. The following year, switch to crops that give nutrients back to the soil, like peas, beans, alfalfa, and clover. In the third season, switch back to crops that take a little bit from the ground, like beets, onions, carrots, turnips, and parsnips. Then start the cycle all over again to guarantee nutrient-rich soil and healthy crops.

Keep eyes open for gardening ideas. Not sure which types of plants and flowers do well in your area? Take a peek in your neighbors' yards and note what's blossoming there.

Plant free seeds in honor of heroes. This nursery will send some annual flower seeds to you absolutely free. The America the Beautiful Fund offers grants of anywhere from 100 to 2,000 fresh seeds to any gardener who is willing to plant a community garden to honor military or community leaders, even friends and family, who have helped make America great. To get an application, write to the America the Beautiful Fund, 725 15th St., NW, Suite 605, Washington, DC 20005.

Secret seed-starting mix. Seeds and soil don't mix. Use milled sphagnum moss to start seeds instead. Add vermiculite to help the moss hold water and provide seeds with magnesium and potassium. And to lighten the mix, toss in perlite.

The latest dirt on planting seeds. When the seed packet instructions say the plants prefer a certain temperature, that's the soil temperature they're talking about — not the air temperature. In fact, soil temperature is more important for seed success than light.

Translate seed packet instructions. The key to following seed instructions is using the last frost date in your area as your transplant goal. So if the tomato instructions say to sow the seeds six weeks before transplant, that means start the seeds indoors six weeks before the last frost is expected.

Plant early during drought. Get seeds in the ground as soon as possible during a drought. Potatoes, onions, garlic, lettuce, peas, and spinach can be sown as soon as you can work the soil. These plants will bloom earlier, miss the high temperatures of summer, and need less water. It's also a good idea to use short-season varieties for your crops. They'll be in the ground fewer days, so they'll need less water.

Test old seeds for planting power. Soak old seeds in a wet paper towel before you sow them. Keep the towel moist for a few days and put it in a warm spot. If the seeds sprout, they are still good. Otherwise, buy new ones.

Encourage your seeds to sprout. For quicker germination, soak seeds for beets, Swiss chard, and peas for 15 to 20 minutes before you sow them. Parsley, New Zealand spinach, and celery seeds require an overnight soak.

Persuade tough seeds to flourish. To help hard-coated seeds germinate faster, soak them in a solution of one teaspoon meat tenderizer and one quart water. Enzymes in the tenderizer will break down the seed's outer shell. After they soak overnight, they're ready to plant.

Give seeds a proper burial. Whatever starting mix you use, don't lay your seed in it until you moisten it properly. Add one part water for every four parts mix. Stir it together until it's wet — but not too wet — all the way through. Then fill your containers a quarter of an inch from the top with this mixture.

> ! Never use garden soil — or any outdoor dirt — to start your seeds indoors. It often contains harmful mold or bacteria and can harden after watering.

Epsom salt to the rescue. Before you sow your crops, toss some Epsom salt into the soil. The stalks will be stronger and the leaves greener. About one cup per every 100 square feet of garden should do the trick.

Seeds love gelatin. Sprinkle some flavored gelatin on your seeds as you sow them. Then water and cover as you normally would. It doesn't matter which flavor gelatin you use as long as it has sugar in it, not artificial sweetener. The sugar provides food for helpful bacteria in the soil. Plus, gelatin has nitrogen, which makes plants grow leafy and green.

Do a little math to find best depth for seeds. You should figure two to four times the seeds' diameter. That's the depth to bury seeds in growing mix. If you sow them in clay or early in the season, cover the seeds a little less.

Let your finger be your guide. Your index finger can tell you how deep to sow a seed. Just stick it into the soil. The depth as far down as your fingernail is right for radishes, lettuce, and Spanish onions. At your first knuckle, plant cabbage, carrots, beets, cucumbers, and squash. Sow bush and pole beans and corn as deep as your second knuckle.

Rake in benefits of wider rows. Instead of planting crops in narrow rows in your garden, try making rows as wide as a rake. That will give you a bigger yield and cut down on weeding and watering.

Plant seeds with ease. Crease one side of a seed packet, tap it, and watch as the seeds fall into place in your garden, one by one.

Sow seeds with a shake. Fill an old salt shaker with seeds to sow them easily, evenly, and without a backache. If you don't have a shaker, make one by poking holes in the bottom of a paper cup.

Go "high-tech" with seed sowing. Planting seeds in your garden doesn't have to be a pain in the neck — not if you make your own seed planter. All you need is a pole of PVC piping about the length of a cane. When it's time to sow, stand up straight and place the far end of the pipe in the soil where you want your seed. Drop the seed in the pipe's other end and watch it plop right in place.

Make your own soil sifter. Dirt clumps and stones are bad news when sowing seeds in your garden. That's where those plastic plant flats from your local nursery come in handy — as sifters. Add a shovelful of soil and shake it wherever you need a fine covering.

Pack your soil into place. A wooden board is perfect for packing the soil after you sow seeds. Just lay it down and step on it. The flat side of a hoe works, too. For potted plants, use the bottom of a smaller, empty pot or your palm.

Keep seeds dry for a long life. Save those small packets of silica gel that come in the box with your new shoes. Stick them in plastic containers or glass jars with your left-over seeds when storing them between seasons. Then place the container in a cool basement or your refrigerator. The silica will keep the seeds dry and help them stay viable for three to five years.

Save seeds till the cows come home. Powdered milk is a natural desiccant, or dehumidifier, for seed storage. To use it, first stack four sheets of tissue paper. Place two heaping tablespoons of powdered milk, preferably freshly opened, into a corner of the tissue stack. Fold the tissue around the milk and fasten it shut using a rubber band or tape. Then place it in a jar with your opened seed packets and seal the jar.

Remember what you planted where. Stick empty seed packets on stakes where you planted the seeds in your garden. Drape them with clear plastic to protect them from the elements.

Use labels as colorful as your garden. Hold onto those wooden stirring sticks after your next house painting project. They make great garden labels. If they have different colors of dried paint on them, each color can represent a different crop. Or write plant names on them with a permanent marker.

Clever use for mini-blinds. Old, bent mini-blinds make marvelous markers for the crops in your garden. Use a permanent marker to write your plants' names on the blinds.

Plant labels made easy. An empty yogurt cup makes up to 10 labels for your garden. First, cut off the cup's bottom. Then clip the sides into arrowhead-shaped strips. Write your plant names on them with a permanent marker.

Hatch new seedlings. Egg containers make terrific seed-starting trays after a few alterations. Start by poking holes in the bottom of each egg pocket. Next, cut off the top of the container and place it underneath the bottom, where it will catch excess soil and water. Then fill each pocket with potting mix, and you're ready to grow.

Plant a seed in an eggshell. For an earth-friendly planting pot, use half an eggshell. Poke a hole in its bottom with a pencil, fill it with potting soil, and lay your seed. When the seedling is ready to be transplanted, lightly squeeze the shell to crack it. Put the whole thing in the soil. The roots will grow through the cracks, while the shell decomposes and fertilizes the soil.

A simple seed starter. Snip off the bottom 2 inches of a milk jug. Punch holes in it for drainage.

Recycled containers love seedlings. The plastic containers baked goods, supermarket salads, and restaurant leftovers come in double as super seed-sowing containers. They are cheap, save space, and come with their own lid already attached.

Another cheap seed starter. Why not start seeds in yogurt containers? They are just the right size, and it's another way to save money and recycle.

Dependable, disposable seed starters. Leftover rolls from toilet paper and paper towels make super seed-starting containers. Cut toilet paper rolls in half and paper towel rolls in quarters. Line them next to each other on a tray so they'll support each other when you plant and water the seeds. When it's time to transplant the seedlings, bury the

Annuals to start indoors

- balloon vine
- bloodflower
- browallia
- coleus
- impatiens
- petunia
- sage
- sweet william
- wishbone flower
- zinnia

containers with them. Make sure to cover all of the roll with soil. Break down their tops if necessary to do this.

Bag cheap seed-starting pots. Cut paper grocery bags into strips 2 inches wide by 9 inches long. Glue or staple the strips into circles. Then lay them side-by-side on a flat tray and fill with potting soil.

Perennials to start indoors
• balloon flower • baptisia • columbine • coreopsis • delphinium • hibiscus • lobelia • lupine • purple coneflower • statice • windflower

Guarantee healthy seedlings with glass. Cover your seed-growing flat with a pane of glass and place it in partial, not direct, sunlight. The glass keeps the seedlings at the perfect moisture and temperature levels.

Put a leaky aquarium to good use. An old aquarium can double as a seedling greenhouse. Stack a bunch of old books or wooden boards in the aquarium. Place your seed containers on them so they'll fit just under the lid. Add the lid and turn on the aquarium light. Leave the lid closed so the air inside stays humid. Once your seeds sprout, open the lid to circulate fresh air. As the plants grow, remove the boards or books to keep the plants beneath the lid.

Make your own mini-greenhouse. All you need are a paper milk carton, a clothes hanger, wire clippers, and a clear plastic produce bag. To start, staple or glue shut the top of the carton. Lay it on its side and cut out the top-facing side. Fill the inside with potting soil and seed. Water it. Next, snip the coat hanger into 8-inch strips. Bend them into arches and plant three or four of these in the soil to make the greenhouse's "girders." Pull the plastic bag over the top of them and underneath the carton. Seal the bag. Finally, place the greenhouse in a spot that's warm and bright yet not in direct light.

Thinning helps seedlings thrive. When your seedlings are 3 to 6 inches tall, it's time for the dirty work — thinning them out. Instead of pulling them, use small scissors to cut them at the base of the stem. This will protect the plants left behind.

Energize seedlings with a pinch. Pinch off the top two leaves of a seedling when it's about 6 inches tall. This prevents it from getting leggy and helps it to become bushy and attractive.

When to transplant your seedlings. It's time when their third and fourth leaves appear, or right before they start to crowd their siblings.

Ease seedlings into the outdoors. Young plants need to be "hardened off," or gradually moved from home to garden. At first, leave them out in the sun for only an hour. Increase it to all-day sunshine over the course of a week.

"Hole" new way to garden. When it comes to gardening, dry areas can be the pits. Adapt to your environment with a pit garden. Just dig a shallow hole, about 5 feet across and 2 feet deep. Fill it with compost and other organic material. Plant around the pit so the roots grow down into the compost. The pit will act like a sponge, holding water for your plants.

Fight weeds with the daily news. Use a layer of newspaper in your garden to help control weeds. Just make sure you don't use colored advertisement pieces, since they contain toxic chemicals that could harm your plants.

How to pick healthy potted plants. Take a peek at a potted plant's "private parts" before you buy it. Carefully pull the plant from its pot and inspect the roots. If they seem healthy and are spread throughout the soil, buy it. But if the roots look cramped or coiled, or if they jut out of the bottom of the pot, find another plant.

Try foolproof pepper plant test. When buying pepper plants at a nursery, take a look at the seed leaves, or first leaves, of the plant. If they are green and healthy, chances are the rest of the plant is, too.

Warm soil encourages healthy plants. Wait until the soil, not just the air, is warm before you plant outside.

Don't stress out your plants. Wait for a sprinkling rain, a cloudy day, or late afternoon shade to plant outdoors.

An easy gauge for soil quality. Grab a handful of soil and squeeze it before planting in your garden. A combination of sand, clay, and organic matter that's best for growing will stick together, but it should break up easily if poked. If the dirt forms a ball, it contains too much clay. Soil that is too sandy will be loose and fall through your fingers.

Try stockings to stabilize soil. Knee-high stockings can come in handy when planting in a deep crevice of a rock garden or on a steep slope where soil, seed, and young seedlings are easily washed away. Make a tube by filling the stocking with soil and tying the open end in a knot. Insert the roll, knotted-side first, into the crevice. Cut a slit in the exposed end, and plant your seed. As the plant grows it will hide its container. On a slope, cut a narrow trench into the hillside, and fill it with a tube of soil placed on its side. Make a long slit, and plant your seeds or seedlings.

Pamper perennials with elbow room. Give perennials lots of space to grow — at least 2 feet between each one. That counts for both seeds and transplants.

Consider best time to transplant. Wait until just before the sun sets to transplant on summer days when the air is hot and the soil is dry. It's a good idea to give the garden soil a thorough watering before you put the plant in the ground. And be sure to fill the plant's new hole with water before you set it in. Early the next morning, give it another drink and continue to do so twice a day for the first week.

The last step before planting. Use a shovel or spade to scarify, or chip up, the sides of the hole before you place your plant in it. This guarantees air and water will get to the plant, and its roots will grow better.

Do-it-yourself mini-greenhouse. A clear plastic milk or juice jug can protect a newly transplanted seedling from inclement weather. Just cut the bottom off the jug, place it over the seedling, and keep it in place until the seedling gets its garden feet. Leave the top off for air and water.

"Brew" healthy plants. Put coffee grounds in the bottom of the hole next time you're transplanting an acid-loving plant. The coffee grounds encourage the growth of acid-forming bacteria.

Keep waiting plants out of the sun. While planting in your garden, place the flats and pots of plants you're not working with at the moment in the shade.

Create shade for tender transplants. Protect new transplants with a makeshift "umbrella." Use bamboo stakes, coat hangers, or any other sturdy stick or pole to hold a square of burlap or rag over your plants.

Rejuvenate dried-out potted plants. It's time to repot a plant when its soil begins to dry out quickly after watering. Another repotting signal is soil that shrinks from the sides of the pot. If you see these signs, take action. Fresh soil provides your plant with a boost of nutrients. If you don't have time for a full transplant, sprinkle a layer of compost onto the top of the old soil.

Rescue a root-bound plant. Transplanting a root-bound plant isn't hopeless. Use pruning shears to make four 2-inch deep slices into the root ball, going from top to bottom, to loosen the roots.

Free up space for fresh veggies. You can still enjoy homegrown, fresh veggies even if you're short on space. Plant them in containers on your apartment balcony or patio. Peppers, tomatoes, chard, and cucumbers seem to do the best with this space-saving gardening technique.

Choose right pot for container gardening. To grow their best, peppers, dwarf tomatoes, and chard need 1- to 2-gallon containers. Regular-size tomatoes, cucumbers, and eggplant require at least 4- to 5-gallon pots. Select containers with 6- to 10-inch diameters for smaller plants, like lettuce, radishes, onions, and beets. And pots with a 4- to 6-inch diameter are perfect for herbs.

Pick deep pots for annuals. Annuals need at least 8 inches of space for their roots during the growing season. Take this into account when planting them in containers.

Be choosy with container plants. If you want to put a tree or shrub in a container, choose a type that grows slowly and stays small. For potted perennials, pick ones that also grow small and aren't invasive. Look on vegetable seed packets to see if they grow small and do well in containers. And whenever you're mixing and matching different plant types in a container, make sure all of them have similar watering and sunlight needs.

Transform junk into planting treasures. Practically anything lying around your yard or garage can work as a plant container. Try wooden barrels, oil drums, old water heaters split lengthwise, trash cans, buckets, fruit boxes, watering spouts, tea kettles, hanging baskets, or even wheelbarrows. Whatever you use, be sure to clean it well. If you're feeling creative, give it a coat of paint. Check to see if it has drainage holes. If not, drill some.

Pretty pots aren't always practical. Double pot if you have a plant container that's pretty to look at but not practical for actual potting. Start by filling the bottom of this decorative pot with several inches of gravel and charcoal. Then pot your plant in a plain clay pot. Make sure this pot is smaller than the decorative pot. Next, place the clay pot with its plant inside the decorative pot. Finish by filling in the space between the two pots with moss, straw, dried leaves, or another colorful filler.

Find pots that retain moisture. If you live in a dry climate, consider other containers besides clay pots. Clay is porous, so moisture can escape easily. That means more trips with your watering can. Glazed, plastic, metal, and sealed wooden containers are nonporous and will keep moisture in the potting soil.

Choose the right color to protect plants. Paint pots white in hot temperatures to keep your plants' roots cool. To warm them when it's colder, paint the pots black.

Freeze frost damage in its tracks. Concrete, wood, and special insulated plastic pots resist frost damage. That's crucial if you plan to pot trees, shrubs, and perennials and leave them outside. Unfortunately, clay pots are not up to the task. They crack when it freezes.

Wrap your plants for winter safety. Plastic bubble wrap makes a great insulation for potted plants left outdoors during the winter. Just line the inside of your pots with it.

Soak old pots super clean. Before you put new plants in old pots, fill a tub with hot water and add one to two tablespoons of bleach for every gallon. Soak the containers in the tub overnight. This kills algae and bacteria and dissolves minerals before they can harm your new plants.

Saturate clay pots before using. Make sure to soak clay pots in water for a few minutes before you plant in them. This will saturate the clay, so it won't absorb water from the potting mix.

Pick up the best potting mix. A 50/50 mix of peat and perlite (or vermiculite) is the best bet when buying potting soil from a store. If you don't know the ratio, pick up the bag. The lighter it is, the better.

Perfect recipe for potting soil. Here's a simple recipe for perennial potting soil. In a container, mix two parts topsoil, one part peat moss, one part sand or perlite, and a few handfuls of organic material.

Coffee filters hold soil in place. Screen the bottom of your pots with coffee filters, small stones, pottery shards, or an actual piece of screen. Water will drain out, but these "filters" will prevent soil from dribbling out with it. Plus, they'll block slugs and other bugs from crawling in.

Install an inexpensive watering system. Place small pieces of sponge in the bottom and along the sides of your pot before putting in your plant and soil. Sponges soak up water and prevent it from flushing out of the bottom of the pot. The roots can "drink" from the sponges whenever they're thirsty.

Think twice before using gravel in pots. Gravel is actually bad for drainage if you put it in the bottom of a pot. It can cause water to pool, which keeps the roots wet. Try using crushed aluminum cans instead.

Take a load off a large pot. For your back's sake, fill the bottom of large planting pots with foam packing peanuts or crushed aluminum cans. You'll need less soil to fill the container, and it won't weigh 100 pounds when you're done.

Improve flowerpot drainage. Place small, flat stones under your pots if you leave them on flat, smooth surfaces like concrete. This little trick helps excess water escape.

Grow an avocado tree. Next time you eat an avocado, save the pit. Stick three toothpicks into the side, about an inch above its flat bottom. Place the toothpicks on the rim of a cup of water so the bottom of the pit touches the water. After a few weeks, a shoot will grow out of the top and roots will grow into the water. When the roots grow into a clump as big as your fist, put potting soil in a 1-gallon container and plant the pit.

Create a home for strawberries. Cinder blocks make great homes for strawberry plants. Fill the holes with a mix of half compost and half potting soil, and place a plant in each. Water frequently and pinch off the runners. Give the plants a dose of liquid fertilizer twice a month.

Pluck berries out of thin air. Grow strawberries in hanging containers. Pick a day-neutral variety like Tristar, which grows its fruit on hanging runners. Then fill a 10-inch hanging container with potting soil and mix in one-quarter cup of slow-release fertilizer. Add several plants and wait for the berries.

Start your tomatoes off right. For healthier tomato plants, sow the seeds in pots that are only half full of potting mix. When the seedlings are about 3-inches tall, add more of the mix. This encourages additional roots to grow and makes for a stronger plant.

Simple way to control tomato pests. Space your plants 6 to 8 feet apart in your garden. That will prevent them from falling prey to pests like dominos, one after the other.

Sink your teeth into a luscious tomato. Basil and tomato make a great team. The fragrant herb repels the destructive tomato hornworm. For a bumper crop of tomatoes, plant some basil around your tomato plants.

Grow veggies in winter. Hardy veggies, like broccoli, cabbage, kale, beets, spinach, and peas, can be "overwintered," which means planted in summer or fall and harvested in spring. If your ground tends to freeze in the winter, you might need a greenhouse or cold frame for best results.

Timing not critical for fruits. You can plant berries and fruits as soon as the soil is dry and workable.

Smart way to plant onions. Leave the necks of your onions sticking out of the soil when you plant them. The sun will start drying them, saving you time after harvest.

Lavish leeks with special treatment. Start leeks in their own 4-inch trench. As they grow, fill the trench with straw. Straw keeps them clean and makes them easy to pull out. They are ready for harvesting when their white stalk is about 5 inches long.

Grow a sackful of potatoes. Burlap bags make great growing containers for root plants, like potatoes, carrots, and beets. Fill the bag with soil, tie it closed, and place it on its side in a sunny spot. Next, cut holes in the bag and plant the crops. Make sure to water it often. To harvest, just cut the bag open.

Pick a peck of home-grown peanuts. To start your own peanut farm, shell four fresh, unroasted peanuts. Fill a 4-inch deep plastic bowl two-thirds full with moist potting soil. Lay the peanuts on top. Next, layer another inch of soil on top of the legumes. Seedlings will appear in no time, and in a couple of months, flowers will bloom. Six months later, you'll have peanuts that'll taste as good as the ones at the ballpark.

The golden rule of planting bulbs. The earlier you get bulbs in the ground, the better. For spring-flowering bulbs — like daffodils and tulips — this means planting in the fall. Bulbs that flower in summer and fall dig springtime planting. Specific dates vary depending on your local climate.

No baths for bulbs. Avoid planting bulbs in areas with poor drainage. They don't like to sit in water.

Guard your bulbs from beasts. Plant a clove of garlic along with your bulbs to protect them from rodent attacks.

Bury your bulbs deeply for better flowers. Place your bulbs in the ground at a depth three times their length. For bigger bulbs, like daffodils, hyacinths, and tulips, that equals

6 to 8 inches. For crocuses, bluebells, and other small bulbs, about 3 to 4 inches does the trick.

Quick way to plant bulbs. Daffodils, tulips, and other bulbs like to be buried deeply, but that doesn't mean you have to dig a deep hole. Instead, only dig down about 3 inches. Bury the bulbs and cover them with soil. Then take mulch, compost, or more soil and mound it on top for another 3 inches of "depth."

Get the most bang for your bulb buck. Plant your bulbs in layers. Just make sure there are about 2 inches of soil between each tier. Use the same variety to guarantee they'll bloom at the same time.

Help a begonia see the light. To plant a begonia tuber, find the little point on its top. That's where the stem will grow from. Plant this tip facing up and slightly under the soil, with several tubers side-by-side. If you can't find the tuber's top, look for the convex, or rounded out, side. At the very least, plant the tuber on its edges. The stem will find its own way out of the soil.

Add a rainbow of color to your lawn. Lift up a patch of grass so you can get under the roots. Insert a few crocus bulbs, sprinkle in some bone meal, and lay the turf back down. Come springtime, you'll have surprising islands of color throughout your yard. Just take care not to mow the blossoms until all their foliage has died.

Grow gads of gladiolus. Plant gladiolus every couple of weeks from January through May (in the South) or April through June (in the North).

Keep the flowers coming. Don't be left without flowers when your tulips wilt at the end of spring. Plant annuals, like petunias and sweet alyssum in their beds, and they'll add some color to your garden come summer.

Spring forward with healthy perennials. Get your perennials in the ground in March, April, and May so they can be acclimated before the hot summer months. Spring is also prime time for dividing and transplanting perennials. Still, you can plant in the summer if you have to. Just make sure to water your perennials once a day for at least a week to prevent them from drying out.

Sweeten the air with flowers. Night-blooming vines and bushes, like nicotiana, moonflower, and four o'clocks, will give you sweet dreams with their sweet smells if you plant them under your bedroom window.

Buy young fruit trees. With fruit trees like apple, peach, and cherry, younger is better. So buy a one- to two-year-old tree instead of a larger, older one.

Treat your trees to a proper burial. Any time in the growing season is the right time for planting trees and shrubs outside, as long as the ground isn't frozen. Just make sure to keep the earth properly watered. However, if you bought a

A tree-buying checklist

- Only buy trees with firm, well-wrapped, moist root balls that don't let their trunks wobble.
- The tree and trunk should also be free of injury from insects and disease, and the bark should look healthy.
- Make sure the branches are well-spaced around the trunk, with 12 to 18 inches between them.
- The main branches should be attached at a wide angle from the trunk and appear stronger than branches at a tight angle.

Of course, all trees are different, and different varieties have other signs of good health. That's why you should always do research when buying a specific variety of tree.

dormant, bare-rooted plant, it prefers an early spring or late autumn planting.

Consider these tree-planting exceptions. Trees that typically have few, but large, roots — like beech, sassafras, sweet gum, sourwood, walnut, and white oak — will prosper if you plant them in the spring.

Preview a tree planting. Help yourself visualize where you want to plant a tree before you actually put it in the ground. Set up a ladder as a stand-in.

Give your trees a perfect shape. Most trees don't come with an even, rounded shape, but you can help yours grow that way if you plant it so most of its branches face away from the afternoon sun. This encourages more branches to sprout on the tree's less-developed side.

Plant smart to avoid tree problems. When planting a tree, arrange it so the section that has the most low branches faces away from high-traffic places, like sidewalks. At the same time, try to place high branches on a side with lots of clearance. You'll save yourself from pruning as the tree grows.

Get a grip on soil moisture. It's essential to have moist soil when you plant a tree, so test the ground beforehand. Using a narrow trowel, dig up soil 6 to 8 inches deep. Hold it in your hand and squeeze. If it sticks together, the soil is moist enough. Otherwise, give the ground a good watering.

Give your sapling room to grow. When planting a burlap-sacked sapling, dig the hole three times the size of its root ball. To help you decide where to dig, place the sapling on the ground where you want to plant it. Outline the area by removing the surrounding grass with your shovel.

Settle the soil around a new tree. A garden hose can help settle the soil around your newly planted tree. Run the water and shove the hose nozzle in and out of the freshly refilled dirt all around the tree.

Help quench your tree's thirst. To keep the earth moist around your newly planted tree, build a ring of soil 3 inches high around the base of the tree to create a basin.

Have a stake in your tree's future. Set stakes firmly in the ground next to young trees. For a thin tree — one that's 2 inches or less around — one 8-foot-long stake will keep it sturdy. Thicker trees could use two or three stakes to hold them up.

Protect your tree with an old hose. Tie your tree to its stakes with an old garden hose and some wire that you can find in your garage. Cut a section out of the hose long enough to reach around the tree trunk. Run the wire through it. Then simply put the hose around the tree and tie the wire to the stake. The rubber protects the tree from getting injured by the wire.

A gentle way to tie plants to stakes. Cut old pantyhose into strips to tie young trees and plants to stakes. The pantyhose won't damage delicate plants, and it'll be easy to remove.

Easy way to recycle large containers. Return those tub-size plastic containers to the nursery after you plant the tree or shrub that came in them. The nursery will be happy to reuse or recycle the containers.

Add nutrients with cover crops. Sow cover crops, like rye, buckwheat, clover, and fava beans, in your garden in the spring. They'll grow fast and crowd out weeds. Come autumn, turn them under or cover them with soil, and they'll add nutrients to the soil.

Fantastic ways to feed plants

Crack the fertilizer code. Confused by the cryptic numbers on fertilizer bags? You don't need a super-secret code book to understand them. Just remember the three numbers refer to the percentages of nitrogen, phosphorus, and potassium, respectively.

Think small to make a big difference. It's healthier to eat several small meals throughout the day rather than one big meal. Take the same approach to fertilizing your plants. In general, feed them lightly and often rather than heavily only once in a while. That way, you know the fertilizer will be used by your plants. Excess fertilizer just runs off into waterways and becomes pollution.

Find the right fertilizer. One fertilizer does not fit all. Resist the urge to use leftover lawn fertilizer on trees, shrubs, annuals, or perennials. It will overload these plants with nitrogen. Their stems and leaves will grow, but at the expense of their fruits and flowers.

Feed plants, not rats. Make sure only your plants are feeding on your fertilizer. Keep leftover fertilizer bags wrapped in thick plastic bags or in solid containers in your garage or shed. That should keep scavenging rodents from getting at it.

Do precise handiwork. Sometimes you don't need to bother with a fertilizer spreader. For rows of vegetables or lone plants, spreading fertilizer by hand is easier. But you should know how much fertilizer your plants are getting. Use a set of scales to measure one of your handfuls of fertilizer. Keep the number for future reference. Remember to wear gloves when handling fertilizer.

Shake off fertilizer burn. Too much fertilizer can harm tender seedlings. For a gentler approach, fill a large saltshaker with fertilizer and sprinkle lightly.

Take precautions when fertilizing. Applying fertilizer can be dangerous. But with the right gear, you should have no fear. Make sure you wear a long-sleeved shirt, pants, boots, and goggles. You might even want to slip on a dust mask. Avoid fertilizing on a windy day, and keep children and pets off your lawn for 24 hours after applying fertilizer.

Choose compost over fertilizer. Just because some fertilizer is good doesn't mean more fertilizer is better. In fact, too much fertilizer can burn plants, stunt their growth, or make them less able to fend off disease. Go easy on the fertilizer. As an alternative, try using more compost to enrich your soil.

Help plants kick chemical habit. You've seen the light and want to switch from chemical to organic gardening. Good for you — but go easy. Your plants might not be able to quit cold turkey. Gradually lessen the amount of chemical fertilizer you feed them, while adding compost and liquid seaweed fertilizer. In about a year, your plants should overcome their addiction, and your garden will be chemical-free.

Scrounge for free compost materials. Sometimes you can't provide all the compost you need, especially when you're just starting your own compost pile. Don't despair. Your town might have a free or cheap compost program. If you're short on compost materials, ask your neighbors for their leaves or grass clippings. See if you can get bales of spoiled hay from local farms or the hay collected from highway mowing. Remember, it never hurts to ask.

A quick guide to making compost

- Alternate layers of "brown" and "green" matter. Examples of brown, or carbon-rich, matter include leaves, straw, sawdust, and hay. Grass clippings, manure, weeds, coffee grounds, and fruit and vegetable peels count as green, or nitrogen-rich, matter. Aim for a balance of browns and greens.
- Make your pile at least 3 feet by 3 feet by 3 feet.
- Water the pile occasionally to keep it moist.
- Turn the pile with a pitchfork once in a while so air circulates through it.
- Wait until your compost is dark, crumbly, and sweet smelling before you use it.

Put paper in compost pile. Shred paper, including newspaper, and add it to your compost pile. Just stay away from glossy magazine pages, and don't go overboard. Too much paper can slow down the decomposing process.

Gather carbon-rich household items. It's easy to find sources of carbon for your compost pile. Just look around your house. Paper towels, napkins, toilet paper rolls, and brown paper bags are just some of the items you can use. Shred or rip them up before adding them to the pile. And make sure the paper towels and napkins haven't been used to clean up anything toxic.

Put cereal boxes to good use. You would be amazed what everyday items can be added to your compost pile. Cereal boxes, used tissues, egg cartons, paper towels, pizza boxes, and junk mail are just some of the things you can compost. Make sure to shred them first so they break down faster.

Scare up some seaweed. Slimy things from the deep don't just make great horror-movie villains. In the case of algae and seaweed, they also make great compost material. Just rinse off the saltwater, and toss them in your compost pile.

Keep pests away from compost pile. Be prepared. Store dry leaves in a barrel, garbage can, or garbage bag and keep them next to your compost pile. When you add kitchen scraps to your pile, cover them with a layer of leaves. You'll keep away flies and other pests.

Patronize pet shops for compost items. Pet shops are a good source for compost materials. Wood shavings often line the cages of rabbits, hamsters, and other small animals. Normally, the shop just throws these shavings away, along with the animal manure. Ask if you can have them instead.

Fetch compost help from pets. You probably get sick of picking dog or cat hair from your furniture. But shedding pets have their good points, too. You can use those clumps of hair to give your compost pile a nice nitrogen boost.

Deliver flowers to your compost bin. Flowers brighten everyone's day. Loaded with valuable nutrients, they can do the same for your compost pile. When the leaves of your perennials turn brown, compost them. And when your annuals get leggy, pull them up and toss them in the compost bin, too.

Grooming leads to blooming. Simply practicing personal hygiene can help your garden grow. That's because fingernail and toenail clippings can be tossed into your compost pile.

Food scraps make great compost. Your kitchen is a treasure trove of valuable items that make great additions to your compost heap. Herbs, grains, bread, freezer-burned vegetables, coffee filters, and tea bags are just some of the things you can feed your compost pile.

Bury dead bugs in compost bin. Splat! Give that dead bug a decent burial — in your compost heap. It might make you feel less guilty about swatting it in the first place.

Choose wisely when composting. Not everything makes good compost. Keep ashes from the grill, meat scraps, bones, grease, milk and dairy products, diseased plants, grass or weeds treated with weedkillers, and dog or cat droppings out of your compost heap.

Build a black bin. Tennis players wear white clothing so they don't absorb heat from the sun. Compost bins, on the other hand, need that heat. So make your compost bin black. Other ways to increase heat include buying an insulation jacket for your bin or insulating the sides with hay bales.

Camouflage your bin. Plant shrubs to screen your compost bin from offended neighbors. Sunflowers, tomatoes, or pumpkins will also do the trick. If your compost bin is made of chicken wire, you can even plant flowering vines to climb it. Whatever living camouflage you choose to plant should spring up in no time, thanks to all the nutrients leaching into the soil from the compost pile.

Let your compost pile breathe. Stick a few perforated plastic drainage pipes into your compost pile to help with air circulation. You'll give the decomposing process a boost without having to turn the pile.

Protect your pile from the rain. Your compost pile should be moist, like a wrung-out sponge, not soaking wet. Make sure to cover your pile in a rainstorm so your "black gold" doesn't wash away.

Guard against nutrient loss. Covering your pile of finished compost with a tarp does more than protect it from the rain. It also prevents valuable nutrients from leaching into the ground.

Plastic is fantastic for heating compost. Speed up your compost pile. Just cover the heap with black plastic. Heat will build up, and the decomposing process will pick up its pace. To make sure the plastic stays in place, hold it down with heavy rocks.

Spark pile with leaves. Waiting for those stubborn plants to break down in your compost pile? Toss in some nettle or comfrey leaves. They'll heat up your heap in a hurry.

Fall for this leaf tip. Here's an easy way to get those leaves from your yard to your compost pile. Spread a large sheet on the ground and rake the leaves onto it. Grab the sheet by the corners and drag it to your compost bin.

Pitch in to save time. Stick a pitchfork in your compost pile, and leave it there. That way, you don't have to fetch one every time you bring kitchen scraps to the compost

Try this easy-to-make compost bin

You can buy pre-made compost bins, but it's easy to make your own. Wooden pallets, cinder blocks, and bricks are all suitable materials. You can even make a compost container out of chicken wire. Just form a cylinder and tie it closed. This method makes it easy to turn the pile. All you have to do is pick up your container, move it to one side, and shovel the pile back into it. A popular composting strategy is to have three bins — one for new compost, one for decaying compost, and one for finished compost. That way, you'll always have available compost. And you'll always be making more. Even if you don't have much space, you can still compost inside a garbage can or drum. Just make sure to punch holes for drainage and air.

bin. It will always be there — all you'll have to do is turn the pile after you add to it.

Composting far from home. Don't forget about composting just because you're not at home, near your compost pile. Remember to save fruit peels or other food scraps from your workday lunch or from snacks while you're on the road. Then add them to your pile when you get home.

Screen your compost. Make your own compost sifter by nailing a one-quarter inch window screen to a wooden frame that fits over a wheelbarrow. This will let you use the compost that's ready and catch the larger chunks of material that need more time to decompose.

"Crate" idea for sifting compost. Don't waste money on an expensive compost sifter. Just strain your compost through the bottom of an old milk crate.

For a simple outdoor worm bin, stack three old tires. Fill with the usual bedding, food scraps and, of course, worms.

Enrich your soil during winter rest. Bears hibernate for the winter. Luckily, soil organisms take no such break. Take advantage of these hard workers by spreading compost over your garden beds in late fall. Cover it with a mulch of chopped leaves, and let the little guys do their thing. By spring, the compost should be sufficiently worked into your soil.

Give compost and soil time to mingle. Add compost to your soil about three weeks before planting. That gives it time to blend with the soil. An even better idea is to mix the compost into the soil several inches deep. Plants will have an easier time establishing roots in the compost-and-soil mixture rather than in a top layer of pure compost.

Dig this easy composting method. Who needs a big, messy compost pile? Just dig a one-foot trench and line it with kitchen scraps, dead weeds, and other plant material. Fill it in with topsoil, and plant vegetables in the trench row next year. The buried material will rot into compost and benefit the plants' roots. Worms will also flock to the buried treasure and leave behind valuable worm castings that improve the soil.

Create compost from the ground up. Eliminate the middleman. Instead of layering your compost materials in a pile then applying the compost to the soil, just layer the materials directly on top of your soil. This method, called sheet composting, takes about two to three months. For best results, use small pieces so they break down quicker.

Make a run for easy compost. When it comes to composting, don't be chicken. In fact, chickens can help make your job easier. Just throw your compost materials into an enclosed chicken run and let the chickens do their thing. Rake out the finished product every few weeks and toss it into your compost pile.

Casting call for worms

Worms turn food scraps into rich castings that make perfect compost. It's easy to harvest the power of these helpful critters. First, you need a bin. Any box with a lid will do. Drill holes in the bottom for drainage and air. Raise the box off the ground, and put a plastic sheet underneath it to catch leaks. Fill the box with bedding or damp, shredded paper. Now you're ready for your worms. Make sure to get red worms, or red wigglers. You can find them at some garden supply stores or order them from catalogs. Once you have your worms, feed them kitchen scraps, like fruit and vegetable peelings, coffee grounds, eggshells, pretty much anything besides meat and dairy products, and just let them do their thing.

Cool tip for worm food. Before you toss those food scraps into your worm bin, pop them in the freezer. Freezing the scraps will soften them, keep away flies, and help your worm bin stay cool.

Keep your worms organized. Worm bins provide a great source of rich worm castings. But they also provide quite a problem. How do you separate the worms from the castings? Try this simple method. Put a mesh bag, the kind used for onions, in a hole in the bedding at the bottom of your worm bin. Place some bedding material and food in the bag, then camouflage most of the bag with bedding. The worms will eventually crawl into the bag in search of food and will easily be transported to a new bin while you collect the castings from the old one.

> Once you set up your worm bin, don't worry about a shortage of castings. The average earthworm produces its own weight in castings every day.

Feed your roses with banana peels. Forget expensive fertilizers for your garden. Old banana peels work just as well for growing fabulous flowers and yummy veggies. That's because they're rich in potassium and phosphorus. Banana peels are especially helpful for roses. Save them until they're crisp and crumbly, cut them into small pieces, and bury them a few inches in the soil around your rosebush.

Hatch a plan for extra calcium. Before you water your plants, throw some crushed eggshells in the watering jug. That way, the soil gets an added bonus — calcium and other minerals — along with the water.

Make potted plants "egg-static." That's not garbage — it's plant fertilizer. Toss eggshells and banana peels into your potted plants instead of the trash can. Banana peels give your plants a boost of potassium and phosphorus, while crushed eggshells provide an extra dose of calcium.

Keep your tomatoes under wraps. Old-time gangsters may have lavished their "tomatoes" with mink wraps. But when it comes to gardening, your tomatoes will prefer a simple banana wrap. Wrap the roots of your tomato plant with a banana peel when you plant it. The potassium will help your tomatoes grow.

Feed your flowers tomato food. Tomato fertilizer isn't just for tomatoes. Use this high-potassium liquid fertilizer to help your annuals flower. Too many leaves and not enough flowers could be a sign that you're overfertilizing. Lay off the high-nitrogen fertilizers and manure, and use tomato fertilizer instead.

Spray your way to better tomatoes. Get more out of your fertilizer. Instead of feeding the roots of tomato plants, feed the leaves. The plants absorb nutrients better that way. For best results, spray the fertilizer on your tomato plants in the morning or evening.

Water your plants with coffee. Leftover coffee is poured down the drain. Your sink doesn't need the pick-me-up — but your plants sure could use it. Let the coffee cool and dilute it with water before pouring it on your plants.

Give plants a coffee break. Don't toss your coffee grounds in the trash can. Toss them in your houseplants instead. Acid-loving plants, like azaleas and camellias, could use a monthly coffee pick-me-up. Just add a thin layer of coffee grounds to their soil.

Throw a tea party for violets. You might enjoy a soothing cup of chamomile tea. But chances are, you never think to offer any to your flowers. Next time, let your African violets in on your tea party. The potassium and tannic acid in chamomile tea will help them bloom.

Tea time for potted plants. Impatient for your impatiens to grow? Try stimulating them with a daily dose of cold tea. Potted plants benefit from the many minerals in this everyday beverage.

Energize plants with club soda. Yuck — flat club soda. Maybe your weird Cousin Ernie will drink it, but most likely you'll just throw it away. Instead, use it as a cheap fertilizer for your houseplants. It contains chemicals they'll love.

Cast a vote for free fertilizer. Most county extension services offer free manure by the barrel or truckload. Other good sources of this valuable resource include farms, stables, zoos, and circuses.

Find use for a goose. Geese come in handy for weeding your garden. They love to chomp weeds, but leave cultivated plants alone. As a bonus, they're also a great source of free fertilizer. Let these hard workers do your weeding — and your manure spreading — for you.

Get help from barnyard friends. Starting a new garden from scratch? First, choose a spot. Then, if you live in the country, corral goats in the area for about three months. These helpful animals will not only kill weeds, they'll also loosen the soil and fertilize it. Now if you could only figure out how to get them to do your planting, too!

Grab a rabbit for your garden. A rabbit's foot may bring good luck — but if you're a gardener, you'll have better luck with the whole rabbit. That's because rabbit droppings make great fertilizer. These tiny, almost odorless pellets are rich in nitrogen and phosphorus. So if you don't own or have access to a rabbit, you'd better hop to it.

Wait for vintage manure. To your garden, manure is like fine wine — it gets better with age. Fresh manure can burn plants. It may also contain weed seeds or insect eggs and larvae. Play it safe and compost manure before using it in your garden.

Fishy solution for plants. One simple liquid fertilizer works wonders for annuals, perennials, vegetables, and even potted plants. Sound fishy? It is. Fish emulsion, or liquid fish, will help your plants grow. Just make sure to dilute it with water before applying it every week or two. You can find fish emulsion at your local nursery or garden center.

Fish tank water full of nutrients. When you clean your aquarium, don't dump the water down the drain. Your fish might be done with it, but it's full of nutrients your plants will love.

Yum ... pond scum. If you have a pond, your plants are in luck. When you clean your pond, gather the algae and scummy water. Then dump it onto the soil around your plants. They'll love the nutrient boost.

Reel in some rose fertilizer. Your next fishing trip might help your garden. After you gut and prepare the fish you caught, bury the scraps under and around your rosebushes. Your roses will go for this fishy fertilizer hook, line, and sinker.

Learn to love lint. You need to empty the lint from your clothes dryer anyway. Might as well put it to good use. Rather than throw it away, till it into the ground around your vegetables or flowers. It will help your soil retain moisture. Or you can just toss the lint in your compost pile.

Revive soil with vacuum bags. After your vacuum cleaner sucks up dust from your house, let your garden do the same. Empty the vacuum cleaner bag in your garden or compost pile. The dust and lint will break down and enrich the soil.

Boost bulb growth. Your bulbs need phosphorus and potassium. Give them both the easy way. When planting, add some bone meal to the hole for a long-lasting phosphorus fix. Then after your daffodils or tulips bloom, sprinkle some wood ashes on them for a healthy helping of potassium.

Coddle your carrots. What's up, doc? For healthy carrots, the answer should be phosphorus and potassium. Give your carrots a cheap boost of these nutrients with hardwood ashes and bone meal.

Friendly fungus among us. They might be hard to spell, but mycorrhizal fungi also work hard for your plants. Known as "fungus roots," they help your trees, shrubs, annuals, and perennials absorb water and nutrients. You can get these powerful fungi in garden centers, home improvement stores, or by mail order.

Rely on rock dust. Here's a tip that rocks. Get some rock dust from your local quarry or garden center. Use it for your trees, roses, lawn, and vegetables to encourage root systems and growth. You can even put some in your compost pile. It will help you save money on fertilizer — and boost your crop production.

Trim your hair to treat your garden. One of the best sources of nitrogen is sitting right on top of your head. Human hair has even more nitrogen than manure does — about 30 times more, in fact. Ask your barbershop or salon for hair clippings for your garden or compost pile.

Great mulch material easy to find. Improve your soil and prevent weeds with organic mulches. Pine needles, sawdust, straw, and shredded bark are just some of the materials you can use. They'll decompose and enrich your soil. Use at least 4 inches of mulch to stop weeds from springing up.

'Tis the season for soil improvement. Christmas is over, but you can still give your acid-loving plants a present. After you take down your Christmas tree, put it through a shredder. Then spread the mulch around your plants. It will help enrich the soil.

Energize soil with cocoa shells. Like other mulches, cocoa shells suppress weeds. Unlike many other mulches, they also provide your soil with nitrogen and other minerals as they decompose. By improving your soil, you help your plants grow. Pretty sweet.

> ! Don't use cocoa bean or cocoa shell mulch if you have a dog. It can poison him, leading to vomiting, diarrhea, or even death.

One-size-fits-all fertilizer. You like do-it-yourself projects. But it's time-consuming to make a different homemade fertilizer for every type of plant you grow. Here's a simple recipe that should satisfy all your fertilizing needs. Mix four parts seed meal (canola or cottonseed), one part rock phosphate or half part bone meal, and half part kelp meal. To adjust your soil's pH, your can also add one part dolomite lime.

Brew a batch of manure tea. This wonderful organic fertilizer fits plants to a "tea." Plop a few scoops of manure or compost in a pantyhose leg, old pillowcase, or flour sack, and tie the top. Put it in a bucket of water. Let it brew for a few days. When you're ready to use this powerful tea, dilute it with water — three parts water to one part tea — and spray it on your plants' leaves.

Try this dynamic duo. Mix chicken manure and sawdust for a potent fertilizer. Either one by itself can harm crops, but the combination creates a perfect balance. That's because the high-carbon sawdust counteracts the high-nitrogen chicken manure.

Make plants comfy with comfrey. Whip up a batch of liquid fertilizer in your garbage can. Just fill half of the can with comfrey leaves. Then fill the rest with water and steep for three weeks. Before using the mixture on your plants, dilute it to half strength with plain water. Pour it around your plants' roots for a natural boost.

Rehabilitate your garden with nettle. Fertilize your plants and keep pests away at the same time. All it takes is this simple solution. Put a pound of nettle leaves in a gallon of water, and let them soak for about a week. Use the liquid to feed and protect your plants.

Serve your houseplants a feast. This might not sound appetizing to you, but for your houseplants it's five-star dining. Mix one teaspoon each of baking powder, saltpeter, and Epsom salt and a half teaspoon of ammonia in a gallon of warm water. Treat your plants to this delicious meal every few months.

Revive plants with vinegar. Apple cider vinegar is chock-full of trace minerals your houseplants need. Mix a tablespoon of apple cider vinegar with a gallon of water to create a mighty tonic. A monthly dose will also do wonders for azaleas and radishes.

Liquidate kitchen scraps. If you live in an apartment or don't have a yard big enough for a compost heap, you can still put your food scraps to good use. Stick your vegetable peels or fruit rinds in your blender, and puree them into a smooth liquid. Dilute with water and pour the mixture on your plants.

Make time for molasses. You've heard the expression "slow as molasses." On the contrary, molasses can speed up your plants' growth. Just mix one tablespoon of blackstrap molasses with a gallon of water for a spray-on boost of potassium and sulfur. For even more help, you can add kelp or vinegar to the mixture.

Pamper plants with tonics. Give your houseplants a boost with a shot of a liquid multivitamin, like Geritol. A tablespoon of castor oil will also do the trick. Try this every few months before watering.

Spark growth with soda. Spur your outdoor flowers' growth with a jolt of caffeine. Combine four parts cola to one part water for a monthly dose of carbonated fertilizer.

Tip your cap to easy fertilizer. You don't have to buy expensive fertilizers or slave over complicated do-it-yourself recipes. Just add a capful of ammonia to a gallon of water. Your plants won't know the difference.

Dish out a dandy fertilizer. Next time you pull dish-washing duty, try this free and easy method of fertilizing your plants. Just pour dirty dishwater on them. Thanks to all the food residue from your pots, pans, plates, and utensils, it's full of nutrients. And your soil will love the phosphorus from the dish detergent.

Slather shrubs with suds. Many old-time farmers say soapsuds make good fertilizer. Keep a tub in your garden to hold soapy water. Use it to water shrubs, flowers, and even vegetables.

Try this tin can trick. Here's an easy way to give your garden the iron it needs. Instead of using a standard watering can, water your plants from rusty tin cans.

Trust rust for great flowers. It's easy to hammer out big, bright African violets. Simply shove some rusty nails into the soil around them. The nails slowly release iron and other minerals that help your plant grow.

Mellow yellow leaves with gelatin. Sprinkle a packet of unflavored gelatin around the base of your yellowing houseplant. The nitrogen will help put the green back in its leaves.

Select a spreader. What's the best kind of fertilizer spreader? That depends on your needs. If you have a small lawn and precision is more important than speed, choose a drop spreader. For larger lawns where speed is key, use a rotary spreader.

Super spreader strategies. Using a fertilizer spreader isn't exactly rocket science. But there are some tricks to keep in mind. First, designate a strip at each end of your lawn to give you some room to turn the spreader on and off as you turn around. Then go back and forth between the end strips, making sure to slightly overlap each row you make. That way, you won't miss any spots.

Effortless way to spread fertilizer. Tired of spreading fertilizer the hard way? Give yourself a coffee break. Make a handy spreader for granular fertilizer by punching holes in the bottom of a large coffee can. A handheld strainer will also do the trick.

Flour power for lawns. When fertilizing your lawn, you don't want to miss a spot. Yet, you don't want to overfertilize and burn your lawn, either. Try this simple trick to keep track of where you've been. Mix some flour with your fertilizer, and use the telltale white powder as a guide.

The ideal time to apply fertilizer. Pay attention to your local weather forecast. It could save your lawn — and save you money. Fertilizer can scorch your lawn if it's not watered in right away. Apply fertilizer to your lawn just before it's supposed to rain. That way, you won't waste water.

Enrich your lawn to thwart weeds. Weeds thrive in poor soil. Make things harder for them in your lawn. Spread about an inch of compost over your lawn and rake it in a few times during the growing season. Your grass will stay healthier and hardier than any invading weeds.

Let lawn hibernate under compost. Here's a two-for-one deal for your lawn. Cover it with a layer of compost or peat moss in the winter. You'll protect your lawn during cold weather and give it a boost come springtime. A half-inch layer will do. To apply the compost, use a manure spreader or rake.

Head for the bat cave. Don't go batty over your brown lawn. Apply bat guano instead. A safe, organic fertilizer, bat guano will help turn your lawn green. As an added bonus, it also acts as a soil conditioner.

Leave healthy lawns alone. Sometimes the best course of action is to do nothing. If your lawn is healthy, you don't have to fertilize it in the spring. It should grow well without any extra help.

Spread out monthly feeding. Did you fertilize your houseplants this month? Hard to remember, isn't it? Instead, try fertilizing them gradually. Dilute the fertilizer to one-fourth the recommended strength, and give your plants a tiny bit of it every time you water.

Feed trees with ease. For trees and large shrubs growing on your lawn, use this simple fertilizing technique. With an auger, punch holes in a circle just beyond the drip line. Holes should be about 2 feet apart. Put fertilizer in each hole, and water thoroughly.

Create a pipeline for fertilizer. Try this easy trick for feeding roses and other flowering plants. First, cut foot-long sections of PVC pipe. Then shove the sections of pipe in the soil near the base of your plants. Pour liquid fertilizer into the pipe every few weeks. Your plants will slurp it up through their new homemade straw.

Special care for all-time favorites

Sun shines brighter at high altitudes. If you live at a high elevation, you might have noticed your impatiens and other shade-loving plants don't do very well. That's because a garden located 3,000 feet above sea level gets about 20 percent more sunlight than one at sea level. Plants that love bright sunlight, on the other hand, should grow quite well.

Do your homework before you buy. You'll make expensive mistakes if you buy whatever catches your fancy at a plant nursery. Before you shop, use a good gardening guidebook to identify plants that will thrive in the conditions of your garden. If your garden center doesn't always have a knowledgeable salesperson available, take your guidebook with you. When you see something you like, check its requirements. And look at the pictures, too, because sometimes plants get mislabeled.

Learn from the experts. If you aren't sure what flowers to plant in your area, visiting garden shows will give you a lot of good ideas. You may be able to get advice about your specific needs and even buy plants you like on the spot. Garden tours can be even better, because you'll get to meet neighbors who will probably be happy to share tips about their gardening successes.

Take a hint from your neighbor. A good, quick way to choose plants for your garden is to look at what grows well in a neighbor's yard that gets similar sunlight.

Looks aren't everything. In planning your flower garden, you may spend a lot of time selecting plants that work well together where color, height, and texture are concerned. But it's equally important to group together flowers that require the same kind of soil and have similar needs for water.

Don't highlight what you want to hide. Unless you can conceal it, don't plant brightly colored flowers near an air conditioner, garbage can, or other unattractive part of your yard. Your eye will follow the color and come to rest on what you'd prefer to keep hidden.

Plan your garden on paper. Filling your flower bed with a variety of vividly colorful annuals may sound like a good idea. But sketch out your plan first using bright-colored markers. It's easier to change your mind about colors that clash before you plant them. If you already have the plants, go back to the garden center for some with white flowers or soft-colored foliage to intersperse and help tone things down a bit.

Create a festive garden quickly. Need to create a beautiful garden for a special occasion? Buy large plants in full bloom, no more than three to five different kinds but lots of each, for a lush, dramatic splash. Plant them close together, 3 to 5 inches rather than the usual 6 to 10 inches apart.

Go "grande" in the shade. As a general rule, large leaf plants require less sun than plants with small leaves.

Leaf size determines wind damage. Plants with small leaves, especially if they are narrow and waxy, resist wind damage better than broad-leafed plants. Also, with less leaf surface, they don't lose as much moisture, so they hold up better in both drying winds and dry soil.

Learn how to grow anything, inside or out, with the help of these great gardening sites.

The Ohio State University PlantFacts database:
plantfacts.ohio-state.edu or plantfacts.osu.edu/web

Aggie Horticulture's PLANTanswer Machine at the Texas A&M University Extension Service:
floriculture.tamu.edu:8080/search.html

National Gardening Web site:
www.garden.org

The Gardening Launch Pad's list of Master Gardeners' programs and extension services:
gardeninglaunchpad.com/extension.html

Watch Your Garden Grow — a guide to growing, storing, and preparing vegetables:
www.urbanext.uiuc.edu/veggies

Clemson University Home and Garden Information Center:
hgic.clemson.edu

The United States National Arboretum:
www.usna.usda.gov

GardenGuides — a growing resource for gardeners:
www.gardenguides.com

Some plants love the heat. For gardens in hot, dry areas, use fleshy succulents and other plants that hold moisture well. Those with small waxy, shiny, or hairy leaves or those with silvery foliage, which reflects light, are good choices. Big floppy leaves tend to dry out fast.

Make a large garden cozy. Warm colors, like orange, red, and yellow, make a large garden space seem more intimate. Cool blues and purples, on the other hand, can give an impression of roominess to a small space.

Help your blue flowers shine. Unlike yellows and oranges, blue and purple flowers can easily fade into the background in your garden. To help them stand out, plant them in full sun beside daisies or other white or yellow flowers.

Show off your blossoms. Pink or white flowers will stand out against a brick wall, whereas red ones will hardly be noticed. To help darker flowers show up better against a dark background, provide the contrast of pale green leaves or white companion flowers.

Red camellias hardier than white. Grow red camellias instead of white if you live where they are likely to be damaged by frost. The red blossoms will keep more of their color, while white ones turn brown. In addition, red camellias tolerate more sunlight than the pink and white varieties.

> ! Maybe it's good that some flowers bloom past children's bedtime. Beautiful and fragrant as they are, blossoms of the night-blooming moonflower, flowering tobacco, and angel's trumpet are poisonous. Keep pets away from them, too.

Which color smells best? When choosing flowers for fragrance, color makes a difference. The scent of the white blossoms of tobacco plants, for example, are more fragrant than the colorful flowers of the same kind of plant.

Create a romantic moonlight garden. If you enjoy an evening stroll in the garden, plant fragrant, night-blooming plants, like white alyssum or nicotinia. The pale blossoms reflect more light than darker flowers, which hide in the darkness. Plants with silvery foliage also shine in your moonlit garden.

Focus on fragrance at nightfall. Flowering tobacco and evening primrose are especially fragrant night-blooming perennials. Or, if you live in a warm area, you can fill the evening air with the scent of mandevilla, jasmine, Peruvian daffodil, and mugwort.

Check cemeteries for survivors. If you want to know which perennials hold up best in your area, check out old graveyards and abandoned houses. You'll see which ones are the toughest survivors, even with neglect. And you just may uncover some heirloom varieties, giving you a lesson in plant history for your locale.

Look for late bloomers. Most people plant lots of perennials that bloom early because that is what's in bloom when they think of planting in the spring. But the garden doesn't have to lose its beauty so soon. Visit public gardens in late summer to see what's still in bloom and plant some of those, too.

Choose perennials with pretty foliage. Attractive leaves will make your perennials interesting, even after the flowers fade. And for more blossoms throughout the summer, mix longer-blooming annuals in the same pot with perennials.

Fill perennial gaps with annuals. When planting perennials, it's important to space them far enough apart to allow for growth until they reach maturity. To avoid a sparse look, fill in the gaps between plants with annuals that complement them. Replace the annuals each year until the perennials have grown in to fill the space.

Be picky about perennials. Perennials come back year after year, making them the perfect plants for lazy gardeners, right? Not necessarily. Many perennials must be divided and replanted frequently. If you want the easiest-to-grow variety, stick with those that self-seed. Just be sure to leave some of the flowers on the stems until they dry and drop their seed for the next season. As an alternative, choose perennials like hostas, peonies, and daylilies. They go for a long time before they need dividing.

Divide perennials while they rest. Don't move or divide perennials when they are busy blooming or growing. As a rule, fall is the best time to transplant those that bloom before late June, and early spring is best for those that bloom after late June.

Some perennials don't need dividing. You can tell perennials need dividing when you see a lot of dead foliage in the center of the plant. Astilbe and asters will need it every couple of years. But some, like candytuft, dianthus, and baby's breath should never be divided.

Bees befriend the garden. Attract friendly pollinators by planting their favorites — bee balm, hyssop, pansies, and mint. They especially like yellow and violet colors. But they don't like tubular flowers since it's hard for them to get inside for the nectar.

Plant flowers deer don't like. Depending on where you live, Bambi's relatives tend to avoid a different set of plants. But, in general, they don't like ferns or ornamental grasses. Plants that have hairy or fuzzy foliage, and those that taste minty, lemony, or bitter, are usually a safe bet, as well. For a specific list of deer-proof plants for your neck of the woods, check with your local extension agent or just ask your neighbors.

Add interest and room to grow. Give bedding plants a more natural look with curved lines or a zigzag pattern, rather than planting them in straight rows. And allow plenty of growing room. If you aren't sure how big your plants will get, allow 12 inches between perennials and 6 inches between annuals.

Fill the air with fragrance. Place pots of fragrant flowers and herbs, like jasmine, lemon verbena, and mint, beside walkways and patios. Twine honeysuckle vines around open doorways and windows where breezes can lift the scent and bring it inside. Water your pleasant-smelling plants late in the afternoon when the weather is dry. Since humidity increases fragrances, as you relax in the evening, you'll enjoy them more.

Simple way to add a splash of color. Old wheelbarrows and wagons work as both garden accents and an easy way to bring some bright color into your shade garden. Just fill them with pots of sun-loving flowers. Roll one into the shade while the other sits in the sunshine. After a few days, trade them out. If neither stays in the shadows too long, the system will work well.

Protect a precious pot. If you have a pretty container you'd like to use as a planter but don't want to put soil directly in it, use a plastic flower pot that will fit inside. If the planter is taller than your plastic pot, place an empty up-side-down flower pot below the filled one.

Build a flower tower. Place pots within pots for a stacked effect. Partially fill a large pot with potting soil. Put a medium-size pot inside before filling it the rest of the way. Do the same with a smaller pot inside the middle one. Then plant flowers in the three pots. The plants will hang over the sides and look very attractive.

Think twice before using Styrofoam. You can use those packing peanuts to save soil when you want to plant shallow-rooted plants in a deep pot. Just fill the bottom of the pot with them and finish filling the last few inches with potting soil. Their light weight makes it easier to move the pot around, too, but they become a problem when you want to change the soil. They won't decay on your compost pile, and if you spill them, they can blow all over your garden. Try plastic soda bottles or inverted plastic flower pots instead. They do the job and are easier to remove.

Resist the urge to plant early. Garden centers generally start displaying their bedding plants long before the last frost is over. If you can't resist the urge to buy early, do restrain yourself when it comes to setting them out in your beds. Frost is likely to destroy them outdoors, so keep them well-watered in a sunny window until the danger passes.

Make a splash and save some cash. You get more for your money when you buy bedding plants by the flat. And a grouping of the same kind of flowers has more impact in your small garden than a mixture of different colors. Even in a bigger space where you want more variety, a repeating border of one plant will tie everything together.

Bigger and "bloomier" isn't always better. When you are shopping for annuals, tall plants or those in full bloom may attract your attention first. But in the long run, you'll have healthier plants if you make bushy, dark greenery your highest priority.

Pinch your plant for healthier blooms. When you buy plants that already have flowers, it's hard to nip them off. But your plants will be prettier if you pinch them back. Remove the top portion of main branches just above a leaf or pair of leaves for a more compact, bushier plant.

Start with healthy plants. When buying bedding plants, avoid those with yellow leaves. Select plants that have dark green, bushy leaves instead. And if the soil in the pots is dry, especially if it's pulling away from the sides, the plants are probably stressed. Reject those and wilted plants, as well.

Pick a fresh six-pack. Annuals that are sagging in their little multipack containers at the store will probably droop even more with the stress of transplanting. Try to take those you buy straight home and remove them from your car rather than leaving them in the heat. Give them a good watering, and transplant them promptly.

Take tender plants for a ride. It's a good idea to "harden off" or acclimate your new annuals before you plant them in the ground. A quick way to do this is to place the pots in a wheelbarrow or wagon. Just wheel them out into the spring sunshine each morning, and roll them into an enclosed porch, basement, or garage before temperatures drop at night.

Neat trick for messy transplants. When you plant flowers in pots that you'll later transplant to your garden, use this handy trick to keep things neat and avoid disturbing the roots. Before you plant, line the pot with several pages of newspaper. Then when the plant is ready for transferring, you can neatly lift it out and plant it, newspaper and all. The paper will decay and become mulch.

Bag seeds as they burst from pods. Sometimes, rather than letting dry seeds from your favorite flowers fall to the ground, it's best to capture them to replant the following spring. After the flowers have died, loosely tie a paper bag around the plant, or use a piece of cloth or old stocking, to catch them when the seed heads pop open. Don't use plastic. It might hold moisture, which could cause them to rot.

Plant peat pots in the soil. Plant seedlings grown in peat pots directly into your garden so you won't disturb the tender roots. Sink them just a little lower in the ground than they were growing in the pot. If the rim of the pot is above the ground, break it off so it won't trap water around the stem. Also, before planting, moisten both the soil around the seedling and the peat pot itself. Then gently break open and remove the bottom of the pot to make it easier for the roots to grow.

Encourage marigolds to return in spring. Don't clean up your garden too quickly when flowers stop blooming in late summer. In mild areas, some annuals will reseed themselves. Marigolds, pansies, and zinnias, for example, will give you a new season of blooms the following spring. But you have to let seed heads develop, dry, and drop their seeds to the ground so they can come up again. For wildflower patches, when the plants turn brown, mow them to a height of about 5 inches. This will scatter the seeds and provide some mulch, too. And be on the lookout for the new seedlings when spring rolls around. Don't mow them or pull them up thinking they are unwanted weeds.

Reproduce success with heirloom seeds. If you like to save flower seeds to replant, start with heirloom seeds for the best chance at getting the same quality the next year. Heirloom seeds come from nonhybrid plants that have been reproducing without major variations for the last 50 years or more. They are pollinated by the wind or insects. Some of your best bets are marigolds, black-eyed Susans, cosmos, and Mexican sunflowers.

Keep seeds cool and dry. An envelope makes a good storage container for seeds you gather to use the next year.

You can write the name of the seed and any information about planting that might be helpful. The envelope, which will keep them cool and dry, is a better choice than an air-tight, plastic container, especially if there's a chance the seeds aren't completely dry when you store them.

Soak seeds for sprouting success. Sweet peas can be planted from seed, but don't just toss a few in loose soil and expect good results. The seeds are hard, so soak them for 24 hours. Next, rub them with sandpaper to make it easier for sprouts to break through the seed coats. Any seeds that don't swell from soaking may need to be nicked with a knife.

Smart way to dry sunflower seeds. When the backs of sunflowers turn yellowish brown and the petals fall off, collect the flower heads in a cloth or paper bag. Keep them in a warm, dry place until the heads are shriveled. Remove the seeds and spread them on an old screen door — or other mesh surface — where air can circulate to help them finish drying.

New twist on classical music. Some scientists say music can help your plants grow, but be careful what you play. In some experiments, rock music killed the plants, while classical caused them to flourish.

Unique use for an old parasol. Until your newly planted seedlings toughen up a bit, they need protection from hot sun. An old umbrella can provide temporary shade during the hottest part of the afternoon.

Shade plants need moisture, too. It's not as hot in the shade, so you might not think as much about watering the plants that grow there. But they need water, too. Mulching is important in shade, as well. And if you set plants close together, the leaves will help keep moisture from evaporating.

Throw an old cover on a new bed. Keep old sheets, table cloths, and curtains on hand to cover your tender plants when temperatures are expected to drop.

Pinch mums for prettier flowers. When new shoots are about 4 to 6 inches long, pinch mums back to the lowest two or three leaves. This encourages more branches. Being bushier, they are less likely to be top-heavy and fall over. They'll need pinching about once a month, but stop when buds start to form — usually around July 4 in zones 1 to 4, earlier in zones 5 and above.

Nip glads for quicker blooms. You can speed up the blooming of your gladiolus for a special bouquet. The flowers open first from the bottom. Pinching off several buds at the top hurries them along.

Cut back petunia "legs." If you have a lot of annuals, it may be hard to keep up with pinching back the leggy ones, like petunias. If you cut back a few stems near the center of each plant every few weeks, you should have some blossoms and some new growth throughout the summer.

Encore performance from summer flowers. When the delphinium flowers fade in June or July, cut the stalk back, leaving just the bottom leaves. You should then get a second flowering in September.

Deadheading prolongs life. When blossoms die, it gives the plant the idea its job of producing flowers is done. So it stops blooming and puts its energy into setting seeds. You can trick it into thinking its job isn't finished by deadheading — or pinching off the dead blossoms before seeds form. If there are still buds on the stems, just remove the dead flower head. If there are no more buds, cut the stems back to the base.

Plant automatic deadheaders. If deadheading doesn't appeal to you, you'll appreciate flowers like impatiens, begonias, ageratum, alyssum, and lobelia. They drop their dead blossoms without any help.

Help tall plants withstand the wind. Globe amaranth is better than most tall flowers at standing up against strong breezes. For less-sturdy tall plants, like delphiniums and gladiolas, make a support using bamboo and string. When flowers are about a foot tall, drive three 4-foot-long bamboo poles in a triangle enclosing four or five plants. Tie garden twine, green yarn, or strips of green fabric around the poles about 10 inches from the ground. When the plants bloom, loop the tie again just below the flower heads.

Support a weak plant with a twig. When you prune your hedges, save some of the sturdy twigs to use as supports for young annuals. As the plants grow, their leaves will cover and hide the sticks.

Great stake for falling flowers. Use an extension-style curtain rod as a support for a tall flower. Just push the rod firmly into the soil and tie the plant loosely to it. As the stem grows, you can adjust the length of the curtain rod.

Gather fragrant blossoms early. Pick sweet peas in the morning while they have dew on their petals. That's when they smell sweetest.

Pick peonies before noon. The best time to cut peonies is in the morning when they are most full of moisture.

Favorite all-summer bloomer. Petunias are among the most popular annuals. That's because, in addition to being pretty, they bloom all summer long. They come in compact varieties for edging borders or planting in dramatic drifts. Others drape beautifully from hanging baskets or over walls. To be sure you are getting this kind, look for the words "cascading" or "trailing" on the label.

Don't smoke around petunias. If you are a smoker, be sure to wash your hands before working with petunias. They are highly susceptible to tobacco mosaic virus. Tomatoes, also, are prone to this disease.

Geraniums for a rainy day. Plants with single blossoms, like maverick and cameo, and those with dark leaves, like rose geranium, do better in rainy climates.

Gorgeous geraniums keep coming back. Here's the secret to overwintering your geraniums. At the end of the summer, gently pull your plants from the soil and brush away any dirt that clings to the roots. Hang the entire geranium — flowers, leaves, and all — upside down in a cellar or other damp place where the temperature stays between 40 and 50 degrees all winter. If the location seems too damp, wrap the plants loosely in newspaper before you hang them to reduce the chances of molding and rotting. The plants will look dead, but don't water them. At planting time in the spring, strip off the flowers and leaves and repot them. Some people soak them for several hours before replanting, but if you water them well, that step isn't necessary.

Color made for the shade. Don't give up on bright flowers just because your yard gets little sun. Plant impatiens, a shade-loving annual that comes in a variety of pinks, reds, purples, and oranges, as well as white.

Don't toss that Easter lily. When the blossoms are gone, transplant your Easter lily for years of enjoyment. Cut off the dead flowers and half the stem. Then carefully remove it from the container. Choose a spot in your garden that gets morning sun and afternoon shade. Loosen the soil at least a foot deep and plant the lily 2 or 3 inches deeper than it was in the pot. Don't look for flowers next Easter. When planted outside, these lilies bloom in the summertime.

Use dampness to your advantage. Siberian and Japanese irises, astilbe, cardinal flower, and candelabra primrose are flowers that love to grow in moist places. River birch and bald cypress trees are right at home there, too. And the evergreen sweet woodruff makes a good ground cover for those areas that never seem to dry out.

Prune and share the Autumn Joy. The beautiful Autumn Joy is a sedum best pruned by cutting off most of the growth in June. New leaves will come back quickly, making a fuller, bushier plant, ready to bloom in late summer. And each of the freshly cut tips can easily be rooted, giving you lots of new plants to share with friends. Just strip off the lower leaves, put the stems into soft soil, and water.

Hang fuchsia to attract hummingbirds. Although fuchsia has no fragrance, hummingbirds love sipping the nectar. Plant these pink, red, or purple beauties in baskets, and hang them where they'll get morning sun and afternoon shade. They like well-drained soil, but appreciate a misting when their leaves get droopy.

Beware of beautiful monkshood. Late-blooming blue or purple monkshood may be just the perennial you are looking for to plant in your shade garden. But wear gloves when handling it so its poisonous sap won't get on your hands.

Daffodils give more bang for your buck. Bulbs, daffodils, in particular, are a good investment in your garden. Buy a few and, in time, they'll fill your landscape. Daffodils, known as "the poets' flower," are easy to grow, and they tolerate any kind of soil, except boggy land. They multiply quickly, yet take years before they need to be divided. What's more, rodents find them poisonous and leave them alone.

Encourage bulbs to thrive. After a bulb has bloomed and faded, snip off — or deadhead — the old blossom. But don't remove the plant's foliage. It will provide food for the bulb next season.

Remove dead blooms. If daffodil and tulip blossoms go to seed, they use up energy the bulbs need — so remove the flowers as they fade. The foliage provides food for the bulbs, so don't cut it back until it turns brown.

Baby your tulip bulbs. For beautiful tulips year in and year out, dig up the bulbs after they finish blooming in early summer. Clean and dry them and store them in a dark, cool place until the fall planting season.

Cool way to keep bulbs from freezing. If you don't have an indoor space to store bulbs over the winter, keep them outside on a porch or under the house in an inexpensive Styrofoam cooler. Just pack them in peat moss and leave the cover open slightly so air can circulate.

Trick bulbs into blossoming. If autumn isn't cold enough in your area, pre-chill your spring bulbs in the refrigerator crisper drawer. Start about eight weeks before planting. The bulbs will "believe" they had a rough autumn and will be itching to bloom.

Give bulbs a new lease on life. When bulbs stop producing flowers, they are said to be "blind." Sometimes you can get them to bloom again by replanting them in rich soil. Most of the time, it's best just to set your sights on new bulbs. On the other hand, if your bulbs have never bloomed, it could be because they weren't planted deep enough. In this case, there's a good chance you'll get blooms if you dig them up and replant them.

How to select healthy bulbs. When you are ready to buy bulbs for your garden, look for those that are big and firm. Examine them closely and reject any that are badly bruised or have an odd smell.

Small bulbs produce prettier blooms. A bigger bulb may blossom into a bigger flower, but a smaller bulb may bloom into a prettier and more fragrant one.

Single daffodils nose out doubles. You may plan to double your money by looking for daffodil bulbs with two "noses." It's true you'll get two flower stems, but these bulbs go "blind" more readily than their single-nosed sisters.

Secret to healthier bulbs. Make sure the bulb packaging says "for naturalizing" if you want to leave your tulip bulbs in the ground year after year. To guarantee the bulbs reappear every spring, dose the bed with a low-nitrogen fertilizer in the fall.

Bargain bulbs may be duds. Specialty catalogs offer a larger selection of bulbs than you'll find from local sources. But be careful about ordering bulbs at what seems like a fantastic price. They are likely to be small and immature and will give disappointing results, especially the first year.

Opt for older bulbs. When buying daylilies, look for those with two fans. That's a sign the plant is mature, so you are likely to get blooms the first year.

Give bulbs a prompt burial. Try to plant those daffodils and other bulbs you ordered from a catalog as soon as you receive them. If you have to delay planting, store them in an open paper bag or cardboard box in a cool location until you can get them in the ground.

Wait to plant tulips. Early to mid-autumn is the best time to plant most bulbs. Tulips, however, should be planted in late fall to prevent a fungal disease called tulip fire. If you live where the climate is mild, you can even plant them in early winter. Don't worry — they'll still bloom on time.

Go deep to plant bulbs. As a rule of thumb, plant bulbs three to six times their diameter. But check the package, or information at the display when you buy loose bulbs, for the right depth for specific bulbs. Deeper is generally better in areas where the temperature in winter gets really low, or where the soil is light and likely to dry out in summer. But don't go too deep or you won't get any flowers. And it's best to plant bulbs with the "nose," or growing end, pointing up. But if you can't tell which end that is, plant it on its side, and it will still grow toward the surface.

Shield bulbs from hungry squirrels. Squirrels love bulbs — especially tulips and crocuses. So at planting time, protect each bulb in a cage made from two plastic berry containers wired or tied together. Surround the bulb completely with soil, making sure there are no air pockets. A simpler solution when bulbs are planted in drifts is to lay chicken wire over the ground above them.

Bulbs bloom without bone meal. The old advice was to put bone meal in the bottom of the hole when you plant bulbs. But now the experts say it's not necessary to fertilize bulbs the first year. And you won't have dogs and rodents, attracted by the smell of bone meal, digging up your bulbs.

Remember where you bury your bulbs. Don't trust your memory when you plant bulbs. Mark the spot with popsicle sticks. This way you won't slice through a bulb while planting something else in that "empty" space.

> ! Check carefully before eating flower bulbs. Although some crocus bulbs are edible, the Autumn Crocus is a lily — not a crocus, and it's poisonous.

Mix bulbs and perennials. Mix spring bulbs and woody perennials in the same beds. The bulbs will give you early blossoms. Then, as they die back, the perennials' leaves and flowers will hide the bulbs' dead foliage. Go slowly, however, putting annuals in areas where bulbs are planted. They require more frequent watering, which doesn't set too well with some bulbs, especially tulips and hyacinths.

Mark bare spots while bulbs bloom. You may notice empty spaces among your spring-blooming bulbs that you'd like to fill in with other plants. While the foliage is still green, place large stones where it's okay to dig. If you don't get around to filling them in before the leaves die back, you'll know where to plant without harming bulbs buried out of sight.

Plant dahlias on steep slopes. If you want to beautify a hillside and avoid dangerous mowing, plant dahlias and daylilies. Planted 5 to 6 inches deep, these bulbs also help prevent erosion.

Eye your calendar before planting irises. Irises bloom in spring. But the best time to buy and plant them is in July through September. Dig, divide, and transplant them anytime in summer or fall. Select a spot with plenty of sunshine and well-drained soil and plant them with the rhizomes just barely visible above ground.

Protect irises from insects. After bearded irises bloom, leave the leaves, but cut the tall stalk. Insects can get in through the hollow stalk and damage the plant.

Mark leaves to keep colors straight. When you plan to move irises of different colors, use a permanent marker to write the color of the flower on a leaf while they are still blooming. The ink will last long enough to get the flowers moved to where you want them without confusion. For more fragile-leafed plants, find yarn that matches the flower color and tie a piece around the stalk.

Have fun with yard art. Create interesting gardens with pots, buckets, and old tea kettles. Or use articles of clothing, like old gardening boots, a canvas hat — even a pair of well-worn overalls with the legs stuffed with newspaper. With a little imagination, you can find all kinds of unusual containers at junkshops and yard sales. In most cases, it's simple to slip plastic pots, already filled with plants, inside these unlikely containers.

Wooden window boxes are best. You have several choices in window box materials, such as plastic, terra cotta, and metal. But wood provides the best insulation for the roots of your flowers. Cedar, although more expensive than most woods, is best of all because it resists rotting.

Potted plants resist disease. Plants in containers need to be watered and fertilized more frequently than in-ground plants, but they are less prone to diseases and insect damage.

Keep containers dirt-free. When planting in containers, lightweight potting mixtures are best. The soil-free kind are especially good. They drain quickly, hold in nutrients, and encourage roots to grow.

Line clay pots with plastic. Terra cotta pots have a natural appeal most plastic containers lack. But they also dry out faster, and the soil temperature changes more than with plastic. A combination of the two, however, may be ideal. Plant in a slightly smaller plastic pot, and slip it inside a clay pot.

Help a dry plant absorb more water. When plants in pots dry out, the soil pulls away from the sides. Then, when you water them, the water races quickly down the sides and out the bottom, leaving the soil dry. The solution? Set the pot in a bucket, tub, or sink half-filled with lukewarm water, and let it slowly soak up the moisture it needs.

Plant some privacy. Your neighbors aren't nosy, but you'd still like your backyard to be a little more secluded in the summer. Line up some beanstalks along your property line, and run strings between them. Plant fast-running beans, like scarlet runner, or perhaps some morning glory vines for a quick screen.

Give flowering shrubs an encore. When the show is over for another season, your flowering bush doesn't have to look dull. Just add a later-blooming vine near the base and train it to run up the branches. Plant the vine in good soil, far enough away that its roots don't have to compete with those of the shrub. And be sure both plants get plenty of water.

Camouflage an eyesore with blooms. Leafy and blooming vines are a good way to disguise an unattractive fence or wall. For maximum coverage, paint it green first, then let ivy, Virginia creeper, or climbing roses scramble over it.

Slow but steady covers the wall. Use vines to transform an unattractive concrete wall into a beautiful focal point for your yard. But pass up fast-growing vines. Climbing hydrangea, with its pretty white flowers, is a better choice than those that quickly cover not only the wall but everything in sight. Just be sure you can give it some protection from hot afternoon sun.

Support vines that don't cling naturally. Grapevines attach themselves to the base they are climbing on with tendrils. English ivy clings with holdfast rootlets. Twiners, like clematis and morning glory, wrap themselves around a post or a tree trunk. But some vines need your help to stay off the ground. For support, screw metal cup hooks into a fence post or trellis. If you need to tie the vine to the hooks, use soft green yarn so it won't show or hurt the vine.

Dry hydrangeas for bouquets and wreaths. Leave the hydrangea blossoms on the bush until they have begun drying and feel like paper. Remove the leaves and hang them upside down in a dark room that's warm, dry, and has plenty of air circulating. In a couple of weeks, they should be completely dry and ready to use. For more vivid color, spray the blossoms lightly with diluted liquid dye.

Protect your home with agave. Agave plants have sharp leaves and grow 4- to 6-feet tall and 10-feet wide. Grow them around your windows and doors, and you are sure to keep intruders away. The fact that they are also fire retardant adds to their popularity in dry regions. In addition, agave plants help prevent soil erosion and are drought resistant. But they can't take the cold. So if you live where temperatures drop below 40 degrees Fahrenheit, don't count on their surviving unless you can bring them inside in winter.

Think ahead when planting a bush. Shrubs are great for shielding your house's foundation, but be careful when planting them close to windows. They could grow too tall or wide and block your view.

Give young shrubs room to grow. Shrubs are easier, and less expensive, to plant when they are small. But leave plenty of space between them to allow for healthy growth and to avoid a crowded look when they are full grown. If you aren't sure how big they will grow, as a rule of thumb, leave 3 to 4 feet between them. While shrubs are small, you can fill the space between them with mulch, or plant annual flowers or perennials that can be moved when they fill in the space.

Plant in threes to please the eye. Avoid dotting your landscape with too many single shrubs of different kinds. Plant the same variety in groups of three for a more-pleasing look. A single plant with showy flowers, colorful leaves, or interesting shape, however, can be a special focal point.

Not all hedges make good windbreaks. Azaleas and rhododendrons make attractive hedges in some landscapes, but don't count on them as windbreaks. They dry out quickly in cold, dry wind.

Give azaleas the right light. Azaleas need at least five hours of sunlight in order to bloom well, so don't plant them in deep shade. Try to plant them where they get morning sun but have some protection from midday and afternoon sun. They like moderation in moisture, as well, so avoid placing them near a downspout or any other wet place. They like acid soil and light pruning.

Be kind to azaleas. Don't plant these flowering shrubs too deep. The upper roots, in fact, should be right at the soil line or just a little lower. If you are transplanting an azalea, be sure to spread the roots out if they have been growing in a circle inside the pot. For lots of blooms, apply 2 inches to 4 inches of mulch and keep them well watered — at least an inch every seven to 10 days. But go very light on fertilizer, feeding them only in early spring. Too much fertilizer can burn them.

Buy azaleas that hold up in heat. Choose azaleas with colorful blossoms for hot regions. White petals wilt quickly in the heat. And buy 3-gallon plants rather than the smaller ones. They have more roots, which will help them survive hot summers.

Pickle your plants. Azalea, blueberry, butterfly weed, fern, gardenia, mountain laurel, and rhododendron are acid-loving plants. Water them with a mixture of 1 pint vinegar to 2 gallons water. Pour it around the base of the plants, not over them. Direct contact with the vinegar can cause the leaves to fall off.

Spare next year's buds. Some flowering shrubs, like lilacs, set the following year's buds while this year's booms are still pretty. So gather flowers carefully. Use clippers to make a clean cut just above the branch where a bud is forming.

Keep protective cages airy. In cold zones, a good way to protect tender shrubs through the winter is to put a cage made of chicken wire around them and fill it with pine straw or leaves. But don't use maple leaves. When wet, they stick thickly together and can suffocate the plant.

Shape a tree from a bush. Topiaries look beautiful, but they can be intimidating for the beginning gardener. Here's an easy way to shape your own. Buy a 5-gallon boxwood and invert a tomato cage over it. Tie any loose wire ends together at the top to form a cone. Trim the bush to match the outlines of the cage. As the bush grows through the cage, use the wire sides as a clipping guide. In a few seasons, your "tree" will be ready to show off. Remove the cage and decorate your boxwood with Christmas lights for a welcoming holiday touch.

Poor watering practices kill grass. In hot, dry weather, you may be tempted to water your lawn every day. But it is far better to give it a good soaking less frequently. In addition, avoid heavy fertilizing. These two practices can cause thatch to build up, making it hard for water to get through to the roots and encouraging damage from disease and insects.

Save money on lawn fertilizer. For a smart, no-hassle way to get nitrogen into your lawn without using fertilizer, leave the grass clippings when you mow. As they decompose, they send a constant stream of nitrogen into the soil. Overseeding with white clover will also put nitrogen into the soil. And using natural corn gluten, a by-product of corn processing, not only increases nitrogen, it kills weeds, too.

Watch out for pets spoiling your grass. If patches of your lawn look scorched, animal urine, particularly that of a female dog, could be the reason. If you catch the animal in the act, take the water hose and flush the area with water. If the pet is yours, feeding it a lower-protein dog food might reduce the amount of nitrogen in the urine, which causes the problem. Adding tomato juice to its diet or baking soda to the water dish could also help. But to be on the safe side, talk with your veterinarian before trying these ideas.

"X" out lawn lumps. Bumps beneath the grass can spoil the beauty of your lush, green lawn. Fortunately, you can level them out easily. In autumn, cut an "X" shape in the mound of turf, loosen it with a shovel, and carefully

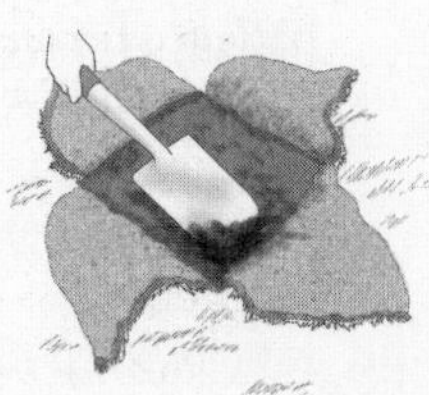

pull it back, exposing the earth below. Scoop out the extra soil and press the grass firmly back in place.

Keep off the wet grass. Walking on wet or frost-covered grass, even sturdy varieties that can take lots of wear and tear, can damage the structure of the soil and also make the grass more susceptible to disease.

Dampen leaves for easy raking. Give leaves a light sprinkling of water before you rake them, and they won't blow away. But don't get them soaking wet, or they will be too heavy to move.

Keep mower blades sharp. A dull mower blade tears the grass, making it easier for disease to set in. Remember to have your blades sharpened regularly.

Refuel with care. If you notice brown spots on your lawn a day or so after mowing, you might have spilled fuel when refilling your lawn mower.

Riding lawn mower warning. Never mow a steep slope with a riding lawnmower, even a well-balanced one. They are too easily tipped over. And a walk-behind mower can be difficult to manage on a hillside, making it dangerous, as well as exhausting. Mowing across rather than up and down the slope will help. Until you are comfortable with any new mower, be sure someone is around to help if you run into trouble.

6 reasons to use a push mower. Are you losing your patience because your lawn mower is hard to start and difficult to maintain? Are your tired of smelling fumes and listening to the noisy roar of the motor? It might be time to switch to a push mower — no fumes, gentle exercise, and cleaner cuts for healthier grass. It's cheaper to operate than a regular mower, and it helps keep the environment clean. Plus, you can mow your grass on Sunday morning without disturbing your neighbors.

Don't mow dormant grass. Grass needs regular mowing when it's growing. But hold off when it's resting. It's likely to turn brown from loss of moisture.

Baby a parched lawn. When the weather is really dry and you haven't been able to water your grass, don't cut it. Mowing dried out grass on dry soil allows the sun and wind to dry it even more. On the other hand, when you do have rain, or after watering, let grass dry completely before mowing. Otherwise, you'll leave clumps of grass that can smother your lawn, and it can leave a mess on your mower blade.

Patch your lawn with plugs. Use plugs and sprigs to fill in small bare areas of an established lawn, but not for planting a new one. The spaces between dry out quickly and are an invitation to weeds.

When to replace your lawn. Follow the 50-50 rule when fixing up your lawn. If more than half of your yard is barren or wracked with weeds, it's more cost effective to start completely over rather than fertilize what's left.

7 secrets for a super-lush lawn

Follow these tips for the best-looking lawn in the neighborhood:

- Select the best grass for your climate and conditions.
- Remove vegetation and loosen, enrich, and level the soil to prepare for a new lawn.
- Lay sod if possible. It's more expensive but more reliable than seed.
- Water new grass often and thoroughly. After roots are established, water deeply but less frequently.
- When mowing, remove no more than the top third of the grass.
- Use a mulching mower and leave the grass clippings to enrich the soil.
- Rake leaves to prevent disease and allow sunlight to get to the grass.

Lucky for you clover is hearty. Maybe your grass has dried up once again in the no-watering days of drought. Or perhaps you are just tired of the work it takes to keep up a lawn. When you are ready for a change, consider planting a cover crop of clover. It requires no fertilizer, tolerates more compacted soil than grass, and requires less water since the long roots go deep. It doesn't hold up as well, however, to high traffic, but it might keep you in a constant supply of lucky four-leaf clovers.

Select the best grass seed for your region. In the South, single-seed grasses tend to work best. Most warm-season grasses just look better planted by themselves. And even if you try planting a mixture, there's a good chance the strongest variety will kill out the others. All northern cool-season grasses, on the other hand, are grown from a mixture of seeds. If one kind of grass fails, the conditions might be just right for another to flourish. What's more, diseases that attack one will often leave another alone.

Grass for the shady lane. For a shade-tolerant grass that grows well in zones 3-8, a fine fescue is your best bet. It often comes mixed with another grass, like Kentucky bluegrass. Before you buy, be sure at least 80 percent of it is fescue.

Unearth a tough native grass. Buffalo grass, a drought-tolerant prairie grass, is so hardy early farmers used it for building sod houses. Today, you can use it for a lush-looking lawn if you mix it with other grasses. For a pretty, natural meadow, plant some wildflowers with it.

Grow easy-care grasses. Ornamental grasses are drought, insect, disease, and deer resistant. If you have well-drained soil and a spot that gets at least 6 hours of sun a day, they may be an ideal addition to your garden. They require little care, but the cool-season types, like blue fescue and feather reed grass, need dividing about every three years.

Bundle up for quick cleanup. Dried, warm-season, ornamental grasses look pretty blowing in the breezes throughout the winter. But in spring, cut them back to prepare them for new growth. To make the cleanup easier, tie the tops together with twine or strips of cloth or pantyhose before you cut them. Then release the whole bundle onto the compost heap.

Good reasons to plant ground covers. Grass might not be the only, or smartest, choice for your yard. Evergreen or flowering ground covers provide continuity and tie together different aspects of your landscape. Best of all, they require lower maintenance than grass and are less dangerous on hillsides, since you don't have to mow them.

Put periwinkle in the shade. To beautify those spots where the sun barely shines, plant a ground cover of perennial periwinkle and enjoy the bluish-lavender blossoms against a background of green leaves.

Just right on the rocks. Sedum, a succulent with star-shaped flowers, and thyme, a member of the mint family, make good ground covers for hot regions with dry, rocky soil.

Make the most of moss. You had hoped to have grass growing in that moist, shady spot, but moss is thriving there instead. Rather than fight it, make it a feature in your garden. To encourage existing moss, in mid-spring spray it with a mixture of 1 quart buttermilk to 2 gallons of water. Keep it moist throughout the summer for lush, green growth. To start moss in a new area, put a piece of moss in a blender with buttermilk and water and mix together. Spread it where you want the moss to grow. You can even "age" pots and garden accessories with this method.

Send moss packing. If you're determined to get rid of the moss in your yard, your best bet is to use lawn sand. But keep this in mind. Although lawn sand will kill the moss, it will come back again if you don't change the conditions that encouraged it to grow in the first place. Moss grows in shady, damp areas, especially those that are poorly fed and mowed too closely. So set your mower at a high level and aerate the soil frequently with a garden fork. Fertilize twice a year, and use lawn sand once a year. Cutting back low-hanging branches on nearby trees to let in more light can also help.

Plant shade trees to save money. To keep your house cool and save money on your electricity bill, shield the sunny side of your home with a fast-growing shade tree.

Invest in fruit trees. Having your own fruit trees can save you money at the grocery store, and they are a good, long-term investment on your property. But a full-grown apricot tree, for example, needs at least 15 to 25 square feet of space. If you don't have that much room, consider planting a dwarf variety. Although the tree is smaller, the fruit is the same size as that of regular trees.

Produce fruit in a warm pocket. If you live in a cool zone, don't be too quick to decide you can't grow some fruit trees and other plants suited to a warmer region. You may have pockets in sheltered areas of zone 4, for example, with conditions more like zone 5.

Grow your own citrus fruit. Citrus trees are pretty easy to sprout from seed. Best of all, you don't have to live in a hot region to grow them. But you do need to plant them in pots that can be moved inside in cold weather. That's not so hard to do with the smallest varieties, which can be grown in a pot as small as 18-inches deep.

Plant a tree for your health. Not only is the exercise good for you, some trees offer natural healing. The bark and leaves of witch hazel, for example, can provide relief when applied externally for hemorrhoids, bruises, and scratches. To make a poultice, boil 5 to 10 heaping teaspoons of finely chopped leaves in a cup of water for about 10 minutes. Cool, strain, and apply the leaves to your skin.

Enjoy trees with bark appeal. Tree trunks with texture and color add interest to the winter landscape. You might enjoy the smooth, gray bark of the flowering ash or the thin sheets that curl away from the reddish-brown trunk of the paperbark maple. Chinese elm, golden willow, paper birch, and red-twig dogwoods are other trees you should consider for their interesting bark.

Match tree size to home site. Before you plant a young tree, give some thought to its height at maturity. Will it eventually shade your property too much? Will it be an unwelcome intruder onto your neighbor's lot? Most home sites can handle trees up to 35 feet high. Dogwood, flowering crab apple, and golden raintree fall into this range. Taller trees, like oak, sycamore, ash, and maple, can overpower the landscape. In 15 to 25 years, they could grow to 60 feet in height, and their branches can spread outward up to 40 feet.

Made for the shade. In the wild, dogwoods are an understory plant, which means they grow beneath the larger trees in the woods. This makes them the perfect flowering trees for a shady yard. For an evergreen that thrives in low light, choose hemlock.

Plan carefully before planting eucalyptus. The eucalyptus tree is among the most fragrant trees, but be sure you know what's in store before you plant one. They can grow as tall as 325 feet, with the fastest growing varieties adding as much as 10 feet a year when they are young.

Move a mighty oak. Oak trees sprout easily from acorns, but not always where you want them. Like other nut trees, they have long taproots and should be moved while they are small. Fortunately, some oaks tend to grow slowly. White oaks, for example, grow about a foot a year, giving you some time to decide where you want to transplant it. But you'll have to move more quickly with a pin oak, the fastest-growing variety. It shoots up more than twice as fast.

Give pecan trees a chance. Pecan trees provide lots of shade and add to the value of your property. But if you are dreaming of pecan pies, don't delay planting. The trees take five to eight years to produce nuts.

Isolate black walnut trees. You may know about the heavy stains black walnuts can leave on your hands and clothing. But did you know black walnut trees produce a substance, called juglone, that is harmful to many plants? These trees are especially a problem for plants that love acid, like azaleas, rhododendrons, and blueberries. And put your vegetable garden with tomatoes and potatoes far from the root zone of these trees — that means at least 50 to 60 feet from the trunk.

Beware of invading tree. When planting a tree near a sidewalk or sewer, avoid the aspen. Its roots produce suckers that can cause damage.

Aggressive roots seek septic tanks. Don't plant willow, birch, aspen, and red maple trees near septic tanks. Their invasive roots can do too much damage.

Calculate your tree's critical root zone. Measure around the tree's trunk at chest height. For every inch around, walk off a foot from the tree. This is the diameter of the tree's "critical root zone." It circles all the way around and includes all of the ground inside this ring. Protect the critical root zone by not sowing, digging, or planting in this area. Just make sure you add some mulch.

Save trees from construction. When building or remodeling, take care to protect the roots as well as the trunks and branches of trees. Driving heavy machinery under and around a tree can compact the soil, making it hard for roots to take up water and oxygen. And be especially careful when digging. As a rule, more than half of a tree's roots are in the top foot of soil. Although it's difficult to know how far out the roots extend, be sure to protect them at least to the drip line.

Send damaging tree roots deeper. Your watering practice could be what's causing tree roots to do damage, like breaking up your driveway. Water less often but more thoroughly, and roots will go deeper searching for a drink, leaving the surface unbroken.

Show support for weak trees. The experts say most trees and shrubs become stronger if you don't stake them. But a tree with a weak trunk might need some extra support. Place a stake in the hole before you plant the tree, and tie the trunk to it with strips of cloth or pantyhose. These will be easy to loosen as the tree grows, and they are less likely than wire to cut into the trunk.

Protect delicate evergreen branches. The weight of winter ice and snow can be too much for the limbs of some conifers. Here's an easy way to protect them. Hold the branches upright, close to the tree, and wrap strips of fabric around them. Most of the snow and rain will slide right off.

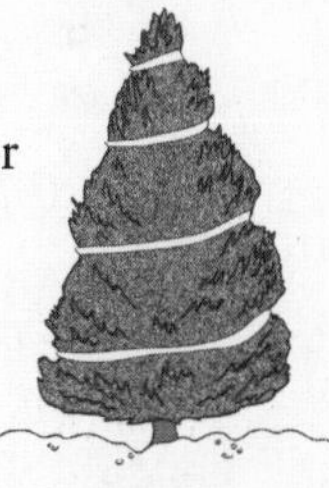

When not to wrap a tree. Old timers used to recommend wrapping a sapling's trunk to protect it from the sun and wind. But today's experts find that wraps can attract vermin, moisture, and disease. Still, if you can't give up wrapping, only do it in the winter. Remove the wrap when the dormant season ends.

Shield tender trees from your mower. A plastic drink bottle, with the top and bottom removed and slit down the side, makes a good protector for tender trees and shrubs. Before you cut the grass nearby, slip the bottle around the base of the trunk. If you bump into it, the lawn mower won't leave a mark.

Know when to call the experts. If you think a storm-damaged tree can be saved, be careful if you decide to repair the damage yourself. Use pruning shears or a saw to remove small branches. Large branches will require a chain saw. Be sure you can stand firmly on the ground and lift the saw no more than shoulder height. Otherwise, it might be best to call in a professional.

Wet and wild watering secrets

Down-to-earth way to soften hard soil. Once dirt gets hard and dry, it often resists getting wet again. Add a teaspoon of dishwashing liquid per gallon of water to overcome its resistance. The soap will break the surface tension on the soil and force it to absorb water. An easy way to do this in a large area is to fill a hose-end fertilizer applicator with soap and run the water through it as you sprinkle the lawn.

Quench thirst of reluctant peat. Potting mix usually has a large proportion of peat moss. Once dry, it seems unwilling to absorb water. To give thirsty soil an incentive to drink, add a drop or two of dishwashing liquid to your watering can. The soap will break the surface tension of the water, allowing it to penetrate and soak the dry moss.

Serve ice to sun-baked planters. Can't reach a hanging plant to water it? Drop a few ice cubes on the soil and watch them melt. They are easier to handle than a watering can. And the slow-water release will give the soil time to absorb precious droplets before they run out the drainage holes.

Save money with a disposable diaper. If you've lusted after the water-absorbing crystals advertised in the better potting mixes, you can save time and money by making your own super-absorbent mix. Just slit a clean, disposable diaper and pull out the cotton stuffing. You can shake it to remove the super-absorbent polymers, or simply mix it in with your potting soil. The same material that keeps babies' bottoms dry will swell and gel, retaining precious moisture in your soil.

Retain moisture with double potting. Unglazed terra cotta makes an ideal container for plants since it breathes, but it also loses water through evaporation. Instead of watering every day, set your medium-size potted plant in a large, decorative, plastic or ceramic planter. Fill the space between the two pots with sphagnum moss and pour water into this outer pot. The clay will absorb enough water to keep the soil damp, but it won't lose any to the outdoors.

Line pots to conserve water. Line your clay pots and moss hanging baskets with plastic before adding potting soil. This will keep water from disappearing through these porous materials. Remember to poke drainage holes in the plastic to make sure the plants don't get waterlogged.

> ! A quart of oil that accidentally spills on your driveway can contaminate up to 250,000 gallons of water if it gets down to the water table. Avoid and contain spills and use proper disposal sites for hazardous waste.

Sneaky way to lower your water bill. One of the best ways to conserve water is to keep plants in groups depending on their individual water needs. Place all the moisture hogs together and water frequently. Plants that need "well-drained soil" and "full sun" will probably appreciate a dry spot. With different watering schedules, you can provide the ideal environment for each plant to flourish — and save water doing it.

Think gray for drought resistance. Some plants advertise their resilience. Hairy, gray, and silver foliage are sure signs a plant is drought tolerant. The color is actually a reflection of the sunlight off millions of minuscule hairs that trap moisture evaporating from the leaves, and return it to the plant.

Catch every raindrop. If you have the luxury of planning the contours of your property, ask your contractor to grade your yard in a bowl shape with the slope at a slight angle. Put plants that need a lot of water in the bottom of the "bowl." Rainwater will fall and run into the basin, trapping water that would otherwise go to the storm sewer. On a smaller scale, you can create mini-basins all through your garden by building berms, or mounds of earth, around groups of plants.

Reuse indoor water for outdoor plants. When you divert water from the rinse cycle of your washing machine, or water your plants with buckets full of bath water — you are making good use of "graywater." Since this water often contains phosphorous and potassium, you can cut back on fertilizing the plants that regularly get a gray bath. Just make sure you use biologically friendly cleaners that are low phosphate or phosphate-free.

Safeguard plants from leaf burn. Soapy water doesn't have to go down the drain. You can pour it on your plants. Just be sure to periodically add some gypsum to the soil to counteract the salt in the soap. This will protect your plants from leaf burn.

> ! Use graywater as soon as possible. When it's left undisturbed, it turns slimy quickly. After 24 hours, dirty water becomes blackwater and should be sent to a sewer or septic system.

Prevent buildup when using graywater. Cycle in some fresh water when you irrigate your yard with graywater — water from the kitchen sink or washing machine that you can reuse in your garden. Every fourth or fifth time, soak the ground with clean water. This will prevent the buildup of salt, soap, and slime.

Spray away pesky spiders. Contrary to what you may have heard, watering a plant from above will not cause leaf burn. So, in addition to the soaker hose that faithfully waters your perennial bed, spray your plants occasionally to wash away spider mites and other creepy-crawlies that might attack the leaves.

Consider this before buying a hose. Don't plant a garden only to discover your hose won't reach. To check the length, tie a string to your spigot and unwind it as you walk to the farthest corner of your yard. The best way to measure the string is by folding it in half, then in half again. Measure this piece and multiply the length by the number of folds. Add 10 feet to that measurement to find the ideal length of hose to cover all your watering needs.

Buy the right size hose. The diameter of your hose makes a big difference in the time it takes to water. To drench a 1,000 square foot garden to a depth equal to 1 inch of rain at an average water pressure of 50 pounds psi will take one hour and three minutes with a half-inch diameter hose. Upgrade to a five-eighths inch diameter hose and you only have to leave it on for 37 minutes. Fastest of all, a three-quarter inch diameter hose will water the same yard in just 24 minutes.

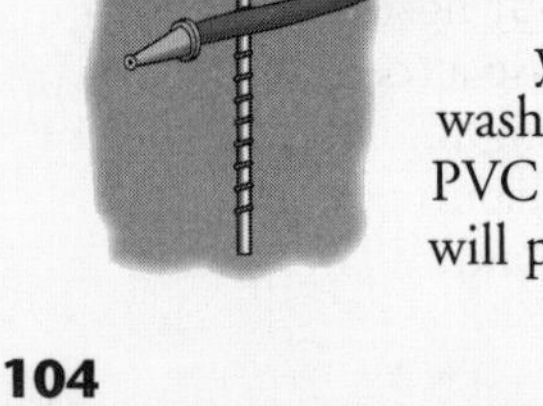

Stake a trail for your hose. Pound a pair of rebar stakes (found at home-improvement stores) into the ground along the outskirts of your bed. To keep your hose from rubbing raw, thread a large washer and then a piece of three-quarter-inch PVC or copper pipe onto the bar. The washer will prevent the pipe from digging into the dirt. Drill a half-inch hole in the bottom of a wooden finial and tap it into place above the pipe. Don't pound it on so tight that the pipe can't move freely. Snake your hose through the guards to keep from beheading your precious flowers whenever you water.

Hide the hose but keep it close. Don't let an unsightly hose spoil the beauty of your garden. Stash it away in a decorative, covered bench. Not only will this make cleanup faster, you'll have a convenient place to take off your garden clogs and store your gloves once the work is done.

> ! Just a few small leaks in a garden hose can add up to 700 gallons of wasted water in one day.

Store your hose in a tire. Constantly tripping over your hose? Give it a safe home. Paint an old tire to match your landscape and coil the offending hose inside. It should be easy to move around the garden and unwind.

Wind hose around wheel rim. Need a cheap, but effective, hose reel? If you have an old, metal wheel rim hanging around, your problem is solved. Bolt the rim to the side of your house or to a sturdy fence, and coil the hose around it. You can spray paint the rim to disguise its humble origins.

Put timers away for winter. Before the first frost hits, remove any timers you installed on faucets in your yard, and turn off spigots. Frozen water can blow timers apart, flooding your lawn in a matter of hours.

Use pressure to clean hose. Flush your hose before you roll it up for the winter, especially if you use a soaker hose or a drip system. Here's how — run a strong jet of water through the hose, turning it on and off in spurts of about a minute. Finally, take the hose end cap off and run water all the way up its length. This will loosen any mud caked in the tiny pores that could clog the hose next spring.

Kink-free solution to hose storage. To keep your hose tucked safely away, cut down a garbage can to half its height and cut a hole in the lid. Run the hose through the hole. The shape of the trash can will encourage the hose to lay in a perfect coil, where it can't kink or crack under pressure.

Patch up a holey hose. For a quick fix, cut a section of excess hose several inches long. Slit it up the side and soak it in hot water. Wrap it around the damaged section and let it cool. The rubber will shrink with the dropping temperature, effectively shrink-wrapping the hole. If the seal is not complete, squeeze some silicon sealant around the edges of the patch.

Fix a leaky hose with wax. This works great for a small hole. Just light a candle and let the melted wax drip on the hole. When the wax hardens, it will seal the hole. For extra reinforcement, wrap a strip of electrical tape over it.

Design a watering system like a pro. Choose the most water-efficient irrigation method for your outdoor space. Sprinklers are only effective on lawns. Drip systems are great for trees and shrubs that need infrequent deep watering. Soaker hoses are easy to install and ideal for plants that need water delivered directly to their roots, like vegetables and perennials. A hose or bucket is the method of choice for container gardens.

Drip hoses save gallons. While a sprinkler may spew out up to 480 gallons of water in just one hour, a 100-foot drip hose will generally only release 60 gallons an hour. On top of that, all this water goes directly where you want it — to the plants' roots.

Leave your drips on longer. Drip systems are tricky. Instead of rating their water output in gallons per minute, as you would for a normal garden hose, these slow emitters are measured in gallons per hour. Keep this in mind when calculating how much water to give your plants.

Take charge of leaks. Keep a close eye on your water meter. If it jumps even though you've been away from home, you might have a leak. Walk by your well when you are the only one home. If the pump turns on and off without provocation, you probably have a leak. Check all pipes, hoses, faucets, and connections if you find a damp or soggy patch of garden. Repair leaks promptly. Your water savings can be significant.

Prevent drowned plants. If you have trouble telling whether or not a plant needs water, try this easy pencil test. Stick the pencil in your potting soil and remove it carefully. If dirt sticks to the pencil, your plant doesn't need to be watered. If it comes up clean, it's time to give your plant a drink.

Let roots take a breath. Many houseplants prefer to sit in dry soil between waterings. It allows their roots to breathe. Don't water greenery that isn't drooping. Stick your finger in the soil to check for dryness. To rewet, fill you sink with lukewarm water and set the plant in it for half an hour. Remove the pot and let any excess water drain away. Now your roots are properly soaked.

Be in touch with your plant's needs. When you water indoor plants, be sensitive to their light conditions. Plants sunning in a well-lit window may dry out faster than those cooling their toes in a shady corner. Be careful to water only when the topsoil had dried out and the leaves show the first signs of drooping. Otherwise, your houseplant's roots may rot.

Prevent runoff with watering plan. Water too much, too fast, and you will flood clay beds. Instead, turn on a sprinkler and time how long it takes for water to pool on the ground. Turn the water off, and time how long it takes to soak in. Now, set the sprinkler timer to water for short bursts of time, resting between them for the time it takes the water to soak in. Watering in four short bursts of five minutes every half hour can save you a lot of water that would run off if you watered your yard continuously for 20 minutes.

Simple ways to cut water bill. Does half your water bill go toward keeping your lawn healthy? Cut your lawn in half, and your bill will shrink accordingly. This spring, expand your garden beds by spreading mulch over the lawn and planting through it. Set garden paths between the beds and leave only a patch of grass. Native plants need far less water than a lawn, and once established, they can be left to fend for themselves during a dry spell.

Water early to save money. Water your garden in the predawn hours. Since there is little evaporation at this time of day, you'll use about 50 percent less water. And unlike evening watering, early hour drenching poses little risk of fungal diseases. The fungi won't have enough time to grow in the wet soil before the sun warms them out of existence.

Arm yourself with a rain gauge. This handy tool can help you keep track of how much water your garden really gets. If you have an automatic sprinkler system, show family members how to turn it off on rainy days.

Water less for a healthier lawn. Grass that is overwatered might have lush, green growth, but the roots are often spindly and shallow. At the first sign of drought, this grass will look parched. Established lawns only need about an inch of water, applied slowly, every week. Water more and you do your grass, and your water bill, a disservice.

Choose fescue over bluegrass. If grass is a must, be sure to select one with modest water needs. Seed or lay sod in the fall when roots grow strong and water is plentiful. Though green growth may be slow, by summer your lawn should be well-established and need watering less often.

Let your lawn go dormant. Many popular grasses, like fescue and bluegrass, can go dormant during the hot summer months. Check to make sure your grass type can handle it, then let your lawn go brown. See if it doesn't perk up again when the rains return.

Stop watering on windy days. Wind can cause up to 300 gallons of water to evaporate from your lawn. To save money and time, you're better off waiting for a calmer day to water.

Retain moisture by keeping grass long. To keep your lawn from becoming a water hog, set your lawnmower blade a notch higher — 3 inches is ideal. Long grass keeps the ground shaded and water loss at a minimum, and longer grass doesn't need as much water to recover.

Give thought to hardy ground covers. The top of a slope is a precarious place for a lawn. Not only does water run away from grass roots, but irrigation and heavy traffic can erode the soil and leave your coverage spotty, at best. Replace your turf with a drought-tolerant ground cover, like sedum, woolly thyme, or creeping Jenny.

Feeding lawns makes them thirsty. Fertilizing your lawn every second Sunday may be the reason it's so green — or it may be all that extra water you have to splash on fertilized ground. To make better use of your resources, add a slow release, water-soluble plant food only once a year, when you aerate. You might be surprised how much water you save.

Save pruning for wet season. Here's a warning from experts at the University of Georgia — if rain clouds haven't crossed your sky in a while, leave the pruning shears in the shed. Once a plant is pruned, it goes into a growth spurt and needs a lot more water than usual. It's best to wait until a plant is fully dormant in the winter. Even then, prune as little as possible. This will keep your plant strong until the rains return.

Take advantage of roof's bounty. You'd be surprised how much water your roof captures. One inch of rain can yield up to 625 gallons of water running off a 1,000-square-foot roof. That's enough to fill a dozen 50-gallon rain barrels.

Find best location for barrels. Installing rain barrels is an obvious way to save water, but finding the best location for them is not so obvious. Go outside during a rainstorm and watch the water run off your roof. If some of your downspouts pour rainwater into your yard, divert the water to your plants. But if a downspout just dumps water on your driveway, install a barrel under this spout.

Turn out the light on algae. If you're installing a large barrel to collect rainwater, buy a dark plastic barrel and set it up in a shady spot. Darkness will keep algae that breed in standing water under control.

Build your own water tower. Keep your rain barrel a cut above the rest — elevate it on a sturdy platform 3 to 4 feet above the ground. Now all you have to do is attach your soaker hose to the faucet, and let gravity do the work for you.

Clever way to collect more rainwater. A half inch of rain falling on your roof will fill a 50-gallon barrel. If you set up a row of barrels, you can collect many times that. Drill a hole near the top of your first barrel and run a hose through it. Drill a hole at the top of the second and connect the two with a short stretch of hose. Connect other barrels similarly in a series. With a system like this, you should be able to irrigate an entire garden for most of the summer with the rainwater you save.

Collect water in a relish container. Rain barrels don't have to be expensive to work well. In fact, a cheap and popular solution is to reuse 55-gallon, food-quality containers, the kind that hold pickle relish and other condiments. Contact a hospital or school cafeteria and see if they will donate a few containers. Just be sure to rinse the barrel well before using.

Make your own rain barrel. Buy a large, plastic trash can with a fitted lid. Elevate it on a stack of bricks so it reaches the downspout. Cut a hole in the lid the same size as your downspout and fit the two together. Drill a hole near the base of the trash can, high enough to fit a bucket underneath. Thread a water spigot through the hole from the outside and attach it with a gasket. Now, when rain fills your barrel, you can attach a hose to the spigot and water your plants.

Keep rainwater clean with pantyhose. If your downspout ends in a rain barrel, try this neat trick to keep the water clean. Cover the end of the downspout with the toe from an old pair of pantyhose or cut a piece of wire mesh to fit over the opening of the pipe. After every major storm, change the pantyhose filter or remove the screen and clean out the leaves.

Handy use for a colander. For a simple sieve to keep leaves out of your rain barrel, follow the advice of the experts at the Chesapeake Bay Foundation. They suggest you use a cheap, plastic colander instead of a screen. Simply cut a hole in the top of your barrel that fits the diameter of the colander. Squeeze some silicone sealant around the edges and fit the colander in tightly. Be sure to check it regularly to keep leaves from blocking the holes.

Give mosquitos the slip. To keep your rain barrel free of mosquitos, pour some cooking oil on the surface of the water. The oil will keep mosquito larvae from hatching and keep adult mosquito populations under control. Since the barrel is rarely emptied during the rainy season, you will only have to do this once a year.

Stop overwatering your garden. Before you turn on your sprinklers, check your rain gauge. If an inch of rain has fallen since the last time you watered, you can skip this cycle all together. If less than an inch sits in the cup, shorten your watering cycle to give your garden only an inch of water.

Measure rain faithfully. To make your own rain gauge, mark a straight-sided water glass in one-inch increments and set it on a post or platform right next to your outside water faucet — where you'll see it. Make sure it's out in the open, not under a tree. Be diligent to empty it every time you water.

Recycle milk with the carton. Before you throw empty milk cartons in the recycling bin, fill them halfway with tap water and swish it around. This milky water makes a nutritious drink for alkaline-loving houseplants and container plants. African violets, especially, enjoy this dairy treat.

Feed plants dinner leftovers. After boiling eggs or steaming vegetables, let the water cool. Then use this nutrient-rich cocktail to water your indoor and outdoor container plants.

Treat plants to aquarium water. The water you empty out of your aquarium is rich in nitrogen and phosphorous, minerals plants crave. Once you have removed your fish, siphon the water into a bucket and lavish it on your outdoor plants.

Water-savvy car wash. No need to waste water when you give your car a bath. Drive it on your lawn to wash it so the runoff can water the grass. Use simple soaps, like dishwasher liquid, which grass can easily neutralize, and move it before you wax.

Recycle pool water. If you need to empty your pool, don't waste the water. Give your lawn and garden a well-deserved drink. Many experts say the chlorine won't hurt plants. Sheldon Hammond, with the Fayette County Extension Office in Fayetteville, Ga., says plants actually enjoy the nutrient boost. Just to be on the safe side, let highly chlorinated pools sit, uncovered, for a day or two so chemical levels can drop. Then use the back-flush pipe to water your plants.

Say "no" to back flush. Screw on a back flow preventer — available at hardware stores — to all soaker and sprinkler lines that run off your potable water lines. These little switches make sure dirty water backed up in the pipe won't pollute your tap water. Double check it every now and then to make sure the little arrow on the valve points away from your house and toward your garden.

New life for a holey hose. Transform a leaky garden hose into a multipurpose soaker hose. Simply puncture the underside of the hose at regular intervals with a hot ice pick. Lay it, pinpricks down, in your garden bed between the plants. Attach one end to your new hose. Plug the other end with a plastic end cap. Cover your soaker hose with mulch and turn the tap on. Water should drip out of the small holes and thoroughly soak your flower beds.

Send your soakers undercover. Sink soaker hoses deep if you install them underground — 6 inches is best. When you add organic matter and till your garden in the spring, the rototiller blades won't nick the pipe and cause a geyser in your backyard.

Soaker hose trick. If your beds border a sidewalk or pavement, install your soaker hose several inches away from the edge. The pavement heats the ground around it, stopping the spread of water. Laying your hose any closer will be a waste of water.

Choose the best sprinkler. A sprinkler that emits water droplets is better than one that produces a fine mist. Large drops don't evaporate easily, so they are more likely to make it to your plant's roots. A mist can float over your plants and evaporate.

Catch fog droplets. In the dry, coastal areas of Chile and Peru, the natives harvest water from fog with a series of nets. Where misty mornings are the norm, you can try this, too. Tightly stretch a fine nylon net between two poles on a slope facing the wind. Use a brightly colored net so birds will see it and not get caught. Plant low-growing plants or lay an old piece of gutter under the net. Condensation will collect on the screen and run off into the gutter where it can be diverted to your flower bed or a holding tank.

Direct rainwater where it's needed. Just dig a trench, about a foot deep, around the beds closest to your house and line it with gravel. Cut a length of 4-inch pipe long enough to reach from the downspout to your trench. In the trench, lay down a slotted or punctured pipe, covering it with dirt. Attach the downspout extension to your slotted pipe and voila — you have a simple, but effective, watering system. The rain from your roof will run down the spout, through the extension, and out the slotted pipe into your beds.

Add a slow-release reservoir. Punch some holes in an empty coffee can and "plant" it along with your tomato seedling. Or cut off the bottom of a soda bottle and punch holes in the cap, setting it upside down next to the roots. Fill your container with water every few days, and let the plant grow around it. Water will slowly penetrate the root zone and keep this moisture-loving nightshade happy.

Try the perfect slow-release system. The Peace Corps encourages farmers in South America to plant pots with their crops. Unglazed terra-cotta pots, especially those with no drainage holes, will "sweat" water to plant roots around them. Try it yourself! Next time you plant vegetables, dig a hole about 20 percent larger than your pot, fill the hole part way with manure, then sink the pot up to its neck in the center and fill it with water. Plant around it. Depending on how fast the water leaches out, it should provide a steady supply of fertilized water to established plants.

Utilize air conditioner runoff. Drip, drip, drip. This slow water torture from draining window units can get under your skin. Harness this power and run a drain line from your air conditioner to a water hungry plant nearby. Impatiens, especially, seem to like the constant moisture and may bloom even in harsh sunlight.

Easy and cheap soaker wands. If you want something a little sturdier than a rubber soaker hose, make some simple, slow-release water wands. Cut one-half inch PVC pipes to fit your beds and draw a straight line down the length of each one. Drill holes every few inches along the line. Fit one end of each rod with a female hose adapter and plug up the other end. When it's time to water, simply attach the hose to the wand and turn it on low pressure. Once one row is done, move on to the next wand.

Save water with a rain chain. Melting ice-cream tends to race down your arm before you can catch it with a napkin. Use this natural motion of liquid to your advantage. Suspend a smooth, sleek, rope or chain from your roof and direct it to your favorite plant. Water that falls on the roof will race down the rope to water the plant. The Japanese refined this idea and invented complex and beautiful chains that hang off their cornices — some that are still in use today.

Know when to stop watering. Scatter empty tuna cans on your lawn and turn the water on. Since these cans are generally an inch high, this is an easy way to see how quickly your sprinkler dumps the required inch of water on your grass. Install a timer and set it to water just until the tins are full.

Impatiens signal when it's time to water. Impatiens can brighten up your yard, but they are also especially useful as watering indicators. These drought-sensitive bloomers droop visibly when thirsty, a good indicator your garden needs watering. You can plant coleus in your vegetable garden for the same effect.

Match watering style to soil. Your soil will tell you how often you need to water. Sandy soil absorbs water easily, but lets it go just as fast. Water it often but in small amounts. Clay soil takes longer to soak up water, but holds on to it. Water it less frequently, but more deeply.

Best way to water on a slope. If your garden is set on a slope, you might have to adjust your watering schedule. Most water will follow gravity straight down a hill, leaving the plants at the top high and dry. Water more frequently and less deeply to keep these mountain huggers happy.

Water only when necessary. You can get away with watering far less if you know when a plant's critical watering periods are. Newly set-in plants need frequent watering, but once established, most flowering shrubs need water only when their blooms are about to burst.

Fruiting plants and vegetables need plenty of water to grow roots, and again when they set fruit. Otherwise, they can live with less.

> ! Keep tender shoots well-watered. A fine mist sprayer works best. If you let their thin, hair-like roots shrivel up, you won't be able to bring them back to life.

Be kind to trees during a drought. Trees may not seem to need much water, but during a drought, lack of water can kill even the most established trees. If you haven't had much rain in the past two weeks, set a running hose within the root zones of your trees and shrubs and water deeply.

Let trees and shrubs breathe. Be careful not to overdo it when you water trees and shrubs. Plant roots need oxygen as well as water, and if the ground around the roots is saturated, the tree will suffocate. Make sure the ground dries out before you water again.

Effortless way to water a tree. There's no need to stand around with a hose watering your tree. To conserve water and give it a good, long soak, set a series of gallon jugs with holes punched in the bottom around the drip line of the tree. Fill these with water and let it seep slowly into the ground — where water hungry roots can drink it up before it drips down to the water table.

Build a moat to hold water. Trees need a lot of water while they get established. To keep water near their roots, build a moat around the base of your tree. The larger the root base, the larger the moat. Turn a hose on low and set it in the basin for a thorough soak. As the tree grows, make sure the moat does, too. Otherwise, the roots will stay in the wet spot, and the tree could get top heavy and topple.

Direct water to tree's roots. Drill holes along a length of PVC pipe, then slip it in with the root ball when you plant your tree. Set the pipe at an angle and backfill the hole so one end of the pipe is above ground. Once you're done planting, fill the pipe with gravel. Now, when your tree needs a drink, you can send water directly to the roots.

Never come home to dead plants again. The next time you take a trip, use this ingenious tip — fill a bucket with water and set it on a tall stool near your houseplants. Anchor one end of a long strip of half-inch cotton rope in the bucket and coil the other end around the base of a plant. If you have more than one, group them around the bucket on a piece of plastic and run a wick from the bucket to each plant. Gravity will slowly water your houseplants for you, and they'll still be lush and green when you return.

Streamline vacation watering. Before you leave home for a week, water your container plants well, then clump those that love water in a cheap, plastic kiddie pool. Fill it with an inch of water. While you're gone, your plants should thrive.

Watch out for dehydrated vines. If you're hiding an ugly fence behind a beautiful screen of vines, you'd better keep them well-watered during dry, hot weather. Wind buffeting the leaves speeds up water loss, and they can soon look bedraggled. A soaker hose might be your best solution.

Get some watering insight. Here's a simple way to tell when your plants need water. Grab a handful of dirt and squeeze it. If it doesn't hold its shape, get out the hose.

Water where it matters. Every drop counts in a drought, so make sure you're watering the neediest plants first. At the top of your list should be hanging pots and porch containers, which need water every day. Expensive, rare, or mature trees and shrubs are next, with vegetables that are forming fruit and perennial beds right behind them. Low on the list should be annuals that are easily replaced and lawns that can tough it out.

Heed the cry of dying grass. Instead of automatically watering your lawn during the dry summer months, wait until it starts showing signs of distress. Common warnings are blades that curl at the tips, leaves that turn bluish green or become dull, and grass that doesn't spring back into place when you step on it. Now you know it's time to turn on the sprinkler.

Win the war on weeds

Boil water to foil weeds. Enough with expensive weedkillers. Choke off these pests with a no-cost solution. Pour boiling water on weeds growing in the cracks of your cement or flagstone walks. It will kill the existing weeds, as well as the seeds waiting to grow.

Terrific, nontoxic weedkiller Household vinegar makes a great — and safe — natural weedkiller. Just pour it full strength into a spray bottle, and use it directly on the leaves and roots of dandelions, bermuda grass, foxtail, thistle, velvetleaf, and other bothersome plants. Heat the vinegar to give it added punch. You might need to spray hardy weeds more than once, but if you keep at it, you could wipe them out for good. Be careful not to spray plants you want to keep.

Household products send weeds packing. Make your neighbors green with envy and save money, too. Mix together vinegar and salt, pour in a spray bottle, and spray directly on weeds. Just don't catch your flowering favorites in the crossfire. Avoid spraying it on weedy sidewalks since it can corrode the concrete.

Put an end to poison ivy. Kill poison ivy without expensive, toxic chemicals. Pour 3 pounds of salt into a gallon of soapy water, stir, and spray it on the leaves and stems.

Make a killer herbicide with alcohol. This homemade spray puts weeds down for the count. Combine 1 tablespoon of rubbing alcohol with 1 quart of water, pour into a spray bottle, and douse weed leaves. For tougher plants, add more alcohol — up to 5 tablespoons.

Give weeds a gin bath. Knock 'em dead with this powerful recipe. Add an ounce of gin, an ounce of vinegar, and a squirt of baby shampoo into a spray bottle full of water, then give weeds a good bath.

> ! Protect yourself while pouring hot water on weeds. Wear closed-toe shoes, long pants, and pour the water from a height of just a few inches to keep it from splashing.

Beware of hazardous weed-killers. Never use gasoline, motor oil, or kerosene as an herbicide. They may kill weeds, but they stay in the ground for years and can even leach into drinking water. One gallon of oil alone can pollute a million gallons of water. Pour them on the ground, and you could poison more than your weeds — you might poison yourself as well.

Stamp out weeds with salt. Rock salt isn't just for ice cream anymore. Sprinkle it in cracks and crevices for instant weed relief. It sterilizes the soil, so keep it away from beloved plants and areas you plan to grow in later.

Crabgrass finally meets its match. Chalk up one more use for baking soda. Sprinkle it directly on crabgrass, but avoid getting it on the surrounding lawn. This solution seems to work best in warm climates where warm-weather grasses, like St. Augustine, Bermuda, and Bahiagrass, flourish. Baking soda may not work as well on crabgrass in colder climates. In fact, it could harm cold-weather grasses. Test it on a small, hidden spot in your yard before going gung-ho. You may have to apply it more than once to kill a patch of crabgrass entirely.

Protect pets with safe weedkiller. People with pets will love this nontoxic weedkiller. Mix together 1 gallon of household vinegar, 1 cup of orange oil, and 1 teaspoon of a mild liquid soap. Spray weeds as needed to control unwanted plants while preserving the environment.

Wash weeds with soap. Clean out weeds with regular dishwashing liquid. Just mix 5 tablespoons of soap with 1 quart of water, then spray weed leaves liberally on a hot day.

> ! Bleach effectively banishes weeds, but think twice before using it. Some experts warn that it will kill all the other organisms, good and bad, it comes into contact with.

Give weeds a sip of soda. Need another use for flat soda? Try pouring straight Coca-Cola on the weeds in your sidewalks. This sticky soda can knock 'em dead.

Stick it to weeds. Give homemade herbicides a boost with your own "spreader sticker." Adding a little soap or a store-bought spreader sticker to certain herbicides may increase their effectiveness. These products help the chemical spread over and stick to leaves. Read all the instructions on an herbicide first, and be extremely careful when mixing chemicals. Try your new blend on a small area to make sure it works.

Save time with portable sprayer. Pour your homemade weedkiller in a portable spray bottle and carry it with you as you work in the garden. Label the bottle clearly so you don't mistake an herbicide for a fertilizer and accidentally spray your prized plants.

Rescue plants from accidental poisoning. Catching your ornamentals in the herbicide crossfire doesn't have to mean certain death. Water them immediately, no more than three to four hours after spraying them, to wash off the poison and dilute it in the ground. The longer you wait, the worse their chance for recovery.

Bag plants before spraying weeds. Having more weeds than good plants makes spraying them simpler. Cover plants you want to keep with a plastic grocery bag, then treat surrounding weeds with an herbicide. Unbag your lovelies once the spray has dried.

Target weeds with killer technique. Spray individual weeds without catching your favorite plants in the crossfire. Cut off the bottom of a plastic 2-liter soda bottle. Set the bottle over the trouble-making weed, stick the sprayer nozzle in the mouth of the soda bottle, and spray away. Let the chemicals soak in for a few seconds before lifting the bottle.

Shield plants from herbicide drift. Protect your plants the lazy way. Shield them with a piece of heavy cardboard. Lean it in front of beloved plants to protect them from drift as you spray nearby weeds. Move the cardboard with you as you go. Be sure to face the same side outward each time. You don't want the side covered in weedkiller rubbing elbows with your darling dahlias.

Use a box to aim weedkiller. Blast those weed clumps taking up space in your yard. Open the bottom of a cardboard box, stand the box around the weeds, then spray away. The cardboard forms a protective barrier between the herbicide and your desirable plants. Have more weeds than lawn? Then set boxes around grassy patches and good plants to seal them off as you spray weeds.

Easy way to K.O. large weeds. Show big weeds who's boss. Cut them back to the ground, and wait for them to sprout again. As soon as you see signs of new foliage, nail them with weedkiller.

4 easy steps to a weed-free lawn. A lush, green lawn never came so easily. First, spray on a pre-emergent herbicide in the spring to stunt weeds before they grow. In the summer, try a different herbicide on weeds that survived your first attack, or pull them out by hand. Apply a last layer of general weedkiller in the fall. Finally, pull up the few weeds still remaining by hand.

Let new grass get a firm foothold. Hold off spraying weedkiller on newly seeded lawn for at least six months. Even if you simply laid new turf, wait until it gets well-established and growing strong before applying an herbicide.

> ! Practice safety when applying herbicides. Wear clothing that completely covers your body, wash your hands thoroughly after handling chemicals, and don't eat or drink while spraying.

Action plan for using weedkillers. Alternate your herbicides to get the most complete weed control. Many herbicides only kill certain kinds of weeds. You may wipe out one type, only to have another weed move in and take over. Switch sprays, especially if you plan to treat your yard more than once in a season.

Check weather before spraying. Apply herbicides on dry, calm, warm days unless the directions say otherwise. Never spray weeds on a windy day. Avoid using weedkillers on hot days or right before rain. Read the herbicide bottle for more specific instructions to make the most of your time and money.

Stomp weeds before spraying them. Herbicides have a hard time penetrating waxy-looking leaves. Boost the power of your weedkiller by crushing these leaves beforehand. Do a victory dance on them, or simply smash them with a shovel. The crushed leaves absorb herbicide better, and you'll have a blast working out your weed rage.

! Always follow the manufacturer's instructions when using an herbicide. Mixing it too strong can harm your lawn and other desirable plants and even prevent it from working at all.

Poison weeds while they are growing. Herbicides work best when weeds are putting out new growth. Schedule your spraying during the growing seasons for best results. Avoid the hottest, driest months since grass and other desirable plants are most vulnerable then to damage from weedkiller.

Rub out weeds in dense gardens. Don a rubber glove, one without holes in it, then pull an old fabric glove over the rubber one. Dip your double-gloved hand in herbicide and wipe it onto the weeds in closely planted beds.

Make a disposable applicator for weedkiller. Wrap a rag around a stick, dip it into the herbicide, and carefully dab it on weed leaves. Just be certain you apply it to the right plants. As always, wear protective clothing and gloves when applying chemicals, such as weedkillers.

Paint away unwanted plants. Add an artistic flare to your fight against weeds. Dip an old paintbrush in weedkiller, and paint the chemical onto weeds nestled amidst precious plants. Then again, don't use the same brush to paint your next masterpiece. Dedicate it to weeding instead.

Mow weeds more often. Mow regularly, especially during peak growing times. You'll have a tidier lawn and catch flowering weeds before they set seed. But don't scalp your grass. Mow high, instead. Longer grass blades shade the ground and stop weeds from sprouting.

Know when to mow 'em. Let weeds grow for two or three days after mowing before you spray them with weed-killer. It will enable them to absorb the chemicals better. Then wait a few days after spraying before you mow again.

Mow down low-growing weeds. Some sneaky weeds lie close to the ground, ducking under your lawnmower blades. Fluff up these lowlifes with a pitchfork or rake before you mow. The taller they stand, the faster they fall.

Guard against trunk damage. Save yourself the heartache of damaging saplings and shrubs when you're whacking weeds or mowing. Cut off the bottom and top of a plastic bottle, and slit it up the side. Wrap it around the base of young trunks while you are working in the area, and slip it off when you're done.

Aerate soil to root out weeds. Aerate high-traffic areas where soil tends to compact, like around sidewalks and pavement. Weeds thrive in this tough dirt, whereas grasses won't dare grow there. Make a point of aerating these areas, or plant a ground cover, like clover, to do the job for you.

Grow a thicker lawn. Go crazy with grass. Put the crunch on weeds by reseeding existing grass in the spring. Aerate the soil, sprinkle on some seed, and water. The thick turf will compete with weedy visitors and leave you with a lush lawn.

Plug lawn holes with peat. If pulling up weeds leaves holes in your yard, fill in the gaps with a little peat moss. Reseed, and you'll have a lush lawn in no time.

Water soil to weed with ease. Let nature make your job easier. Wait until after a good rain to weed, or wet the ground yourself. You'll have less trouble pulling plants out of damp soil.

Set out buckets for easy weeding. Take some of the hassle out of weeding. Hide old containers around your plant beds within easy reach. Each time you walk into your garden, pull a few weeds and drop them in the bucket.

Slow and steady wins weed battle. Don't try to weed all at once. Spread it out to make it more manageable. Pull a few plants each morning or evening, or set small goals, like weeding the garden a foot at a time. Tackle these pests early in the season, and you'll have less work later on.

Make weeding fun. Let young grandchildren gather your weeds. Make a game of it, or pay them a penny per pull. Dandelions are perennial favorites with children. Ask your grand kids to pick a yellow bouquet for you before the weeds go to seed. You'll have fresh color in your house, fewer unwanted plants in your yard, and a wonderful time with children.

Do away with weeds while you're away. Make sure your yard looks as pretty when you return from vacation as it did when you left. Ask a neighbor or friend to stop by and weed for you while you're gone, and offer to return the favor.

Wait to water after weeding Let any weeds you left on the ground dry out in the sun first. You don't want the plants you just pulled coming back to life in your freshly watered garden.

Master the grab-and-pull method. Grab weeds near the base, and get your fist around as many stems as you can hold. Pull the plant up slowly, so you don't break off the roots or stem. Hardy perennial weeds can grow back from a broken piece of root left in the ground.

Separate plant roots from weeds. Take care when pulling up large weeds in your perennial beds. The roots may have intertwined with those of your prized plants. If that's the case, pulling out the weed could damage or uproot the plants around it. Break this choke hold by digging up both the weed and the plant at the start of spring and gently separate the root systems. Try to remove all of the weed root, then replant your perennial.

Pull a pest, sow a plant. Combine fresh planting with early weed pulling. Yank a weed and drop a new plant in its place. Pulling out the weed breaks up the soil and leaves a ready-made hole just the right size for a new plant.

Get to the root of weed problems. When digging up perennial weeds, get the whole root. Each piece of root you leave in the ground can grow into a new plant. Save yourself a headache later by getting all of it the first time. Otherwise, you may have to dig up the same pest again in a few weeks.

Weed store-bought plants. Planting just a few weed seedlings hiding in a store-bought plant opens the door for a full-fledged weed invasion. Pull the weeds in container plants before giving them a home in your garden, and you will solve this problem before it crops up.

Continue after harvest to stop seeding. You've been weeding all summer, and you never want to see another hoe. Don't give up yet! Weed once more after harvest. Like all other plants, weeds want to set seed before the cold settles in. Catch them before they complete their mission, or you'll have a planting bed full of them again next season.

Give your back a break. Save your back later with good gardening technique now. Never bend over at the waist to weed. Squat low, letting your knees and thighs do the work.

Garden without pain. Lend your body a helping hand. Wear knee pads while weeding to protect achy joints. A back brace and a sturdy walking stick are also worthy investments.

Pull tough plants with pliers. Take a hint from your dentist. When persistent weeds won't come out by hand, get your pliers and go to work. This tool can help you get a grip on the worst weeds.

Tweeze your weeds. Eyebrow tweezers serve double duty. They make perfect tools for plucking tiny weeds and are handy for getting hard-to-reach weeds in small places.

Dig up deeply rooted weeds. An old, serrated apple corer can help you win the weed war. It digs down deep and cuts the roots at the same time, and it's little enough to reach small spaces.

Nail weeds with a handy tool. Hammers have a new purpose. Dig the clawed end of a hammer into the soil, grab the weed at the base, and pull out the plant like you would a nail.

Fork over weeds. Dig into those uninvited garden guests with an old, but sturdy, fork. The tines make great grippers for pulling up pesky weeds.

Cheap tool helps weeds disappear. Invest in a dandelion digger, also called an asparagus knife, for pulling weeds with long taproots. Slip the pronged end under the weed and pop it out of the ground. No fuss, no muss, and no damage to your grass.

Dig out weeds with a screwdriver. Forget expensive specialty tools. Go after weeds with an old screwdriver. The small, flat blade is perfect for prying weeds out of cracks in driveways and between paving stones. It's also great for loosening tough weed roots before pulling them out by hand.

High-tech pruners cut plants to the quick. Invest in a pair of clippers that automatically dispenses herbicide onto its blades when you squeeze them. The blades then wipe weedkiller on the open cut of a stem, sending the poison straight into the plant. Sound too fancy? Dip your regular weed clippers in herbicide each time you make a cut. Wash them well with soap and water afterward to avoid accidentally poisoning other plants.

Compost weeds wisely. Composting returns valuable nutrients to the soil, but be careful about tossing weeds on that pile. Only compost weed roots and seed heads if your compost pile gets hot enough to kill them, about 160 degrees. Make sure it heats evenly, too. Weeds could hide and survive in cool spots within the compost heap.

Toss weeds in your salad. Dandelions, chickweed, lamb's quarters, purslane — you may not want them in your garden, but they can add taste at your dinner table. Check a wildflower field guide to find out which weeds are edible, and what they look like. Then eat away at unsightly weeds.

Water plants with weed tea. Put those weeds to work. Place the roots of bothersome plants in a gallon jar of water. Put a lid on it, and let it ferment for up to a month. Strain the mixture and use it to water your vegetables and return nutrients to the soil.

Rent a goat to clear out weeds. Farmers use the most organic weed control in the world — animals. Chickens and cattle nibble weeds while supplying manure. Some geese, called weeder geese, have been raised to turn overgrown land into a fast snack. You can even rent goats to clear a large weedy area. Consider creative alternatives, and find out what living weed-eaters are available near you.

Bugs battle invasive plants. Biological control is the use of natural predators to keep weeds in check. It can certainly work, but you need to know which bugs to buy before you set them free in your backyard. Contact your local extension service to find out what biological controls they recommend, or visit www.invasivespecies.gov, a government Web site with information on state and federal programs for controlling aggressive weeds.

Copper nails kill woody weeds. Nail weeds where it hurts. Try driving copper nails into the stems and trunks of woody weeds. You may not kill the whole plant at first, but old-timers swear by this uncommon remedy.

Cook weeds with a flamer. Flame your weeds, but don't set them on fire. Gas torches called weed flamers heat the sap inside plant cells, causing them to burst and eventually die. Heat weeds for two to three seconds as you walk slowly by with your flamer. The plants may not look singed, but rest assured you've read these weeds their last rights. Within a day or so, you'll have the satisfaction of watching them die.

Remember fire safety when flaming. Fire and drought don't mix. Avoid flaming during dry spells or in otherwise fire-prone areas. Some mulches can catch fire, too, so stick to flaming weeds in cleared, open areas with plenty of room between the weeds and the plants you are cultivating.

Young weeds burn best. Flaming works to control both annual and perennial weeds, but for the best results, flame plants when they're young and most vulnerable. It takes less time, less fuel, and less aggravation.

Stop weeds naturally. Spread corn gluten meal on bare ground wherever you want to keep problem plants, like crabgrass, dandelions, and purslane from popping up. Check your local nursery and garden supply store for this nontoxic product.

Nix weeds with newspapers. Weeds won't grow where the sun won't shine. Old newspapers provide a natural sun block that keeps your garden weed free but still lets water through to your plants. Simply spread several layers of paper in your garden, and weigh them down with stones or mulch. Cut slits in them when you're ready to plant. Eventually the paper will break down and add organic matter to your soil.

Protect fallow gardens from eager weeds. Lay overlapping pieces of cardboard on unused beds, cover with 3 or more inches of bark, and let the bed rest during winter. The cardboard should turn to rich mulch come spring, and you'll have a weed-free, well-rested garden.

Mulched beds lay weeds to rest. Lay a thick blanket of mulch to keep weeds from sprouting. A layer of grass clippings, bark, straw, leaves, or other natural material blocks sunlight and air weeds need to grow. Plus, mulches return rich nutrients to the soil as they decay, so they feed your plants while protecting them from competing weeds.

Look for weed-free products. Know what you are getting — or getting into. Buy only certified weed-free seeds and mulches from reputable gardening stores. Overseeding your lawn or laying a thick mulch won't help a bit if the answer to your weed problem is full of weed seeds.

Choke off weeds with plastic. Prepare the bed just before growing season by clearing it of weeds and leveling it. Put down a layer of heavy, black plastic and poke holes in it for water to drain through. Weigh down the edges with stones, or simply add a layer of mulch on top. The plastic will block sunlight from struggling weeds, while warming the ground for the growing season.

Kill weeds with sunshine. Till a new bed when summer is at its peak, then mix in your usual composting materials. Water your plot and cover the ground with a clear plastic sheet for several weeks. The sunlight and water will coax weed seeds into sprouting, but the plastic will trap the heat and bake them while they are still young and vulnerable. Be warned that in colder climates the plastic may not trap enough heat to bake weeds. Instead, it may stay just warm enough for them to thrive.

> ! Leaving black plastic down for more than a few months deprives the soil of air and water, so pull it up at the end of the season.

Proven alternative to black plastic. Landscape fabrics can succeed where plastics and mulch fail by suppressing weeds without damaging soil structure. These fabrics let water and air pass through to the ground, while barring weeds from sunlight. Unlike black plastic, landscape fabric can stay down for more than one season. Cover it with a little mulch to beautify the area, and you have a low-maintenance weed control system.

Avoid this mistake. Limit the mulch you pile on landscape fabric to about 1 inch. More than that, and you create a comfy bed for weeds to take root in. These problem plants can actually sprout in deep mulch and root to the fabric, damaging it when you pull the weeds out.

Roll out the red carpet. Or beige, or blue, or brown. Cut left over carpet into long runners and lay them between the rows of your garden. The carpet will keep weeds from sprouting, and the cushioning could make kneeling easier on your joints. Choose carpet without foam backing.

Otherwise, you'll find yourself "weeding" bits of plastic out of your garden for years to come.

Stall them with a quick fix. Weeds keep growing whether you have time to pull them or not. Buy yourself a break by hiding them. Plunk a birdbath, brick, or even a piece of wood right on top of them until you have time to deal with them for good. Meanwhile, you'll deprive them of light and the ability to run rampant over your yard.

Block invading weeds. Seal off garden plots with a thick layer of heavy-duty plastic edging. Bury it along the perimeter of your garden, leaving the plastic top poking up slightly above the ground. It forms a wall around precious plants that weeds just can't climb.

Keep an eye on the edges. Guard against garden invaders by paying close attention to the edges of your beds. Unwatched perimeters can let in encroaching weeds or let out sprawling plants. Lay mulch along bed edges, or fence weeds out with stones, wood, and other hurdles.

Shady way to discourage weeds. Let your shrubs and trees develop a wide canopy instead of trimming them back extensively. The shade they create acts as a natural weed barrier, blocking the sunlight these unwanted plants need to thrive.

Pave garden paths with sawdust. No more walking on weeds! Dig up your garden walkways several inches deep, then fill them in with a thick layer of sawdust. This material acts as a natural herbicide by tying up the nitrogen in soil so weeds can't grow. For this same reason, don't use it around plant beds.

Bar weeds with a heavy barrier. Lay several sheets of heavy, nonasphalt roofing paper on paths, then cover them with stones, tile, or other paving material. Unwanted plants can't break through this thick barrier, so you'll never have to weed your walkways again.

Outsmart weeds in stone walkways. Why fight plants between paving stones? Plant them there, instead. Low-growing herbs, like thyme and chamomile, thrive in stone pathways, acting as a delicious-smelling carpet that crowds out undesirable weeds.

Design a weed-proof walkway. Put down a liner, such as landscape fabric, then pour 2 inches of sand on top of that. Lay your stones and fill in the space between with more sand to keep weeds from cropping up.

Crowd out weeds with cover crops

Cover plants add lush greenery and color to any landscape, as well as smother uninvited plants. Ground covers compete with greedy weeds for sunlight and water. Some even produce natural herbicides that keep weeds from growing. Ask the experts at your local nursery what kinds of covers would work best in your garden.

Fed up with grass? Get lucky with clover. These hardy plants make thick, cushy ground covers just perfect for choking out weeds. Clovers are drought tolerant and never need fertilizing. And best of all, the low-growing varieties, like white dutch clover, rarely require mowing. Plus, the roots aerate compacted soil and add nitrogen back into the ground.

Tidy gardens intimidate weeds. Regularly whip over beds with a rake or hoe to clean up small, shallow-rooted weeds. This bit of housekeeping will control your weed population and give your garden a neat, well-kept look.

Save seedlings from careless hoeing. Hoeing may get rid of weeds, but a slip of the hand can injure desirable plants, too. Slide a piece of plastic pipe over the stems of seedlings while you hoe nearby, then remove the pipe when you're through.

Secret for smart hoeing. When hoeing weeds, use short, shallow strokes. Otherwise, you may churn up more fresh weed seeds or injure nearby plants.

Cut weeds to the ground. Chop-chop! Chop off the top growth of undesirable plants until they stop coming back. This method works especially well on hard-to-beat perennial weeds because they store energy in their roots. Every time you cut off their tops, the roots spend some of that energy growing new foliage. Cut them back enough times, and eventually you'll wipe out their savings.

Till twice before planting new bed. Lure weeds out into the open. Till once, wait a week, then till or hoe again. The first tilling brings buried weed seeds to the surface. Waiting a week or more gives them time to germinate. Add water to help them grow. Once they start sprouting, hoe them down or till again. Just till shallowly the second time so you don't churn up more weed seeds.

Work your garden at night. Tilling your soil at night might keep weeds from cropping up the next day, according to some experts. Tilling brings weed seeds to the surface, then quickly buries them again. In the process, some get enough sunlight to start germinating. The result — a fresh crop of weeds a week later. Nighttime tilling denies these seeds the light they need, so they may never sprout.

Working the soil sprouts more weeds. Deep digging may breed more weeds than it destroys. Tilling and plowing can bring long-buried seeds to the soil surface, as well as chop weed rhizomes into many small pieces, each of which could grow into a new weed.

Harvest an early crop of weeds. Growing an early garden full of weeds could lead to healthy crops later. Prepare your beds for planting, and water as if you had sown seeds. Wait a week for young weeds to sprout, then lightly hoe the topmost layer of dirt. This will cut off weed seedlings without churning up more buried seeds. Repeat this process for particularly weedy soil if you have time before the planting season.

Stir up beds to beat weeds. Controlling weeds early is the key to keeping a neat garden. Stir the top soil occasionally in a new bed to uproot young weeds before they take hold. Keep at it for a few weeks, and your new plants will begin to defend themselves, shading the weeds and winning the competition for sun and water.

Put the squeeze on weeds. Plant beds and individual crops as close together as you can. As they start to grow, they will naturally create shade and crowd out weeds.

Start seedlings indoors. Give young plants a head start in the battle against weeds. Raise seedlings in containers indoors. Once they are well-established, transplant them to outdoor beds.

Plant fast-growing vegetables. Weeds grow fast, but some vegetables grow faster. Plant veggies, such as beans, squash, cucumbers, potatoes, and tomatoes, that are likely to outgrow weeds. With a little help early on, these fruitful plants will get a firm foothold and successfully overpower weeds for sunlight, nutrients, and water.

Rotate crops to counter weeds. Weeds are creatures of habit. They love thriving in the same place year after year. Rotate your crops to throw them off stride. Change the kinds and heights of plants you grow in different sections of your garden each year. For instance, plant aggressive, fast-growing plants where you grew small, noncompetitive plants the year before to give weeds a run for their money.

Rotate weed-beating veggies. Tall or shading vegetables can work wonders against weeds, but remember to rotate your crops about every two years to give the soil a rest. Swap out weed-blockers, like cauliflower, corn, and tomatoes, with smaller, nonshading plants, such as lettuce and carrots.

Never let weeds set seed. Whether by pulling, clipping, mowing, or tilling, catch weeds before they go to seed. Pinch off flower heads on annual weeds, and pull perennials as soon as you see them. With a little persistence, you might outlast your weeds.

Experiment with clover. You might consider white clover a weed, but a living mulch like this holds big benefits for fruit-producing plants. Living mulches smother other weeds, and at the end of the season, you can plow them under to feed the soil. Worried about it overtaking your garden? Plant a cover that will die off at season's end, like crimson clover. Ask the experts at your local lawn and garden center to recommend a living mulch for your vegetable garden.

Winter covers keep weeds at bay. Sow a cover crop in your garden near the end of the growing season to establish it before winter. Grasses, like rye, hairy vetch, and oats, help suppress weeds during the fall and winter, saving you valuable time spent weeding come spring.

Outsmart cover crop seeds. Till in cover crops before they go to seed. They make excellent green manures, and plowing them under before they form seeds will stop them from sprouting up later as unwanted "weeds" in your garden.

I.D. your weeds. What some people consider a weed may be a home or meal to desirable insects and animals. Some weeds are even effective folk remedies for rashes, stings, and other ailments. Get to know the plants in your yard before deciding you don't want them there.

Know your enemy. Is it an annual or perennial? Broadleaf or grass? Knowing what kind of weed you're dealing with will help you figure out how to defeat it. You might simply mow or pinch back annuals but dig up perennials roots and all. Different herbicides may also work better on certain kinds of weeds. Learning the nature of your pesky problem puts you one step closer to solving it.

> Jewelweed, *Impatiens pallida* or *Impatiens biflora*, may dry up poison ivy rashes. For quick relief, crush a jewelweed stem and rub the sap directly on the rash. See your doctor immediately if you notice any adverse reactions.

Uproot poison ivy. Feeling brave? Get to the root of your poison ivy problem. Experts say pulling it up by the roots, especially the small plants, is one of the surest ways to route this threat. Clear out as much of the roots as you can, even after you kill the top growth. Don't bother composting it. Instead, place it in double-bagged garbage bags and set it out with the trash.

Rub out poison ivy itch. When you have a brush with poison ivy, look around for plantain. This weed may be an eyesore in your lawn, but it offers soothing relief for poison ivy rashes. Pick fresh leaves and crush them by hand, or chop them in a blender. Rub the moisture from them on irritated skin.

Make your own disposable gloves. No need to pay an arm and a leg for special gear. Put long, plastic bags, like the kind used for bread, newspapers, or groceries, over your hands and secure them around your arms. Double-bag your hands for extra protection. When you are done rooting out your poison ivy, carefully slip the bags off and turn them inside out. Be careful not to touch any part of the bags that came in contact with the ivy.

> ! Whatever you do, don't burn poison ivy! Never set fire to any part of this plant, including the roots. Breathing in the smoke can trigger serious allergic reactions.

Dress for safety and success. Always wear long pants and a long-sleeved shirt when dealing with poison ivy. Wash your hands thoroughly when you finish, and launder these clothes separately. Take care when handling the clothing. There's a good chance it's covered with urushiol, the irritating oil from the poison ivy.

Handle "contaminated" tools with caution. Carefully wash any tools you used to cut back poison ivy. Avoid touching any trees you stripped of ivy, as well, since the irritating oil could still cling to the bark.

Simple steps to halt moss. If moss in your yard has you wringing your hands, try these five tactics. Aerate the ground, and work on improving your soil's drainage. Prune shady branches to invite more sunlight, and avoid cutting your grass too short. Finally, feed your lawn a healthy fertilizer, especially come fall. Your yard will love all the attention, and you can wave so long to mossy infestations.

Give unruly bamboo the ax. If bamboo is trying to take over your yard, starve it into submission. Start by cutting back all of the shoots to ground level. Wait and watch for new ones to sprout, and cut them down as soon as you see them. Be ruthless, and keep at it. Invasive bamboo is persistent, but with time you can declare victory.

Fish keep ponds clean. Left unchecked, pond weeds look unsightly, and they can harm the fish living there. Researchers have discovered an organic solution — grass carp, weed-eating members of the minnow family. These fish control pond weed growth and can even be caught and eaten once they've done their job. Your local extension service or conservation department can tell you whether grass carp could work in your water.

Learn to accept weeds. Weeds happen. Gardens and yards will always have them. Accept the few you can't get rid of. Otherwise, gardening may become more of a chore than a joy.

Divide plants and conquer cuttings

Consult calendar to take cuttings. It's always the right season to start plants from cuttings. In late spring, when plants shoot up and branches have leaves of various sizes, take softwood cuttings. These root easily but need a lot of care. In late summer, when the leaves reach full size and the branches begin to stiffen, take semi-hardwood cuttings. In the winter, when there is no sign of growth and the branches have grown bark, take hardwood cuttings. These will root next season. Herbaceous cuttings, from soft-stemmed plants like coleus, mums, and dahlias, can be taken anytime and will root readily.

Get clean cut with clean knife. Make a clean cut when snipping off stems and branches to propagate new plants. Use a thin, sharp knife or sharp pruning shears so you don't get jagged edges. Before you cut, sterilize your tool with rubbing alcohol or bleach to avoid transmitting diseases to the new growth.

Cut out confusion. It's important to plant your cuttings right side up, but once you strip the leaves off a branch, it's hard to tell which end is which. In the future, cut the top end of the branch with a straight cut and the bottom end at an angle. Then you'll know at a glance which way is up.

Trim leaves to foster roots. Even after you take a cutting, its leaves continue to produce food for the developing roots. But too many leaves can be harmful. Keep some leaves on your shoot, but cut them in half. That way, the plant doesn't waste energy feeding leaves when it needs to concentrate on growing roots.

Better wet than dead. Any cutting you try to propagate needs one thing above all others — moisture. Keep the rooting medium damp, not waterlogged, and you'll give your cutting a fighting chance of survival. Mist the leaves or cover the tray in plastic so humidity around the plant stays high. Otherwise, your plant will dry out and die.

Test roots with tender tug. Here's an easy way to tell if a cutting has developed roots. Give the leaves a gentle tug. If they resist, your cutting is on its way to adult planthood.

Simple steps for semi-hardwood cuttings. To take a semi-hardwood cutting from plants like rhododendrons, azaleas, and lilacs, look for new growth that has thickened and grown a layer of bark. Cut right below the node where a leaf or bud comes out, and strip all but the top leaves. Dip the cutting in a rooting hormone, and stick it in a tray of moist peat moss and vermiculite. Cover and keep the soil moist but not soggy. And be patient. Fast-rooting cuttings, like lilac, take four to six weeks to develop roots, but rhododendrons can take up to 14 weeks.

Grow a bush from a blunder. Accidentally rip a branch off your favorite bush? If it came off with a tiny bit of the main branch, you can use it to start a new shrub. Trim the bark "heel" down a bit and remove any leaves from the bottom half of the shoot. Dip the tip in rooting hormones, tap off any extra powder, then plant it in a sterile mix of sand and peat moss. Wrap the pot in a plastic bag to keep the soil moist, and wait for the roots to grow.

Roll up cuttings to save space. Mums and geraniums are easy to propagate. Cut a 6-inch strip of plastic and run a

2-inch layer of damp sphagnum moss along it. Lay your cuttings, already dipped in hormone powder, in a line with their leaves above the edge of the plastic. Fold the plastic over lengthwise and roll up your cuttings. Tie the plastic bundle just below the leaves to hold in the moisture. Set it in a sunny window and watch for roots to show through the moss. Remember to keep the moss damp or the cuttings will dry out.

Prevent damping-off naturally. Damping-off is a devastating disease not only to the tiny seedlings it kills, but also to the gardener who one moment is rejoicing over the miracle of spring's first growth and the next is heartbroken over the dead sprouts. Preventative measures against damping-off fungi include using clean, sterile tools, containers, and soil to start your seeds. A couple of natural fungicides you can sprinkle on the seedbed are cinnamon and chamomile tea.

Damp soil promotes damping-off. The fungi that cause damping-off live where air meets moist soil. If your propagating seed bed is kept constantly moist by overwatering, these fungi thrive. As your seedlings grow, decrease moisture at the soil surface. Don't sprinkle when you water. Instead, soak the soil and wait until it is almost dry enough for plants to wilt before watering again. This keeps surface soil dry as long as possible and discourages fungal growth.

Save seedlings from damp doom. While seeds are germinating, cover your seed container with a piece of glass or a plastic tent to keep moisture from evaporating. But the same warm, moist conditions that help seeds sprout also favor the fungus that causes damping-off, a disease that makes seedlings turn black and die. So once seedlings start poking through, remove the coverings to allow air to circulate and soil to dry out.

Slice and dice perennials in season. The best time to divide and multiply your plants depends on where you live. In cold climates, it's best to divide them in early spring so the new transplants have the whole summer to grow strong before winter. In milder climates, fall is the ideal time to divide perennials so they can grow roots in milder weather before the punishing summer takes its toll.

Pep up perennials. If your perennials look sluggish, they probably need to be divided. It's just another way to care for them properly so they can rejuvenate their growth. Signs to look for are smaller flowers, dead places in the center of the clump, sparser foliage, and lackadaisical growth. Most perennials should be divided every three to five years, some never need dividing, and certain chrysanthemums do best when divided every spring. The best rule is to watch for the above signs and, if they're doing fine, leave them alone.

Pick the right time to divide perennials. Divide perennials when they're not blooming. Otherwise, all their energy goes toward producing flowers. They might not be able to develop new roots, too. In general, divide fall bloomers in the spring, and spring and summer bloomers in the fall.

Plan ahead when dividing perennials. Water plants to be divided a day or two ahead of time, and get the site for the new divisions ready before you dig. Cut any foliage back to 6 inches from the ground to limit water loss and make division easier. Use a shovel or spading fork to dig around the plant. Work your tool in under the clump, and lift it gently out of the ground. Then cut it into manageable-size parts, discarding dead or weakened growth.

Inspire your iris with division. If your iris looks fatigued, dig it up and divide its roots. Do this every three to five years. First trim the leaves to about one-third of their height. Then dig up the root ball and separate healthy rhizomes from any old and rotten parts. Dig a hole 5 to 6 inches deep. Mound the soil at the bottom and set the rhizome on it, spreading the roots over the mound. Fill the hole until only the very top of the rhizome is above ground. By next spring, your irises will be blooming beautifully.

Double fans mean better blooms. When you cut up your iris rhizome, look for "Y" shaped roots — two young nubs connected to an older and larger section of the tuber. Each small rhizome usually has a fan of leaves. This is the best root form to find, since it will produce more blooms the first year. Plant a triangular grouping with the fans pointing outside the triangle and the roots pointing in.

Grow bulbs from bulblets. Bulbs duplicate themselves by making tiny bulblets every season. Once their flowers have finished blooming and their foliage turns yellow, dig up your bulbs. Gently separate the bulblets from their parents, and plant them directly in the ground. They may not bloom the first year, but by the second, they should grow large enough to form a flower.

Salvage suckers. You like the clean look of well-pruned crape myrtle — and can't stand the little suckers that pop up around the roots of the tree. Instead of cutting them down to the ground, carefully dig them up with a handful of roots and pot them. Let them grow the first season in a sunny but sheltered corner. Once they grow their own root base, you can plant these crape myrtle volunteers where you want them.

Bury a branch for more hydrangeas. Ground layering is an easy way to propagate hydrangeas. Just take a branch from the main plant, bend it over, and bury it in the ground. Before you bury the branch, cut a notch in it or scrape a little bark off the underside. Make sure at least one leaf node will be underground. Use a brick to hold the branch down and retain moisture. When the branch forms its own roots, cut it loose and pot it like a cutting.

Copy your clematis. If your clematis is the envy of the neighborhood, share it with your neighbors. Strip the leaves from one of the lower branches while it's still attached to the vine. Dig a shallow trench and gently bend the branch down into it. Cover with an inch of rich soil and weigh it down with rocks. Eventually, little shoots will pop up wherever there were once leaves on your branch. When each sprout grows its own roots, cut the branch into small pieces. Pot the new vines and give them as gifts.

Plant the leaves of African violets. African violets can be propagated simply by planting a leaf. They are called whole-leaf or petiole cuttings. Just remove a leaf, making sure you have up to an inch and a half of the petiole — or stalk — of the leaf. Stick the leaf into moist rooting medium until the blade just touches the surface. When new growth is obvious, transfer the plant gently into another pot.

Propagating with cut-up leaves. Propagation using part-leaf cuttings is used for plants with thick, fleshy leaves and can be done two different ways. You can slice a full-grown leaf down the middle, discard the rib running from the stem to the leaf's tip, and place each leaf half cut-side down in a seed tray with rooting medium. For plants like *Sansevieria* (snake plant), cut its long leaves horizontally into 3- or 4-inch pieces, and insert them bottom-side down into the medium.

Slash veins to spark new begonia. Produce new begonia plants from split-vein leaf cuttings. Remove a leaf from your plant and make cuts across the big veins on its underside. Anchor the leaf cut-side down into your rooting medium, and new plants will form at each cut.

Whip up a willow rooting mix. Nature gave the willow tree more than its fair share of growth hormones. Take advantage of them to make your own rooting solution. Simply cut 6 inches off the fresh tips of a willow tree with swollen buds. Soak a handful of stems in two quarts of boiling water for a few hours, until the water turns light brown. Strain out the plant material, let the water cool, and bottle it. You can keep this willow tea in the refrigerator for up to three months.

Speed up rooting with warm soil. Take a tip from professional nursery men, and heat your soil to speed up rooting of propagated cuttings. But keep the air around your rooting flat cool. Air temperatures warmer than 70 degrees encourage fungus and bacteria growth and also stimulate leaf growth at the expense of the roots. Warm the soil without heating up the air by setting your flat on top of the refrigerator or a heating pad.

Heat soil to hurry roots. Roots grow faster when soil temperatures are around 70 degrees. If you're propagating cuttings outside, try setting your planting tray on top of a manure-filled hotbed. Just dig a hole about 2 feet deep and fill it with manure. The manure heats up as it decomposes, providing cheap, natural warmth for the new roots.

Reserve solid food until baby is grown. Wait for your cutting to grow a nice bundle of roots before you start feeding it. Fertilizer attracts bacteria, and nasty green things might invade your pot before your baby has roots to protect and nourish itself.

Bury hardwood cuttings for easy callusing. If you live where the ground freezes, cut hardwoods early in the cold season, and overwinter them in the basement. Cut woody tips about 6 inches long with at least three buds on them. Bundle a handful, all pointed in the same direction, and tie with a rubber band. Then bury them in a box of damp sand.

Make sure to keep them moist while they form a round bump on the bottom. This is the callus from which the roots will grow. In the early spring, plant the cuttings in a trench outside, and keep them moist as they grow roots. By the following fall or spring, your cuttings should be ready to move into the garden.

Foil wet leaves with foil. Some houseplants will root from stems placed in water. But keeping the leaves dry can be a problem. Solve it by covering the top of a glass of water with a piece of aluminum foil. Punch holes in the foil and drop the stems through the holes. That keeps them upright, with their bottoms wet and leaves in the air, while the new roots form.

Solve rooting headaches with aspirin. Toss some aspirin in the water before you add your cutting. Aspirin contains a natural clot buster that keeps the cutting from scabbing at the end. This helps the stem absorb water to feed the leaves. It also encourages roots to grow quickly.

Water roots take longer. When propagating leaves and stems in water, maintain the water level and change it if it turns green. When the roots begin to appear, transfer your cutting to a pot filled with very moist potting mix. You'll probably find that cuttings rooted in water take longer to get going than with other methods.

Turn your umbrella upside down. It's easy to propagate your exotic umbrella palm or papyrus. Simply cut off a healthy head, flip it upside down, and stick it in a glass of water to root. Once small shoots appear between the leaves, plant your new palm — right side up — in potting soil.

Produce houseplants from produce. To create an attractive hanging houseplant, just open your refrigerator. Cut the 2-inch top off a large carrot and hollow it out. Hang it upside down in good light and fill the hollow area with water. Fernlike leaves will grow upward from the inverted top as long as you keep filling it with water. Try the same thing with beet, turnip, or parsnip tops.

Remove risk of rot. Let your cactus or succulent cuttings dry out before you plant them in a starting tray. This will help prevent rotting.

Write it down to get it right. Keep a propagation journal to track the progress of your seeds and cuttings. It will help you identify successes and mistakes so that each year you get a little better at producing new plants for your garden. Keep track of dates and weather conditions, identity of seeds or host plants, techniques used in planting or taking cuttings, and the results of your efforts. Then, before you start next time, review what you did last year and how it turned out.

Grow flowers from the root up. Poppies, daylilies, and peonies can be propagated from root cuttings. In the winter, when the plant's asleep, dig up its entire root ball. Cut off the newer roots and replant the root ball in its original spot. Trim your cuttings to about an inch and a half in length. Push them into sandy potting soil until their tops are level with the soil. New shoots will emerge in the spring, when you can plant them outside.

Pick a winning rose donor. Vintage roses, the kind that still grow in cemeteries around the country, are among the easiest to grow from cuttings. Miniatures, ramblers, and other roses that grow on their own rootstock are also good choices. New hybrids that are less than 17 years old cannot be legally propagated. They are also harder to grow since they're often grafted onto the roots of a different rose bush. Once you get them started, all roses should mature in two to three years.

Start rose cuttings early in cold zones. If your winters are harsh, start propagating your roses in May. Take cuttings from green branches with wilting flowers and developing rosehips. Remove the flowers, hips, and leaves except for the top two leaves. Slit the outer bark of your cutting about an inch from the bottom. This "wound" will encourage the plant to grow more roots. Dip it in rooting hormones, and plant it in a pot of moist sand covered with a plastic bag. Place it in a bright but sheltered spot. It's critical to keep your cutting moist until you see new growth, then you can plant it in the garden.

Make a homemade planting tray. You don't have to buy any special equipment to propagate your own plants. Simply punch holes in the bottom of a plastic tray, fill it with airy, moist potting soil, and slide your cutting in. Bend two wire coat hangers into hoops, and stick a hoop into the soil at each end of the tray. Cover the whole thing with a clear plastic bag or plastic wrap. Punch holes in the plastic for air, and you have a top-notch starting tray without spending a dime.

Hold in humidity with plastic. When rooting stem cuttings, it's important to give them a humid environment. Put several cuttings in a large pot and cover them with a bottomless milk jug to hold in the moisture. Another method is to set the pot inside a large, clear plastic bag. Take the top off the milk bottle or poke holes in the bag for ventilation.

Keep soil moist with clay pots. Give your cuttings the steady, gentle moisture they need to put down new roots. Start with two clay pots, one larger than the other. Plug the hole in the smaller pot and place it inside the big one. Fill the space in between the two with a damp potting soil mix, and press your cuttings into the soil. Then fill the inside pot with water. The water will seep slowly through the pot and keep new roots from drying out.

Pot rooted cuttings for stronger plants. Once your cutting produces roots 1 to 3 inches long, transfer it to a pot with potting soil. The fragile roots it develops in the rooting medium are not strong enough to sustain it in a landscape setting. Moving to a pot first will help the root system get bigger and stronger and increase the plant's chances of survival. It's also important not to leave a cutting in the rooting medium too long. The lack of nutrients will stunt the plant.

Label now to avoid headaches later. When starting seedlings in containers, label each pot or flat. Include the date, type of planting, and any other information you think is important. It makes it much easier to keep tabs on what you're growing.

Pick the right light for strong seedlings. Most seeds don't need light to germinate, but keep them moist so they don't dry out and die before they become seedlings. Then that's the time to make sure they have plenty of light. If seedlings don't get enough light they grow leggy — with weak, spindly stems — while reaching out trying to find light. Most houseplants germinate well with artificial light. Just keep the light source close to the plant, usually less than 12 inches away for fluorescent lamps.

Transplant small seedlings for better results. When you're propagating from seed, it's better to move them to a larger container when they're small, since small seedlings suffer less transplant shock. Wait until the first true leaves appear, and then lift them out of the tray with a spoon or flat wooden stick. Handle seedlings by the root ball rather than the stem, and replant them at about the same depth they were growing before. Firm the soil, and lightly fertilize.

Turn a glass into a greenhouse. Create a miniature greenhouse for seedlings with an ordinary drinking glass. Start your seeds in premoistened potting soil and cover them with the glass or a plastic cup. Keep the pot in a warm place to promote germination and growth. The cup provides protection from cold air and holds in moisture. Just make sure the cup or glass is clear so light can get through.

Paint on pollen for super squash. To get a good harvest of squash, melon, or zucchini, you need some help from local bees. The bees move pollen between the male and female flowers that grow on each vine. If you live in a bee-free zone, you can hand-pollinate with an artist's paintbrush. Carefully pick up the golden pollen from a male flower, then brush it on the center of the female flower. The male flower usually has a long stem, while the female flower has what looks like a tiny fruit under the bloom. Only pollinate freshly opened flowers because they get less receptive as they age.

Score more ferns with spores. In the woods, you may notice some ferns look like they're covered with little brown bugs. These are actually fern spores, and you can propagate ferns from them. Shake a frond over a white paper towel to collect the spores. Sterilize some potting soil in the oven for a couple of hours, then sprinkle the spores on the damp soil. Cover with clear plastic. The soil should turn green in a few weeks. Within months, you'll have little fronds you can pot up individually.

Handle hollyhocks with care. Think twice before you transplant hollyhock volunteers that sprout in your yard. These flowery perennials have long, straight taproots that can't be cut. If you decide to move hollyhocks, prepare their new home by digging a hole and watering it well. Dig carefully around the root ball and lift it out of the ground, along with as much of the original soil as possible. Keep your transplants watered until they resume growing. With any luck, they won't even notice they've been moved.

Weather-wise gardening

Consider climate within zones. The Plant Hardiness Zone Maps for the United States and Canada, found on pages 362 and 363, are helpful in figuring out which woody and perennial plants will survive where you live. But other climate considerations within your zone — such as when and how much it rains, length and severity of winter, and how long and how hot the summers are — are just as important. Use all of this information to pick plants that will thrive rather than merely survive.

What's your day like? As you fine-tune your efforts to find plants that will give maximum performance in your particular environment, consider how long the days are at your latitude. Plants rely on the amount of daylight to tell them when to grow, when to bloom, and when to get ready for winter.

Find out what your plants need. The amount of heat and light from the sun's rays is an important factor in a plant's performance. Even though it is supposed to do well in your Hardiness Zone, a plant still needs a specified amount of sunlight. If cloud cover, rainy days, and amount of shade don't give your garden the right amount of light, it could be difficult for your plants to survive. Also, keep in mind plants grow best within a certain range of temperatures, and that band may be wide for some and very narrow for others.

What to plant in sun or shade. Sun and shade are two big considerations when deciding what to plant where in your garden. Flowering annuals, many perennials, and vegetables, like tomatoes and beans, need lots of sun. In general, showier plants need more energy, which they get from sunlight. If they don't get enough, they are weaker and less fruitful. On the other hand, shade-loving plants, like hostas and ferns, will wilt and lose their lush green color if they get too much sun.

Learn from your plant. Here's an old tip to help you decide which of your plants like sunshine and which don't. Those with big leaves, like hydrangeas, rhododendrons, and hostas, need less sun than plants with tiny leaves, like herbs and sedums.

Be aware of your growing season. To grow vegetables and other annuals successfully, you need to know the length of your growing season — the number of days between the last frost in the spring and the first frost in the winter. Compare that number of frost-free days to the "days to harvest" number on the seed packet to see if you have time for your crop to grow and mature. Use your area's average frost-free date in the spring to help determine when to plant.

> **Know your zone**
>
> One of a gardener's basic tools is the U.S. Department of Agriculture's Plant Hardiness Zone Map. It divides the country into zones based on average minimum temperatures. If you live in Canada, check out the Plant Hardiness Zone Map for Canada. (Both maps can be found at the back of this book.) Plants are rated on their ability to withstand cold. By comparing the plant's rating to your zone, you'll know if you can expect it to make it through the winter. This system is one of a gardener's first tools in deciding what permanent plants to grow, based on their winter hardiness.

Welcome native plants for best results. Choose plants for your landscape plan that are native to your area. Native plants grow better and need less maintenance. They have evolved over time to function at peak efficiency according to regional characteristics that include climate; soil; and timing of rainfall, drought, and frost. They need less fertilizer, pest protection, and watering and attract beneficial insects, native songbirds, and butterflies. Non-native species often don't do well because they can't deal with the heat or cold or length of the seasons. Sometimes, plants adapted to a harsher environment do so well they crowd out everything else.

Pay attention to microclimates. Pick locations for your plants according to the characteristics of the microclimates within your yard. For instance, the north side of your house is shady most of the day, while the south side gets full sun all day long. The east side is sunny in the morning, while the west side heats up about midday and stays hot all afternoon. Match these sites with the requirements of the flowers you want to grow.

Southern exposure usually best. Most of the time, a gently sloping south-facing garden plot is ideal. It gets full sun and the slope encourages water drainage and air circulation. But, depending on how high your average annual temperatures are, you might be getting a spot that's too hot. Ironically, in cooler climates, a southern exposure

Check out a helpful map before planting

Heat can damage some plants just as much as cold does others. To help understand where it gets hot, the American Horticultural Society has created the AHS Heat-Zone Map. This map shows the annual number of "heat days" — days above 86 degrees (30 degrees Celsius), the point where heat starts to damage plants. It ranges from zone 1, where it doesn't ever get above 86 degrees, to zone 12, where more than 210 days per year are heat days. Look for heat zone designations on seeds and plants to see if they can stand the summer in your garden.

may cause problems with winter kill due to thawing and refreezing in the colder months.

Jump-start spring with a warm wall. To give your flowers an early start in the spring, put them in front of a south-facing brick or concrete wall. That time of the year, the sun travels low across the southern sky and warms the wall, which naturally soaks up the heat and radiates it back out overnight. Combined with the wall's protection from the chilly north wind, you get an area with a climate that is several days — or even weeks — ahead of the rest of your garden.

Information you need to know

Whether you've just moved or if you've been in the same place all your life, you need to know these three basic pieces of information about where you live:

1. The local average annual rainfall.
2. First and last frost dates for your area.
3. The average low temperatures and your USDA Hardiness Zone.

These are the starting points in deciding what and when to put in a garden suited to your own particular environment.

Discover a warm spot in your yard. A microclimate you might overlook is the area next to your house, which will be hotter and dryer than the rest of your yard. This area is usually protected by the roof overhang or eave of the house and won't get much watering from rainfall. Reflected heat from the side of the house and heat retained by the foundation also make it warmer. Be sure to give extra water to these areas and choose more heat-resistant varieties for summer plantings. In the winter, close to the house might be the place where less-hardy varieties will survive.

Northern slopes stay cooler. If you live in the North, stay away from north-facing slopes for your gardening. They get less sun and are cooler than surrounding areas. They also stay moist, and snow cover stays there longer. On the other hand, if you're in the South, a gentle northern slope might be just the ticket — it will need less water and stay cooler on the hottest days of the summer.

Beware of low places. Avoid putting plants in low-lying pockets of ground, especially in northern climates or at higher elevations. Cold air settles in these little hollows on cold, clear nights and then doesn't circulate well. It all adds up to frost on the pumpkin, or whatever else is growing there, while surrounding areas remain unfrozen.

Manage sunshine with leafy trees. Deciduous trees are a good way to manage the climate in your yard. Their leaves provide shade from the hot summer sun, and in the winter, their bare branches let the sun through to warm the chilly landscape. Prune away low-growing branches so you get good air circulation at ground level. Avoid gardening directly under the tree's canopy. The roots make it hard to till the soil, and the tree competes for water with your other plants.

Pruning protects wind-blown trees. Strengthen your trees with proper pruning, especially if you live where high winds are common. Take out small, inside branches that can catch the wind and break off the larger limbs. Then the wind can pass through the tree instead of blowing it down. No matter where you live, keep dead and damaged limbs pruned to reduce the energy load on your trees. Good pruning practices will also pay off when snow and ice storms add undue weight to limbs and branches.

Keep out the cold with a windbreak. Protect your home with a windbreak on the north or west side of your house — whichever the direction of prevailing winter winds. It gives shelter to your house and yard and can lower your heating bills as much as 20 percent. Use tall, dense evergreens, like Douglas fir or spruce, that keep their needles year-round. Fill in around the foundation with evergreen shrubs, like yews and junipers, to stop cold air.

Create an effective windbreak. The most effective windbreak is not a solid wall but a fence or line of trees that lets some air pass through it. Low pressure develops on the sheltered side of a windbreak and actually sucks air coming over the barrier downward, creating swirling turbulence in the area you are trying to protect. By letting a little air through the windbreak, the low pressure is reduced, and the wind you're blocking stays up where it can blow over your garden instead of dropping down into it.

Strengthen garden with a windbreak. A windbreak minimizes damage to your garden from drying summer winds and destructive winter winds. Less stress means more and better flowers and vegetables. Stiller air means more bees to pollinate blossoms. Walls around plants mean warm protection from late frost in the spring. Use natural buildings and fences for windbreaks or plant trees and shrubs. Make sure you don't create too much shade and remember that living windbreaks compete for soil nutrients and water.

Summer winds wilt plants. The combination of summer wind and heat causes moisture to evaporate quickly from plant leaves, especially young or small ones. If the roots can't absorb and distribute water quicker than it escapes, the leaves wilt. One of the best solutions for this problem is to grow native plant varieties that are adapted to the weather conditions of your area. Another is to establish root systems ahead of time that can stand the stress by watering deeply and less often. When it gets hot and windy, keep plants well-watered and provide extra shade and windbreaks.

Stop wind with sunflowers. Protect your cutting garden from harsh winds with a flower you won't cut, the sunflower.

With their large leaves and thick stalks, these yellow-petaled beauties provide fast-growing, sturdy protection from stiff breezes that dry out and rip off leaves from your more delicate bloomers. Plant two or three rows on the windward side of your garden and mix in vines, like sweet peas or morning glories, to climb the stalks and provide a denser barrier.

Inexpensive way to make a cloche

It's easy and inexpensive to make a tunnel cloche. All you need is plastic sheeting and some half-inch PVC pipe, about 9 feet for each support. Cut the pipe to the length you need. Saw off both ends at an angle and push them into the ground, bending the pipe to form an arch over your garden row. Insert an arch about every 3 feet. Then spread your plastic over the arches and anchor it at the bottom. Use enough plastic to close up the ends if it frosts. Otherwise, leave them open for air circulation. At the end of the season, take off the plastic and store it for use next year.

Get growing quicker with a cloche. Cloches originally were bell-shaped jars placed over individual plants, but today you can use clear plastic to make cloches that cover many plants at a time. Use tunnel cloches to extend your growing season during those chilly spring days when you're afraid you started your garden too soon. Like a mini-greenhouse, a tunnel cloche protects tender young plants from frost, wind, rain, birds, and pests. Cloches also hold in heat and humidity and keep rain out, so you need to provide for ventilation and supplemental watering when you use them.

Extend your growing season. For gardeners living in cooler climates, floating row covers are an easier alternative to cloches and cold frames to extend the growing season. Made from lightweight sheets of synthetic fabric, these covers warm the soil and provide frost protection during early spring and late fall. Light and water can penetrate the fabric, but heat and moisture are trapped underneath. The material is light enough to literally float on top of your crops, which means it doesn't need bulky framework. Plants just push it up as they grow.

Use empty bottles for "hot caps." Make individual cloches — sometimes called hot caps — from empty soda pop or milk bottles. Cut off the bottom and stick them in the ground over young plants to create a greenhouse effect of warmth around them. Leave the caps off for air circulation unless you expect a frosty night. Then replace the caps to hold in more heat. If wind is a problem, choose milk jugs over pop bottles so you can drive a stake through the handle to anchor them down.

Stretch season with a cold frame. Lengthen the gardening season by starting seedlings early in a cold frame and transplanting them later. A cold frame is a bottomless box with a clear top. It uses the sun's rays to create a warm, toasty environment before it's warm enough for plants to survive out in the open. Most cold frames are homemade from wood with an old window for a top. The frame should be tilted toward the south to catch more sunlight. It also needs to be airtight and easily opened from the top. If you put your cold frame next to your house, it'll pick up even more heat from the foundation.

Make a cold frame from straw. Make a quick, simple, and inexpensive cold frame from bales of straw and an old storm window. Just stack the straw to form a frame to fit the window. Stack two layers of bales on the north side and only one on the south to give the top the proper tilt. You now have a well-insulated cold frame for the spring and a supply of mulch for the summer. All you have to store is the window and you're ready for next year.

Switch cold frame to hot bed. If it's too cold for a cold frame, then turn your cold frame into a hot bed by heating it up. For an organic heater, add some manure to warm the soil. If you're not up to the smell, just get an electric heating coil. Most heating coils come with a thermostat so you can have it exactly how hot you want it.

How to make a raised bed

You can make a raised garden bed simply by raking tilled soil into a pile and leveling off the top. One reason for raised beds is to avoid soil compaction, so keep them small enough to work them without stepping in them. Make paths between several beds and use the soil from the paths to raise the beds. If you have poor dirt, bring in new topsoil for the raised beds, or work in soil amendments to make it better. Your beds can remain flat-topped mounds or you can enclose them with wide boards, bricks, or other materials.

Lift lid to cool off the heat. Don't burn up little seedlings in your cold frame when the weather gets warmer in late winter and early spring. A cold frame's job is to trap warm air and give your seeds a boost. But when the cover is down on sunny afternoons, it can get hot enough under that glass to fry your tender young plants. When it's above 45 degrees outside, lift the lid to keep the temperature temperate and provide air circulation inside the frame. Just remember to put it down again early enough in the evening to keep it warm at night.

Skip a step with portable frame. Most folks use cold frames to hold pots and flats of seedlings until it's warm enough to transplant them. But if your cold frame is portable, take it into the garden, start your vegetables from seed, and skip the whole transplanting process. Just prepare your seedbed as you normally would and set the cold frame over it to get the soil warm enough to germinate the seed. Then sow your seeds and leave the frame in place until the plants are far enough along to survive without it.

Save plants from frosty nights. If unexpected frost catches your growing plants, the young buds and tender shoots are likely to pucker up, turn black, or drop off. The usual cure for frosted fronds is to pull them up and start over, so keep track of the weather forecasts during transitional temperature periods. If a freeze is predicted and your plants are vulnerable, cover them for the night with burlap, plastic sheeting, or even newspapers — just enough to keep frozen moisture from forming on the plant itself.

Water keeps garden warm at night. Keep your garden warm at night by using passive solar heat. Put large cans, buckets, or even barrels of water around your garden on sunny winter or early spring days. They'll absorb heat during the day and release it slowly at night. To make it work even better, paint the buckets black and put them inside a tunnel cloche or cold frame.

Fight frost with a fine mist. If a frosty night is in store and you can't get your new garden plants covered up, turn on the sprinkler before you go to bed. As water turns to ice, it gives off heat and keeps plants warmer than the air around them. It's important to keep the sprinkler going from the time the temperature drops below 33 degrees until the sun warms things up the next morning

Raised beds warm the soil. Warm your garden soil sooner in the spring with a raised bed. By raising the planting level of your garden, you work the dirt above ground level and allow it to stay warm while the rest is still frozen. A raised bed also gives you better drainage and avoids soil compaction. This technique is very helpful where winters are long and cold, but it's not as good in warmer, dryer climates because the soil can warm up and dry out too much.

Cozy cover warms raised bed. Turn your raised bed into a mini-greenhouse with a cozy cover for added warmth and protection. The soil stays warm in a raised bed just by being higher than the ground, but a clear plastic roof will use solar energy to heat it up even more. It also holds the heat through chilly late autumn and early spring nights.

Tires make great weather beaters. Use old car tires to protect plants from the weather. They're good windbreaks and also make a fine raised bed for tomatoes, peppers, eggplant, and other vegetables that like it warm. Stack the tires two or three high. Put a mixture of fertile soil and some stones, to promote drainage, in the tires. The black tires soak up heat to help you get a head start on spring. But you better watch out later in the summer. Your tomatoes will probably need extra water when it gets hot because of the heat retention.

Get a jump on spring. Do you wait until all risk of frost is past before you start planting your garden? Well, you don't have to. Sure, warm-weather plants won't grow when it's cold, but there are lots of vegetables that actually prefer the cooler temperatures of early spring. These include lettuce, spinach, radishes, onions, carrots, beets, Swiss chard, peas and the cabbage family crops — broccoli, cabbage, Chinese cabbage, cauliflower, kohlrabi, and brussels sprouts. Plant salad crops, like lettuce and radishes, every 10 days and harvest them well into the summer. Then start planting them again to grow while it's cool in the fall.

Hide asparagus from frost. Asparagus is the first thing you can harvest from your garden in the spring. It starts poking through as soon as the soil temperature gets to about 50 degrees. However, the tender spears are very susceptible to frost, so be alert for cold snaps after a premature spring warm-up. If temperatures are predicted to drop below freezing, mulch new asparagus shoots with newspaper or leaves. Then remove it the next day when the sun comes out. Frost-damaged spears won't recover, so snap them off and let the plant put out new shoots.

Give pea patch a head start. Peas are difficult to transplant, but here's a way to start this early spring crop indoors. Take a length of plastic gutter, fill it with seed sowing material, and plant your pea seeds. When they're a few inches tall and have plenty of roots, clear out a shallow trench in your garden. Then slide the pea plants off the gutter and into the trench without disturbing the roots. Pat down the soil and cover your pea plants with a transparent covering or floating row cover if it's still too cool for them.

Some like it hot. Just because your plants are in the ground first doesn't mean you'll have the first tomato in the neighborhood. Warm-season vegetables, like tomatoes, peppers, okra, and eggplant, don't do well when it's cold. If you set them out when the soil is colder than 70 degrees, it may take several months for them to start growing normally. Plants planted later will actually grow faster, so be patient and wait until it's warm enough. If your plants are suffering a relapse because of cold weather, pull them up and start over with healthy transplants.

When is the right time to plant?

Plant potatoes on St. Patrick's Day, set out tomatoes anytime after Memorial Day, and always plant by the sign of the moon. These and many other time-honored "truths" about gardening may or may not work. Each crop has its own requirements and each locality has its own climate. Use these factors along with the advice of local experts and your own experience to determine the best time to plant. You'll find that this year's weather patterns and soil temperature will have more to do with it than dates on the calendar.

Baby your bean seeds. Snap beans, either the bush or pole variety, are a snap to grow if you keep your eye on the thermometer. A warm-season crop, beans need to be planted in full sun after the soil heats up above 65 degrees. If it's cooler than that, they have a hard time germinating and may even suffer seed rot. Ideal growing temperatures for snap beans are between 70 and 85 degrees. Hotter than that causes blossom drop and pollination difficulty. If it doesn't get too hot, they'll usually come back when it gets cooler and set on more pods.

Give seedlings a boost. In hot weather, don't let the soil in your seedbed dry out and crust over after you've sowed your seeds. The little seedlings will have a tough time breaking through the hard surface and many won't make it. Soak the seed trench thoroughly before dropping the seeds to speed up germination and give the roots a path to follow. Then cover them with dry dirt. If you have to water the seedbed, sprinkle it often or cover it with newspaper to keep it from drying out.

When to put out annuals. A good way to tell when to put out your bedding plants is to watch the flower beds in parks, shopping centers, and other public places. Professional landscapers know the best time to get things growing. Transplanting needs to happen as early as possible to get the most blooming time, but if there's still a risk of frost, you could be in trouble. Annuals need warm soil to grow well. Cold weather will slow them down and put them behind later-planted flowers.

Relieve stress on transplants. To make transplanting a success, take steps to reduce stress on the new seedlings. Wait until all danger of frost has past, and work up your soil a few days before you actually put out your plants. Water them in their old containers a few hours ahead of time. Avoid the heat of the day when transplanting. Wait for a cloudy, misty day or until late in the afternoon when the sun is low.

Harden off, then transplant. Toughen up the seedlings you started inside the house before you transplant them outside. The process, called hardening off, prepares young plants for the transition from their stable, incubator-like environment to the wind, sunlight, and fluctuating temperatures of the outdoors. Start out by setting the seedlings outside for a few hours in a sheltered area. Leave them out longer each day until they can stay out all night. A week or two of hardening off will acclimate them so they'll do well after transplanting.

Do your homework to find best blooms. There is an endless list of flower species and varieties, each one with its own unique climate requirements. If you want the best bloomers for your flower beds, do some homework before buying seeds and plants. Label information is often sketchy, so use other references to see if the variety you're getting will flourish in your climate. Just because plants are for sale locally doesn't mean they are perfectly suited to the area. And remember — information in catalogs is usually based on the weather where the catalog comes from.

Unbloomed bedding plants best. The best summer bedding plants to buy are the ones that haven't bloomed yet. Look for bushy, bright-looking plants. If they already have flowers and buds, pinch them off at planting time to encourage more abundant blooms later on. Remember that these plants have been started in a greenhouse and may not be ready for the outdoors.

Swooping swallows predict rain. Waiting for it to rain before setting out transplants? Watch for swooping swallows. When they're flying low, it's a pretty good bet it's going to rain. That's because the insects they feed on are no longer being carried high in the air by warm thermal currents rising from the ground in clear weather. When rain is approaching, the insects fly lower and so do the swallows.

Use natural basin to hold rainwater. Protect new shrubs and thirsty plants from the ravages of dry weather by planting them in basin-like depressions. These basins retain rainwater and provide more moisture for their new roots. You can create the same effect by clearing a circle of mulch from around the base of the plant. This not only provides a little well to hold water, it gives the roots a better chance to absorb oxygen.

Protect houseplants from sunburn. While some plants need a lot of sunshine, others — especially houseplants — are more adapted to a shady scenario. So if you put your houseplants outside in the summer, take care not to give them too much direct sun. Plants grown in low-light conditions will burn easily if moved suddenly into sunshine. Discolored or dead leaves are symptoms of plant sunburn. Set your houseplant in the shade when you take it outside and gradually give it more sun until you know how much it will tolerate.

Double up for more spring color. Keep color longer with a mixture of blooms in your spring flower bed. Just plant low-growing annuals or perennials on top of your bulb beds. The bulbs will poke through first and, about the time they're finished, the other flowers will break out, covering up the leftover foliage from the bulbs.

Allow bulb foliage to die naturally. When your spring bulb blossoms have faded, it's time to prepare for next year. Cut off the dead flowers but leave the green leaves. This is when they soak up sunshine and make food for next year's blooms. It takes about six weeks for the foliage to yellow and die back naturally. If you don't let them have their day in the sun, you probably won't have any flowers next year.

Let annuals soak up the sun. Sunshine is important for growing annual flowers. Their entire life span is less than a year, so they need to soak up lots of energy in a short time to make their beautiful blooms. Plot the sun's passage before choosing the flower bed for your annuals. They need six to eight hours of midday sun every day. Early morning and late afternoon sun is not as intense and doesn't do as much good. Keep in mind the changes that the seasonal movement of the sun, cloud cover, and progress of leaves on the trees will bring.

Heat up your garden with color. Torch lilies, also called red hot pokers, provide dramatic summer color in your garden. *Kniphofia*, its proper name, is a perennial with several varieties that bloom at different times during the summer. A British favorite, *kniphofia* grows in zones 5 and warmer. It puts out flower spikes that range in color from ivory and orange to coral red and grow 2 to 5 feet tall. Leaves are blue-green to medium green. If you have enough room — they can spread up to 3 feet — plant several varieties and have blooms all summer long.

***Kniphofia* needs sunny climate.** *Kniphofia* grows wild in South Africa, so it likes full sun and mild winters. It doesn't do well in shade, and even though it's an evergreen, it tends to take a beating in the winter. Shelter your plants from the wind and mulch the crowns when it gets cold. Keep water out of the crown in winter by tying the foliage together. *Kniphofias* will survive drought periods in the summer, but they do better when they have lots of water.

Leggy mums need more sun. For chrysanthemum plants full of blooms, make sure they get plenty of sun. Mums love sun, and if they don't get enough, they'll turn out leggy — with tall, spindly stems and fewer flowers. If your mums look like that, see what you can do to eliminate shade in the area or move them to someplace sunnier. They need at least four or five hours of direct sun a day. Some chrysanthemum varieties are naturally leggier than others. If that's the case, make sure you pinch them back regularly during the summer.

Grow ground cover in shady places. Ground cover is one solution for areas too shady to grow grass. There is almost an endless variety of ground covers and most are less demanding than grass. It's a good way to add contrasting color and texture to your yard, too. Ground cover won't take a lot of wear and tear, but you can lay stepping stones or a mulch-filled path through that area. When planting ground cover, be sure and space the plants correctly — too much space and it won't fill in, too little and it chokes itself out.

Lend pollination a hand. Bad weather while your fruit trees are blooming can be bad news when it comes time to pick the crop. Continued heavy rain, unseasonable cold, or heavy wind during prime flowering season not only knocks blooms off the tree, it also drives away honeybees and other insects that pollinate the blossoms. Poor pollination results in small fruit that drops off instead of growing. One solution is hand pollination, using a cotton swab or artist's brush. Check with a fruit tree expert at your local extension office or garden center on the pollination requirements of your particular variety.

Safeguard trees from hot winds. When moisture evaporates from tree leaves faster than the root system can replace it, wilting, scorching, and scalding of the leaves can occur. Hot, windy weather is the main cause of problems, and young trees whose root systems are not fully developed are the prime targets. Keep an eye on your trees and shrubs, and don't let them dry out in hot weather. Choose varieties to plant that are adapted to your particular climate. Put more sensitive plants where they have adequate shade and shelter from the wind.

Buffer young trees from sunscald. Protect new trees from sunscald by wrapping their trunks in winter. The condition affects young, thin-barked trees, especially when they are transplanted from shady to sunny areas. Sunscald is due to heating and freezing of the bark and shows up as dead patches on sun-exposed trunks and limbs — usually on the south or southwest side of the tree. Evergreens and shrubs show scorched foliage. Use tree wrap specified for sunscald and keep the white side out. Remove it before summer because it's a good place for insects and diseases to hang out.

Hot weather causes bitterness. Heat stress can turn the taste of some vegetables bitter. Cucumbers and eggplant are particularly prone to this condition. They will produce wonderful, sweet-tasting fruit all spring, but stress from hot weather or low moisture will suddenly produce a bitter compound that seriously offends your taste buds. When this happens, the plant's useful life is pretty much over. You can try harvesting only smaller, somewhat immature fruits, but they'll never taste the same as when the plant was healthy.

Bolting ruins plant's taste. When cool-weather crops, like lettuce, spinach, and members of the cabbage family, send up long-flowered stalks from the main stem, it's called bolting. A plant bolts because nature tells it to go to seed. When that happens, the taste deteriorates and gets bitter. Bolting is usually caused by several days of too cold temperatures — 40 to 50 degrees — early in the plant's growth, but it doesn't actually happen until warmer weather. Cutting the flower stalks will not stop the poor flavor, so the best thing you can do is avoid setting out your plants too early.

Shade tomatoes from direct sun. Tomatoes, peppers, and other hot-weather plants need the sun for warmth. But direct sunlight on their fruit causes sunscald, which results in soft white or yellow patches that attract black rot and other fungus diseases. The plant's protection is its leafy foliage, so limit pruning and keep leaves healthy to avoid sunscald. If ripening fruit is exposed to direct sun, find a way to shade it. Peppers and tomatoes that have sunscald are still edible if you cut away the bad parts.

Cut back tomatoes before frost. Make the last days of summer in your tomato patch count. Prune new growth, blossoms, and small, very green fruit about three weeks before the first frost is due. It takes 40 to 50 days for the standard tomato to go from blossom to maturity, so what you cut away won't have time to make it. The remaining tomatoes can take full advantage of the nutrients supplied by a root system at its peak. Fully formed leaves also supply nourishment, so don't prune them.

Make the most of green tomatoes. Just before the first frost hits your tomato plants, take mature, green tomatoes inside to ripen. These are the ones that are good-size and have turned light green to white. Ripen them in well-ventilated, open cardboard boxes at room temperature. It should take about two weeks at 70 degrees, but check them every few days and cull out those that spoil. Small, dark green fruits will not ripen satisfactorily, so use them for pickles, relishes, green tomato pie, and fried green tomatoes.

Heat up the soil with stones. Use large, flat stones for multipurpose mulch in your tomato, watermelon, and other heat-loving-plant patches. The stones soak up heat from the sun during the day and radiate it back into the soil at night. They also keep weeds from popping up.

Sterilize soil with solar power. If your garden plot needs to be purged of weeds, fungi, bacteria, and insect pests, get rid of them with solarization, a process using the sun's rays and clear plastic. Here's how to do it. Ready the ground for planting, dig a trench around the bed, and water it. Spread a sheet of plastic and anchor it into the trench with the backfill. It takes four to six weeks to sterilize soil and is best done in the middle of the summer. Check with your county extension agent about how effective solarization is in your climate.

Start winter garden in summer. Start growing cool-weather vegetables in the summer for harvest into the fall and early winter. Plant seeds outdoors from late June to early August or transplant seedlings early in September. This gives your winter crops the chance to establish a good root system before frost sets in. There are more than 40 vegetables suitable for a winter garden, including varieties of broccoli, cauliflower, spinach, beets, carrots, peas, and onions. Depending on your particular climate and the crops you choose, you can harvest fresh garden vegetables almost all year-round.

Strengthen soil for double cropping. If your weather allows you to grow cool-season vegetables both spring and fall, beef up the soil between plantings during the summer. Spread granular fertilizer after removing the spring plants and work in extra organic compost before the fall planting. Consider a soil test while you're at it. Broccoli, cabbage, and cauliflower — the staple of winter gardens — like alkaline soil, so you might need to add some lime.

Buckwheat preps winter garden. If your climate is warm enough, you'll have a section of garden for both early spring crops and late fall/winter crops. In between, plant buckwheat as a cover crop. This fast-growing, warm-season succulent protects and improves the soil surface, chokes out weeds, and helps prepare the ground for transplanting. If the soil is above 55 degrees, it will germinate in just a few days and grows to flowering in just four or five weeks. Mow it or till it under within a couple of weeks after that to keep it from going to seed.

Fall frost sweetens kale. Kale is a cool-weather vegetable that should be grown in your winter garden instead of the spring or summer. Frost prompts kale — and other brassicas — to make extra sugar as a sort of antifreeze protection. Kale that hasn't been frosted tastes pretty bad, but people who grow their own beginning in late summer or fall love to eat it. It's a vigorous grower you can start from seed a couple of months before first frost. You'll have a delicious fall harvest of a different and very healthy vegetable.

Plant pansies anywhere. The pansy is often called a flower for all seasons. No matter where you live or what your weather, pansies will thrive sometime during the year. Grow them during the summer in the North and all through the winter in the South. Technically a perennial or biennial, they grow year-round in California and other regions with moderate to mild winters. They produce abundant blooms, come in a bright variety of colors, and are relatively free from pests and disease, which make them an increasingly popular flower.

Add fall color with pansies. In climates with hot summers and freezing winters, grow pansies as annuals in the cool spring and fall. In the South and Southeast, set out pansies after the summer heat has broken to beautify your garden all winter. They can even survive a sudden cold snap, especially if you cover them with a cardboard box or sheet of plastic overnight. They'll last through late winter and early spring until it gets too hot for them.

Colorful kale looks wonderful in winter. The ornamental flowering kale, not the kind you eat, is a wonderful source of winter color. It's easy to grow and, with highly colored leaf rosettes that vary from white to cream to rose to purple, it gets showier as the weather gets colder. Ornamental kale is usually sold as a spring bedding plant, but it actually does better in cooler fall weather or in winter temperatures above 20 degrees. Start them from seed in early spring or late summer or transplant seedlings. For a showy flowerpot or window box, mix ornamental kale with pansies.

Help chrysanthemums weather winter. If you live south of USDA Hardiness Zone 5, you shouldn't have any trouble getting your chrysanthemums through the winter. But where it's colder, pay closer attention to these pretty fall flowers when temperatures start to drop. Make sure they're in a relatively sheltered, well-drained spot away from cold, dry winds. The right amount of moisture is important — dried out mums will die in the winter and too much wetness on their shallow roots will cause them to rot. Other overwintering alternatives are raised beds, mulching, and cold frames.

When to plant perennials. You can transplant perennials any time of year, but the best time is in the autumn when the air is cool and the ground is warm. In the fall, the growth cycle concentrates more on the root growth necessary for a long, productive life. They'll also bloom the following summer, while spring-planted perennials don't usually bloom the first year. If you live where fall is a short season and winters are harsh, wait until spring. Perennials generally stand up to cold weather better than hot, but they need several weeks of mild growing weather to get started.

Plant spring bulbs when it's cool. Spring-flowering bulbs have to be planted in the fall. If they don't get a proper "cooling-off" period, they might not bloom at all. Exactly when you plant depends on where you live. The rule of thumb is the colder your climate, the earlier you plant. Put them in as soon as nighttime temperatures stay around 40 to 50 degrees, but make sure they're in before the first frost. Bulbs need about six weeks before the ground freezes to put down good roots.

Mulch protects against winter sun. You might think your garden would welcome a warm, sunny day in the midst of subfreezing winter weather. But that's not the case. When the ground thaws and then freezes again, the roots of your overwintering plants heave up out of the ground, resulting in damage and serious setbacks in the spring when the plant is ready to start growing again. Protect your perennials and other shallow-rooted plants from heaving with 5 inches of mulch, applied after the ground freezes, to keep it from warming up too fast.

Insulate with winter mulch. In the summer, mulch holds moisture and discourages weeds, but winter mulch is an insulator. Mulch vulnerable plants before the first frost to protect them from low temperatures. But for hardy perennials and biennials, wait until the ground freezes to lay down your mulch insulation. These plants start sprouting when the ground warms up. However, the first thaw is often a "false spring," followed by more freezing temperatures. Mulch protects plants from these weather fluctuations and keeps them cold until it's safe to sprout.

Best time to tidy up. If you have mild winters, it's a good idea to clean out your perennial beds and borders in the fall. It looks neater and gets rid of dead growth where pests and diseases like to hibernate. But if it stays cold long enough to kill off the bad stuff, you might wait until spring to tidy up. Birds can eat the leftover seeds, and the dead growth will help protect the foliage underneath.

Avoid wintertime drought. Drought can be a wintertime problem because roots can't absorb moisture from frozen ground. Avoid this by watering thoroughly in the fall and continue until the ground freezes. Mulching helps keep the ground moist and at a more even temperature. Pay particular attention to evergreens, rhododendrons, and other year-round plants.

Help prepare plants for winter. Hardening off isn't just a spring task for preparing transplants. Perennials and shrubs also need to harden off in the fall to get ready for the rigors of winter. Start lengthening the time between waterings in late summer to toughen the plant and stop new growth that will be damaged by the first frost. Stop deadheading and allow the plant to go to seed — a signal to plants that it's time to go dormant for the winter. Nature helps this process with shorter days providing less light and cooler temperatures.

Select flowering trees carefully. If your flowering trees and shrubs aren't performing as well as you'd like, take a look at your cold weather. Most species need a certain cooling-off period in the winter to stimulate their fancy spring blossoms. Others are winter-hardy only to a point — too much cold will nip their buds before they can bloom. These problems are likely when cold-climate trees are grown in the South or warm-climate trees in the North. Get the most out of your ornamentals by matching the plant's climate requirements to your own Hardiness Zone.

Find shelter for rhododendrons. It's just as important to protect rhododendrons from winter warmth as it is to keep them from getting too cold. Winter sun may bring them out of dormancy too soon. It's also important to keep them out of the wind. Rhododendrons and other evergreens with broad leaves lose a lot of moisture through their foliage on bright, windy days. Rhododendrons have varying levels of cold hardiness, so get varieties that match your climate. Then plant them in a sheltered spot — they need shade in the summer, too — or be prepared to put up windbreaks and sunscreens for winter protection.

Give evergreens a winter blanket. Broadleaf evergreens, like rhododendron, camellia, azalea, and some varieties of gardenia, are easily damaged by rapid freezing and thawing. Cover them with blankets for protection against severe winter cold. To prevent the blanket from touching the leaves, drive some stakes around the plant and drape the blanket over them. Remove the blanket when the temperature rises, but leave the stakes in place in case it gets cold again. You can also use burlap, sheets, or any other cloth material, but don't use plastic. It cuts off air to the plant and also gives a greenhouse effect when the sun comes out.

For best color, buy trees in fall. If you want trees and shrubs with the most stunning fall foliage, shop for them just as the leaves are beginning to change color. That way you can see for yourself which plants will put on the best show. Fall color depends on many climatic conditions, including night and day temperatures, light intensity, and length of day. Large retailers don't always stock the particular variety best suited to their area, so it helps to see what it's really going to look like. Autumn is also a good time to plant trees, and they might be on sale.

Best time to transplant a tree. The best time to transplant trees and shrubs is when they are dormant, from late fall to early spring. Transplanting is a traumatic experience for plants. Trees seem to stand it better in late autumn when they lose their leaves. Just remember to wait for a good, hard freeze. You can successfully move a tree from then until it leafs out in the spring. You're usually OK even when the buds turn green but wait until fall once the leaves start to develop.

Stop winter tree girdling. Animals and rodents turn to tree bark for food when winter covers everything else with snow and ice. They chew and gnaw your trees, destroying essential cells just under the bark. This girdling can seriously damage or even kill the tree. If you can't keep deer, rabbits, mice, voles, and squirrels away, install tree guards around the trunks. Or get rodent repellents that can be sprayed or painted on the tree.

Shake snow off limbs. Few sights rival the beauty of a fluffy, wet spring snow. The morning sun sparkling on the snow-laden branches of hedges, shrubs, and trees is a winter wonderland to behold. But don't admire it too long — get out and shake the snow off the limbs before they snap off or sag so low your landscaping is permanently disfigured.

Snow can help – and hurt – your garden. Snow is good for your garden. It holds a lot of air and works like mulch by forming a blanket of insulation against below-freezing temperatures and protecting tender shoots from the wind. And while you're dealing with snow, get it off your garden paths, sidewalks, and driveways with a shovel. If you use salt or other snow-melt products, the chemical runoff will wash into your garden and poison the soil.

Flush out salty soil. Salt burn keeps plant leaves from getting enough water, turns them brown, and eventually kills the plant. It is common where there's low rainfall and overfertilized or alkaline soils, where lots of road salt is used, and along the seashore. If your microclimate is salty and you have plants that are not adapted to dry or saline conditions, irrigate the ground heavily about once a month to leach the salt out of the soil and give your plants a chance to get enough moisture. Hose down oceanfront plantings with fresh water to remove salt from the foliage.

Salt burn or wind burn? You can distinguish salt burn from wind burn by the type of leaves that are turning brown and dying. Wind burn affects young, new leaves, and salt burn attacks mature leaves first.

High pressure boosts air pollution. If you can't figure out why your plants aren't doing well, the problem could be air pollution. It happens gradually, and the initial effects sometimes aren't noticeable. Damage from air pollution includes dead or discolored leaves and stunted growth. It's worse during the warm, humid, clear, still weather that comes with high barometric pressure. The biggest pollutants are ozone, most common in the eastern United States, and smog, more prevalent on the West Coast. The best defenses against air pollution are healthy plants and resistant varieties.

Keep hanging baskets moist with ice. Hanging baskets dry out fast in hot weather — so fast you often need to water them twice a day. If you can't get to your baskets that often, give them a steady supply of moisture by using ice. Freeze water in small plastic bottles and turn them upside down in the basket. You can also put ice cubes in a plastic bag with holes punched in it or just scatter ice cubes in the basket. The slow melting keeps the compost moist and doesn't run off or drip through the basket.

Produce bigger, better veggies

Start right for great asparagus. The secret to a long-lasting, productive asparagus bed is patience and a lot of elbow grease. To prepare the bed, dig a trench about 12 inches wide and 12 inches deep. Layer compost at the bottom and plant the soaked asparagus crowns about 18 inches apart. Cover them with compost and water well. As the spears grow, shovel dirt into the hole until it is full, then top with compost and mulch. Fertilize once or twice over the summer and keep the bed weed-free. Wait two years to harvest your spears, then pick them regularly thereafter.

Triple your asparagus bounty. If your area enjoys mild summers, you can stretch asparagus season into the fall. Start by planting them in a large, rectangular bed. In the early spring, harvest only from the first third of the patch. Let the other two-thirds grow ferny. In eight weeks, switch to the second third. Cut off the wispy growth and harvest the new shoots. Let the section you picked first grow full-size fronds to feed its roots for next year. Finally, cut down and harvest the last patch in mid-summer. You should be able to bite into tender stalks until frost sends the plant into hiding.

Harvest asparagus carefully. One of the sweetest rites of spring is collecting tender asparagus spears from an awakening garden. Make sure you take a sharp knife for your harvest, and trim off the spear just below ground level. You can also snap it off near the base of the plant, being careful not to damage the roots. Remember, asparagus should be harvested only from its third year on. Any earlier, and you will weaken the plant.

3 reasons to combine tomatoes and asparagus. Plant tomatoes around your asparagus bed as soon as you finish harvesting the spears. Tomatoes protect the feathery fronds from asparagus beetle and will keep the extensive root system cool. Asparagus return the favor by repelling nematodes that kill tomato plants.

Destroy insects' winter time-share. If you see spotted beetles that look like ladybugs hanging out in your asparagus patch, squash them without mercy. These are asparagus beetles. To keep them from coming back, every winter cut all brown asparagus fronds to the ground. Otherwise, these pesky beetles will lay eggs in the dry stalks and destroy your long-awaited spring harvest.

Build a teepee for tasty peas. Don't throw away all the branches you pruned off trees and shrubs in the fall. Stick some in the ground when you plant your bush peas or gently poke the long, twiggy branches in a loose teepee around the seedlings before your beans start running. The vine will race up the poles and produce a bumper crop of flowers and pods.

Give beans a running start. Like all runners, beans need a lot of water to finish the race. To make watering simple, dig trenches between your rows and pile the dirt around your seedlings. Lay the hose down at the beginning of the trench and flood it, and your beans should be well-stocked for the run of their lives.

Separate feuding legumes and lilies. Beans of all kinds detest members of the onion family. So don't plant peas next to leaks, broad beans around garlic, or peanuts near shallots.

Beans need relatively dry, compost-rich dirt to flourish, and onions compete for the same soil.

Think spring for fall harvest. Vegetable gardening is an exercise in futuristic thinking. If you want to harvest broccoli, brussels sprouts, or cabbage in the fall, you need to plant your seeds in the spring. In most of the country, May is an ideal time to sow seeds of slow-growing fall veggies.

Harvest sprouts from the ground up. Brussels sprouts are one of the strangest-looking vegetables to populate the veggie patch. Pick the tiny cabbage-like sprouts when they are about an inch in size. In the excitement of harvest, don't forget that these mini-cabbages ripen from the lowest heads to the highest ones. So pick the bottom ones first.

Extend sprout harvest. Once brussels sprouts start developing, speed up the harvest by picking off all the leaves on the bottom 7 inches of the central stalk. Just remember to leave some at the top to nourish the plant. The cabbage will immediately put all its energy into growing taller and producing more sprouts. Keep picking and pruning until winter puts an end to the harvest.

Cultivate cabbage on solid ground. Cabbages are rugged and actually thrive in conditions other vegetables hate. Dig and fertilize your cabbage bed for your tender seedlings earlier than the others, then trample all over it. By the time you plant, the ground will be good and hard, just the way cabbages like it.

Cabbages like tough love. Your cabbages will grow too fast, drink too much water, and then crack — unless you prune their roots. Do this by spinning their head half a turn around, tugging it slightly out of the ground, or digging a spade about 6 inches around its stem.

Stop club root with rhubarb. Sacrifice a rhubarb pie for your cabbage patch. Instead of mixing the red stems with strawberries, strip the leaves and plant the stems in a ditch around your cabbage patch to prevent club root. This nasty little disease can wipe out your entire cabbage patch by spreading from one plant to the next. But rhubarb will catch it before it spreads and save your patch from certain death.

Get two heads for the price of one. For all the trouble that goes into raising cabbage, you should get double the pay. Here's how you can. Keep an eye on your spring planted cabbage. Once the head reaches a reasonable size, cut it off right above the highest set of loose leaves. Leave the roots, stem, and bottom leaves intact. When a small ring of heads appears around the stem, side dress your cabbage with compost. If you want another full head of cabbage, thin the heads to just one healthy specimen. Otherwise, let them all grow, and you'll have a collection of small heads to grace your fall table.

Mark the spot with radishes. Mix about 20 percent radish seeds in with 80 percent carrot seeds. Radishes are quick to pop out of the ground and mark where the more tender and slow-growing carrots are hiding. And since they are soon ready to harvest, you can have them out of the ground before your carrots need the space.

Safeguard carrot seeds. Keep manure away from your carrot seeds when you plant them. Whether it's fresh or rotted, manure causes carrots to get "leggy" and take on all sorts of odd shapes.

Shield carrots from the sun. It's easy to grow carrots, but don't let a large, green canopy fool you into pulling them up before they're ready. They may still be small underground. If you spot part of the orange root peeking out before it's time to harvest, mulch it heavily or mound dirt around it. This orange top will turn green and bitter if left out in the sun — a condition nicknamed "green shoulder."

Blanch celery for milder flavor. For celery that's white, tender, and mildly flavored, cut off the top and bottom of a half-gallon milk or juice carton. Slip it over your celery plant, and let the stalk grow through the top.

Use tin for tender celery. To produce long, white, tender stalks of celery, cut the bottom and the top off a clean tin can and place it over the developing stalks. This wrap will shade their tender shoots from the sun so they stay white and supple. Light glinting off the silver sides will also confuse aphids and keep your stalks whole for harvest.

Three's company in the corn patch. Corn, beans, and squash grow so well together Indian tribes call them the "three sisters." Tall cornstalks support trailing beans and shade squash, while squash keep the ground cool. Beans replenish the soil with plenty of food for the others. Squash vines also repel corn pests, including raccoons, who don't like climbing over prickly leaves. Plant your corn first to give it a head start. Once the corn is about 12-inches tall, plant beans around it. Then intersperse squash seedlings between the beans at regular intervals.

Enhance your melon harvest. The creeping morning glory vine may be the plague of your flower garden, but in your melon or corn patch, it's a gift. Indians planted morning glory vines with corn and melons to increase their production.

Attract super bugs with flower power. Flowers look great in the vegetable garden, but they are much more useful than their innocent beauty suggests. Take borage, for instance. Its tiny, blue, star-shaped blooms attract green lacewings. These, in turn, become aphid lions. As their name suggests, these valiant little bugs eat plenty of veggie-chewing pests and are worth their weight in gold. So plant borage among your vegetable rows, and you'll entice this friendly lion into your garden.

Give pests something to bite into. If you have a persistent pest problem, don't spray — give trap crops a try. Trap crops are bug-appealing plants that keep pests occupied and away from the plants that really matter. For instance, sunflowers will draw stink bugs and aphids away from your vegetables. Nasturtiums are irresistible to aphids, and a patch of smart weed can keep Japanese beetles too busy to notice fruit nearby. If you don't have a pest problem, be careful with these tasty lures. They may attract the wrong kind of attention to your garden.

! Ask your local extension agent if the Southern corn rootworm is a problem in your area. If so, don't plant corn with pumpkins. After destroying the corn, the adult worm wreaks havoc for pumpkins.

Pick corn at peak of perfection. It's easy to tell when corn is ripe for the harvest. Simply pull back some of the silky hair and poke the kernels with the tip of your nail. If they press down and don't pop, you've left them on the stalk too long. If they pop and ooze a clear liquid, you're still a few days shy of harvest. But if they pop and a milky white stream shoots out, fire up your grill — the corn is ripe. Check your corn frequently. The heads are perfectly ripe for only about a week.

Easy trick for prettier cauliflower. If you want a snowy-white cauliflower, you have to keep the developing head hidden from the sun. You can blanch the heads by pulling up a few of the outer leaves and tying them over the tiny white crown with a rubber band. Under cover, this vegetable develops quickly. In a week or two, you should have a crispy, white head ready for harvest.

Plant cukes with corn. Cucumbers love the cool shade that tall stands of corn provide. In return, cucumbers scare raccoons away with their unpleasant smell, keeping your corn safe.

Encourage cukes to climb. To get the most cucumbers from your vines, train them to grow up a trellis and keep the branches about a foot long. Pick the cucumbers when they are still young and tender. Just remember to harvest your crop regularly. If you leave mature cucumbers on the vines, your plant will stop producing.

Attract good pests and repel bad. For a bug barrier with a touch of color, plant marigolds and bee balm around your cucumber bed. The roots of marigolds give off a gas that kills nematodes burrowed in the soil. And bee balm attracts bees, who pollinate the plant, ensuring a rich harvest.

Be prepared when Jack Frost departs. Every year, toward the end of winter, call your local county extension office to find out when they expect the last day of frost. Count back to start your seeds so they will be an inch or two tall right after the last frost. The sooner you can get those seedlings adapted and growing in the ground, the faster your harvest will come.

Don't stop to ask for directions. Ask a farmer and he may swear vegetables should be planted east to west, while his neighbor plants his north to south. Instead of trying to follow conflicting directions, plant your garden so each plant gets just the light it needs. Usually, this means planting the tallest vegetables on the north side so they don't shade the rest of the garden. But if you grow cool-weather vegetables, like lettuce, afternoon shade is exactly what they like. If you're trying to grow on a slope, you have little choice but to plant across it, no matter what direction the slope faces.

Wider rows work better. Neat rows of lettuce, carrots, and radishes are the standard of many old-time gardens. But break with tradition and you may find your harvest increasing dramatically. Instead of one narrow, straight row, plant in an area as wide as your rake. Just mark it off with string, then sprinkle your seeds loosely. Greens that grow this close will keep down weeds, preserve water, produce more, and last longer as they stay cool and resist bolting.

Scatter many seeds for mixed salad. Rustle up a mixed planting to save space in your veggie patch. Pour your lettuce, radish, and carrot seeds into an old coffee can. Add some sand so it spreads evenly, then punch small holes in the lid. Sprinkle the mix on a prepared bed and cover it with a thin layer of dirt. As the veggies sprout, thin those that are too close together and add the cuttings to your salad bowl. The mixture of close-growing vegetables should confuse pests and keep weeds under control, but you may spend a wee bit of time hunting for your salad.

Double your crops with less work. Double your space and halve your weeding time by planting different crops together. Lettuce, spinach, beets, and onions are quick to mature. Plant them with slow-growing vegetables, like cabbages, carrots, and corn. They will keep weeds down but be out of your way before the larger plants need the dirt they are growing in.

Build up bed for better harvest. You can plant earlier than your neighbor and enjoy a longer, more fruitful harvest simply by planting in raised beds. A raised bed drains and dries much quicker than the ground nearby. Because of its small size, you can custom build your soil, plant your vegetables closer together, and harvest a bigger crop. The only problem is that improved drainage means your bed can dry out fast in the full heat of summer. So make sure you install a watering system and mulch these beds well, and you will reap the bounty soon after.

Simple steps to a thriving bed. To create an instant garden, lay down an old wooden ladder and fill the spaces between the rungs with fertile soil. Plant shallow-rooted vegetables, like lettuce, spinach, leeks, radishes, and herbs, in the compartments. It's a quick way to put together a tidy garden.

Rotate crops to frustrate pests. Divide your garden into four zones and rotate your vegetable crops among them. Moving them keeps pests under control and prepares the soil for the next crop. For example, start your rotation with the cabbage family since they need rich soil. Follow with a crop of beans, which replenish the soil with nitrogen. Peppers, potatoes, eggplant, or tomatoes can come next since they are greedy eaters. Follow with vining veggies — squash or cucumber. By now, the soil is poor but loose, just perfect for onions, garlic, carrots, parsnips, or celery.

Grow bigger eggplants. To grow supermarket-size eggplants, wait until four fruits start swelling, then pinch off all other buds and flowers. Eggplants that come along later won't have time to develop before the season is over. With a limited crop, this nitrogen-hungry plant can put all its energy into four winners, instead of a slew of losers.

Easy way to harvest. No need to invest in an expensive harvest basket when you can make one out of a gallon milk jug. Simply cut out a large, square hole opposite the handle and punch some holes in the bottom of the jug. String your belt through the handle, and it will free up your hands for the harvest. Once you collect your bounty, stick the jug under water and rinse your vegetables before bringing them inside.

Reap and rinse outdoors. Why bring dirt from your garden inside? Rinse your vegetables outside and let the dirt stay where it belongs. Just remove the bottom of an old wooden produce box and replace it with chicken wire. When you harvest your vegetables, pack them loosely in the box and cart it over to the hose.

Keep overeager crops under control. Some root crops, like horseradish and Jerusalem artichokes, can quickly jump out of their beds and become pesky weeds. To get rid of them, don't wait until fall to harvest. Strip the leaves or dig up the roots from spring to late summer. With constant stress, the roots will not be able to grow big enough to make it through the harsh winter. By next spring, your problem should be solved.

3 reasons to grow kale. Kale can pretty up your plate, protect your vision, and it grows well in cold weather. To enjoy the best flavor of this hardy, healthy treat, harvest it after a frost. Pick leaves from the center of each stalk. Don't bother with the bottom leaves — they are too tough to eat. Leave the undeveloped tender leaves at the top to grow next week's harvest.

New twist on growing leeks. Follow an old European tradition to grow leeks with a long, white stem. Dig a trench a foot deep and pile the dirt to one side. Plant your seeds about 8 inches apart and cover them lightly with soil. When the stalk is as thick as a pencil, mound dirt around its base to hide it from the light. As the plant grows, keep adding dirt until you are ready to harvest. Keep dirt loose and leave a bit of the crown showing or the plant will die. By late summer, this "poor man's asparagus" should be ready for harvest.

Leaf through lots of lettuce. Plant lettuce multiple times throughout the year. But keep an eye on romaine and other loose-leafed varieties, which grow faster than heady types. Turn over any lettuce you don't harvest in time.

Sow a gourmet salad. Spring salad, or mesclun as the French know it, is a refreshing and colorful mix of lettuce, endive, chervil, and arugula leaves. You can easily grow these trendy greens. Just mix together the various seeds and sprinkle them on a prepared bed. Sow only enough seeds to produce greens to feed you for a week. Plant another batch the following week for a continuous harvest. Once they are a few inches tall, chop down the greens to within an inch of the ground and fertilize the bed. Your greens will be ready to pick again in a month.

Sow summer salad greens. It may defy reason, but you can grow lettuce even in the hottest season. Just sprinkle seeds on a prepared bed in the shade of taller vegetables — tomato and pepper plants are ideal. Cover the seeds with a half-inch layer of fine dirt and lay a piece of damp burlap on the soil and keep it constantly moist. Once the seeds poke through the ground, remove the burlap and mulch the seedlings heavily. Make sure they get an inch of water a week. Harvest the greens while the leaves are still tender.

Grow veggies under wraps in winter. You can enjoy fresh, home-grown salad fixings even in the dead of winter. In late fall, set up floating row covers over your carrots, parsnips, turnips, leaf lettuce, or parsley. Stuff them full of straw to insulate the veggies from frost. Remember to mark where the rows are. Roots and tender greens will continue to grow slowly under cover so you can harvest them all winter long. Just be careful to harvest all your carrots before spring, or they will sprout flower heads and grow bitter.

Arrange greens instead of flowers. Bring new meaning to the words "fresh produce" with a salad centerpiece. Sprinkle lettuce seed on some potting soil in an old salad bowl or a low clay pot. Keep it moist and put it in a sunny window. When the greens grow a few inches tall, set the bowl in the center of your dining table. Make this unusual arrangement the cornerstone of a salad bar, and your guests can simply pick what they want directly from the bowl. For season-long munching, plant a bowl every week and grow the greens under lights.

Tipsy tops signal onion crop ready. There should be no question when onions are ready to harvest. When the bulbs are large, the green tops simply fall over. Pull them out of the ground and let them sun for a couple of days before storing them in a cool, dry place.

Tobacco and tomatoes don't mix. Do you use tobacco? Be careful to wash your hands before you touch your tomato or pepper plants. Both of these nightshades are sensitive to the tobacco mosaic virus. To be on the safe side, plant resistant varieties of both.

Fire up the pepper patch. Slip a box of matches in your pocket when you head out into the garden to plant peppers. When you dig a hole, throw in a few match heads and cover them with a layer of dirt before plugging in your transplant. These plants will gobble up the sulfur that's released, but don't let their tender roots touch the matches before they mellow a bit.

Clever way to double your peppers. There's a delicate balance between a strong pepper plant and a bushy one. You don't want a bush with too many branches, but a single stem plant will only produce a few peppers. If your plant has shot up and still hasn't developed more than one stem by the time it's a foot tall, pinch off the uppermost leaves and let a second stalk form along the main stem. Two stalks mean double the peppers.

Pep up your peppers. Spray your blooming pepper plants with a mixture of one tablespoon Epsom salt and one gallon of water. Then spray them again 10 days later. The magnesium in the Epsom salt will encourage the peppers to grow.

Cut cleanly for healthy plants. It might be tempting to just pick ripe peppers and eggplants right off the vine, but if you twist, pull, or rip them off their stem, you risk permanent damage to your plant. Instead, get some really sharp clippers or a knife and cut them off cleanly.

Grow super spuds in straw. If you do one thing this fall in anticipation of spring, set out some alfalfa hay bales in your vegetable garden. By the end of winter, they will be partially decomposed and ready to use as instant planters for potatoes and tomatoes. Simply dig a hole in a bale and fill it with dirt and compost, then plant your seedling. As it breaks down, the bale will feed the growing plant. Many gardeners are surprised how easy it is to harvest spuds from the disintegrating straw.

Clever way to grow potatoes. Use an old trash can. Pick one with drainage holes in the bottom or drill some. Fill the can with 6 inches of soil and stick in the seed potatoes. Top them off with 3 inches of mulch or soil. When leaves appear and the seedlings are 6 inches high, add another layer of soil, and continue this until the can is full of soil. Simply lay the can on its side and shake to harvest your crop.

Great use for old tires. Try this and you'll be surprised how quickly your crop rolls in. Fill an old tire with dirt. Plant several seed potatoes, cover with more dirt, and water well. As the plant grows, stack more tires on top of the first one, and fill the space around the vine with straw. Potatoes will soon sprout all along it. You'll know it's time to collect your spuds when the flowers die or the vine yellows and shrivels up. Break down your tire tower carefully, and collect the clean potatoes from the layers of straw.

Comfort food needs comfrey. Layer withered comfrey leaves in the ditches between your potato mounds. Spuds are fertilizer hogs and love the ready supply of potassium in these plant leaves.

Separate spuds from squash. Don't mix potatoes with squash or tomatoes. Potatoes block the growth of squash vines, and they share a weakness to the same blight that attacks tomatoes.

Crown your regal pumpkin. To grow a pumpkin fit for a king, build it a throne. Form some wire mesh fencing into a large tube shape and secure it. During the winter, fill the tube with all the makings of great compost — grass, fruit and vegetable scraps, paper, and leaves mixed with generous amounts of dirt. In the spring, sow pumpkin seeds on top of the compost heap, and your plant will quickly cover its throne. When it fruits, pinch off all but one healthy specimen. Water and feed it regularly, and you'll have the king of the pumpkin patch sitting in your backyard.

Soak seeds to wake them. Nature has a way of making sure vegetables don't sprout before their time. Beetroot seeds, for instance, are covered with a coating of natural chemicals that slows germination. In the wild, this coating would be washed off by rain, but if your seeds come out of a packet, rinse them well with water, then soak overnight before planting.

Keep horseradish confined. Horseradish is easy to grow and adds a healthy wallop to otherwise bland dishes. But be careful — it can take over your yard. To keep it contained, plant it in a galvanized pipe or a bottomless pot. Sink the pipe in the ground and fill it with fertile soil. Plant the root thick side up and firmly pack down the soil. Be sure to remove the entire root, along with the pipe, at the end of autumn, or next spring, the horseradish will return with a vengeance.

Save seedlings from an early death. Young spring plants are in danger of getting eaten by birds. To keep your vegetable seedlings safe from beady eyes, cover them with plastic mesh baskets, the kind strawberries and mushrooms come in. By the time the plant pushes up against the roof of its cage, it won't be tender or interesting to the birds any more.

Trade achy back for a planting stick. For a quick and easy way to dig holes at exactly the right depth for each vegetable seed, simply wrap a rubber band around the handle of your hoe. Turn it upside down and adjust the rubber band so it marks the exact depth for corn or bean seeds. Now simply go down the row and push the stick into the ground to the correct depth. You can easily switch to a different seed — just adjust the height of the rubber band and start a new row.

Pick spinach off a vine. Spinach shoots up in early spring, but by summer, the delicious green has gone to seed. To enjoy fresh greens from your garden all summer long, grow Malabar spinach. Not a true spinach, this vine is originally from India. It loves the sun and tastes surprisingly like its namesake. To harvest it, pinch off the tender leaves, and let the older, tougher ones nourish the plant.

Why you need to grow basil. Antony and Cleopatra, Napoleon and Josephine, Sonny and Cher — of all the famous couples throughout history, none was as successful as basil and tomatoes. Though basil will grow anywhere, plant it next to a tomato plant, and this fragrant herb will fight off tomato pests and encourage the fruit to grow large and juicy. They even taste well together. Thick slices of tomato with fresh basil and mozzarella cheese are a favored side dish at any Mediterranean table.

Help tomatoes grow more roots. Buy the tallest, healthiest tomato seedling you can find at the nursery, then bring it home and strip all but its top leaves. Tomatoes grown in pots have a root base that is only the size of the pot. When you plant that naked branch lengthwise in a ditch, it will grow roots all along the stem. With a huge root base to pull from, your tomato plant will be the largest, most fruitful plant you have ever seen.

Rotate tomato plants. Don't plant your tomato plants in the same spot every year. Rotating their location helps prevent soil diseases.

Amazing way to boost tomato harvest. Build a Japanese tomato ring in your backyard if you want monster tomato bushes and a bumper crop. First, prepare a round bed in a sunny spot, about 6 feet in diameter. Wrap 10 feet of cattle wire into a cylinder and center it in the cleared bed. Fill it with alternating layers of fertilizer, compost, and shredded leaves, then soak it well. Plant four tomato plants around the cage and tie them to the wire trellis as they grow. Water the compost pile regularly. The tomato roots will find water and plentiful food in the pile.

Pet your tomato plant. To keep your tomatoes stocky and compact, brush them gently with an open palm every time you pass them by. Experts at Cornell University discovered that touching tomato plants keeps the seedlings more compact and better suited to produce tomatoes than their leggy cousins. This works best when the plant is still young.

Cut leaves to trim disease. To keep leaf diseases at bay, trim off all the greenery below the fruiting branches of your tomato plant. Since most diseases come from leaves close to the ground, this should delay or even stop them from ruining your whole crop.

Help your tomato plant grow strong. If you want a strong tomato plant, don't let it rush into fruiting. Keep pinching off the flowers until the plant is bushy and at least a foot tall. Also, pinch off the suckers — new growth that pops up between the stem and an existing set of leaves. If left alone, these growths will form their own branches and could weaken the plant.

Secret for juicy tomatoes. For the sweetest, juiciest tomatoes ever, add powdered milk to their water. Milk is a great source of calcium, which nourishes the plant and can help prevent blossom end rot — the bane of a tomato grower's existence.

Amazing cure for blossom end rot. To give your tomatoes all the calcium they need to prevent blossom end rot, "plant" a small piece of wallboard or gypsum board in the ground close to their root zone. With plenty of calcium to pull from, you shouldn't find any more infected tomatoes.

Fool the birds to save tomatoes. Hang red Christmas tree ornaments on your tomato plants before the fruit appears. Birds will approach and peck at the ornaments. With any luck, they will assume your tomato plants produce ornaments instead of tomatoes and won't return when the real thing is on the vine.

Put an end to boring tomatoes. Be careful not to be too eager when you feed your tomatoes. If you give them too much nitrogen too early, you'll have beautiful, leafy bushes but watery, bland fruit. Wait until the fruit starts showing before you side dress your bushes with a low-nitrogen fertilizer.

Shed light on fruiting vegetables. Peppers and tomatoes need radiant heat to produce large, full-flavored crops. You can ripen tomatoes faster with aluminum foil. Simply cover the ground under the plant with strips of foil, or drape a nearby fence with a wall of silver to keep developing fruit nice and toasty. Foil mulch will also squelch weeds and keep viruses away from your plants.

Tomatoes love red light. Strange as this may sound, spread a red plastic mulch around your tomato plants, and they will start producing like there is no tomorrow. Studies done at Clemson University show that red plastic reflects red light onto the leaves, fooling the plant into believing it is in competition for sunlight with other tomato-bearing plants nearby. It will then put more energy into shoots than roots, and you should harvest a bonanza. Just be sure to keep the soil evenly wet and fertilized, since so much fruit above ground can compromise the roots below.

Pick early to avoid cracks. If your tomatoes tend to crack, they absorb more water than their thickening skin can hold in. Pick them three to four days before they are perfectly ripe — usually when they start turning pink. Leave them in a warm, dark place, and they will turn a brilliant red without straining their skins.

Plant an easy-to-grow tomato. If your cool, wet climate gives your tomato plants fits, try cherry tomatoes next season. These small but hearty plants will grow no matter where you live.

Suspend vines on a horizontal trellis. Give your vines a bed to lie on. Suspend a square frame covered with chicken wire about a foot over your seedlings. The trailing vines will quickly find their reclining trellis and spread out, shading their own roots and keeping them moist and cool. You can easily apply fertilizer and mulch under the spreading canopy and harvest clean veggies from the overhang. Bugs don't like the breathing space and should be easy to spot once they arrive.

Support squash with pantyhose. Dress your heavy vining vegetables in pantyhose, and they will stay free of insects. Simply tie two ends of a pair of pantyhose to a trellis, forming a hammock to gently support each squash or melon. As they grow, the pantyhose will stretch, so there is no need to adjust the tension. These hammocks discourage birds, snails, worms, and other munchers from boring into your precious harvest.

Protect veggies with milk. Sprinkle outdoor plants with the water you swish around in an empty milk jug before recycling it. Tomatoes, eggplant, peppers, and potatoes love milky water because it kills the tobacco mosaic virus. It also protects cabbages from cabbage worms.

Bury a bucket for a quick soak. Save time watering. Simply punch holes in the bottom and along the sides of a clean five-gallon bucket and mound soil around it. Plant larger vegetables, like tomatoes, potatoes, squash, melon, and beans, around the hill that hides the bucket. Fill it with water and the drainage holes will release water slowly right where it's most needed — at the roots. To feed and water at the same time, dump a shovelful of manure in the bucket and fill with water as usual. The manure tea will fertilize the soil, assuring you of a lush and tasty crop.

Bushels and bushels of fruits and berries

Simple way to beat the bare years. Do your fruit trees bear bushels of fruit one year and almost none the next? When fruit-bearing is sparse in alternate years, it's called biennial bearing or alternate bearing. You may be able to break the cycle if you thin even more fruit than usual from the trees during a heavy-bearing year.

Thin high-hanging fruit by taking a pole. Got a broom handle or a long pole of similar thickness? Wrap the end with part of a rubber hose or a thick covering of tape, and you can use it to thin fruit off the top branches of your fruit trees.

Wrap a fig tree for winter. People who live north of the fig's natural range can still grow fig trees. Some gardeners grow them in the ground, while others put them in containers. As winter cold approaches, fig wrapping becomes all the rage. Intrepid gardeners trim and prune their trees. Then they wrap them in several snug layers using burlap, newspaper, blankets, rugs, or cardboard. If you try this, gently tie each layer closed with rope. Experts warn against using plastic garbage bags and black plastic as a final layer. Instead, give your fig a raincoat of tar paper so everything inside stays dry.

Grow full-size apples on mini-trees. Growing dwarf apple trees is a great idea for home gardeners. Although the tree is only 6 to 10 feet tall, the apples grow full-size. Harvesting and caring for the tree is made easy by its small height. Even better, dwarf trees bear their first apples at least two years earlier than standard-size trees.

Don't flush flavor out of fruit. For the tastiest apples and pears, don't water your fruit trees too much. The excess water can also make soft fruits, like figs, split open as they ripen.

Set trap for apple maggots. Protect your apples from apple maggots by making traps from plastic balls, like the kind craft stores sell to decorate as Christmas ornaments. Paint the balls red and coat them with a sticky substance, like Tangle-trap, you can find at a plant nursery. Hang five to eight traps on an average-size tree. Check them every two or three weeks. If they are completely covered with dead insects and other blown-on debris, clean them off, reapply the glue, and rehang.

Mix up an apple worm brew. A few minutes in your kitchen could keep the worms out of your apples. Here's how. Before your apple blossoms open, grab an empty milk jug. Pour in one quart of vinegar, a quart of water, and one cup of sugar. Top it off by stuffing in a banana peel. Hang this "tree ornament" without its cap in the middle of the tree. Make one for each tree to help keep your apples worm-free.

Keep apples safe. Are you afraid when you bite into an apple with a blemish you'll find a worm? Make sure apple maggots don't get to the fruit before you do. When apples are about half an inch in size — before the flies emerge, usually around July 1 — put a clear plastic bag over each one and secure it with a twist tie. Cut off the bottom corners so any moisture inside the bags can drain out. Although the sun shines through the plastic to help them ripen, these apples may not be as red as unprotected ones.

See red for better berries. For larger, sweeter strawberries, mulch with red plastic rather than black. It's no joke! The USDA says so.

> ! Before you buy a black currant or gooseberry plant, check with your local extension agent. Some states ban or restrict currants and gooseberries because both shrubs can host white pine blister rust, a hazardous tree disease.

Stop bingeing birds with curtains. Are the birds getting more berries from your bushes than you are? To keep birds and other hungry animals out of your fruit vines and berry bushes, try this. Cover the vines and bushes with old, sheer curtains. The curtains will stop those eager nibblers with no harm done to creatures or plants.

Give blueberries new mulch for Christmas. You know your blueberries need mulching before January's cold weather sets in, but you can't possibly take the time to track down new mulch until after Christmas. Fortunately, the mulch you need might already be sitting in your family room. Once your holiday celebrating ends, break down your live Christmas tree and use its branches for mulch. Evergreen mulches increase the soil's acidity, and blueberry bushes insist on acidic soil. But you don't have to wait for the Christmas season to arrive. Your blueberry bushes may appreciate an evergreen mulch anytime they need protection from winter cold.

Treat blueberries to well-aged sawdust. What may look like old, rotting sawdust to you looks like a mouthwatering dessert to your blueberry plants. New sawdust just won't cut it. To please your blueberries, sawdust needs to be old enough to rot a little. Give your blueberry bushes a mulch of well-aged sawdust, and you may be surprised at what they can do. Just make sure you don't use sawdust from chemically-treated wood.

Mix blueberry varieties for better harvest. If you're planting blueberry bushes, why not plant at least two varieties? After all, blueberry varieties from the "rabbiteye" group won't even produce berries if you just plant one bush. They need to cross-pollinate to grow berries. But, even if you don't grow rabbiteye blueberries, consider growing more than one variety anyway. The "highbush" varieties are able to produce berries with just one bush, but you'll get better results if you plant two highbush varieties.

Pick blueberries at their sweetest. Experts say blueberries may not be completely ripe until one to three days after they turn blue. Could it be worthwhile to wait a day or two before harvesting those berries? Why not put it to the test? Clean and taste a few berries the day they turn blue. No matter when you decide to harvest most of the bush, tag a few of the newly blue berries and leave them on the bush for taste-testing. Sample several berries on each of the next three days. When you're done, you'll know exactly when to pick to get the best-tasting blueberries.

Try a trellis for simpler blackberry harvesting. It's easy to see why trailing varieties of blackberry work well on a trellis, but consider one for the erect varieties, too. When erect varieties are on a trellis, they're both easier to cultivate and easier to harvest.

Pick "dull" blackberries for delicious flavor. Don't pick blackberries before they're at their best. Here's a trick to help you decide when to pick. Pay close attention to whether your berries are shiny black or dull black. Glossy berries aren't quite ready to pick yet, but duller berries are ready to snatch.

Isolate garden blackberries from wild. Plant garden blackberries well away from any wild-growing brambles of raspberry or blackberry. Your blackberry plants are more likely to become infested with diseases or pests if they're close to wild berries.

Bag grape clusters just like apples. Bagging doesn't just work for apples. If your grapes are likely to be raided by birds or other pests, slide a paper bag over each cluster and tie the sack shut. Check the bunches for ripeness from time to time until the grapes are ready for harvest.

Grow sweeter grapes. Plant your vines where they'll get the most sunshine, and you'll be rewarded with sweet grapes. A south-facing wall or slope is ideal. And if you grow them in rows running north to south, your plants will receive the most sunlight and will be more protected from wind damage, as well.

Encourage cats to stand guard. Attract cats to your yard by planting catnip. Birds will keep clear of your yard and your fruit trees.

Grow your own mangoes. Start by eating one. Clean off its husk, or seed, and pry it open. Inside, you'll find a pit. Place this in a sealable plastic bag filled with moist peat moss or sphagnum. Make sure the pit is covered with the mix and check it every day to see that it's moist but not soaked. Finally, move the pit into a pot when it has roots at least 4-inches long.

Grow fruit outside its hardiness zone. Don't give up hope if your climate isn't right for your favorite fruit. You may still be able to grow it in a container. Lemons, limes, figs, tangerines, and apples are among the fruits you can raise in a good-size planter.

Scare off fruit-snitching squirrels. The fruit in your garden must be good or the squirrels wouldn't steal it every year. This year, stop those four-legged fruit thieves by making a fuss. Get a dozen pie tins and string them from the lower branches of your fruit trees — and make sure the wind will catch them. The rattling and clattering they make will send squirrels scampering somewhere else for easier pickings.

Prop heavy fruit branches. Heavy limbs of fruit can split from the trunk and do serious damage to your fruit trees. To remedy the problem, prop up the branches that are sagging dangerously low. Use 1-inch thick boards with a "V" cut into the end and place them directly under the branch. You might need to place one in the middle and a second one toward the end of the limb.

Select hardy fruits for cold zones. Most stone fruits — those with pits, like peaches — grow best in warm climes. But if you are a gardener in one of the cooler zones, chances are you'll be more successful with sour cherries, apricots, and plums than with peaches and sweet cherries. And it seems changes in temperature can cause as much damage as low temperatures. To help keep temperatures stable, wrap trunks with thick plastic or cloth in the late fall and remove them in spring. Some fruit tree growers find painting the south side of the tree trunk with

Choose a fruit worth the wait

If you're trying to choose which fruit trees to plant in your yard, remember that fruit trees don't bear the first year after they're planted. If you planted a fruit tree seed, here's how long you'd have to wait for fruit from various trees. For apples and apricots, expect a 2 to 5 year wait. Peaches take 3 or 4 years to bear. The wait for pears and plums ranges from 4 to 6 years. Sweet cherries take the longest — 5 to 7 years. If you buy the tree as a sapling, the wait may be shorter. What's more, the dwarf versions of these trees usually bear a year or two sooner than the standard-size trees.

white interior latex paint helps keep bark temperatures moderate.

Tidy up fruit trees. Keep the ground under fruit trees clean of weeds, leaves, and fallen fruit that could harbor disease and insects. Remove any infected fruit immediately and put it in the trash, not the compost. And don't leave rotting fruit on the tree after harvest.

Train branches with a clothespin. While your fruit tree is still a sapling, coax its branches to grow outward so they spread at a good angle from the trunk. To do it, take a spring-type clothespin — or two clothespins clipped together — and wedge it into the fork formed by the branch and the trunk.

Encourage fruit trees to produce. Strange as it may seem, "whipping" your fruit trees with a rolled up newspaper will help them yield more fruit. That's because it loosens the vessels that carry sap to the leaves and buds. And don't worry, this really does hurt you more than it does them.

Mix the right cherry trees to get fruit. Some sweet cherry varieties need another cherry tree nearby for the pollination that leads to fruit. Yet, these snobby cherry varieties are also picky about which other trees they'll work with. To clear up confusion, experts divided the varieties into groups. A variety refuses to pollinate any cherry in its own group but will pollinate a tree from any other group. Bing, Lambert, and Napoleon are in one group, but Van, Venus, and Windsor are in a separate clique. Black Tartarian and Early Rivers are in a third group. Contact your local extension agent for information about sweet cherry groupings in your area.

Give your peach tree a trim. Right after planting a peach tree, trim it down to about 30 inches high and lop off all the branches. As harsh as it sounds, pruning the tree down to this "whip" shape can get the tree off to a very good start.

Deck citrus with lights on frosty nights. Expecting frost tonight? Help protect your citrus trees by stringing old-fashioned — the big bulb kind — outdoor Christmas lights in their branches. Leave the lights on all night. This might also work for other kinds of fruit trees.

Grow melons in a small space. You can grow watermelons, cantaloupes, and pumpkins in a small city garden. Just let them run up a fence or sturdy trellis. When the fruits are small, slip each one inside a length of pantyhose and tie the ends to the fence or trellis. The stockings will stretch as they grow and keep the fruit from falling to the ground.

Hold in heat for sweet melons. Warm up your melon beds, and you'll get sweeter cantaloupes, honey dews, and watermelons. Lay black plastic over seedlings and cut holes for the vines to climb through. The plastic will not only trap and reflect heat to the plant, it will also keep weeds under control.

Is it ripe yet? When the underside of a watermelon turns from white to yellow and the tendril closest to the melon dries and turns brown, it's time to pick it. Cantaloupes let you know they are ready by turning darker and slipping easily from the vine.

Sow a pretty pumpkin patch. Would you like to have some flowers blooming among your pumpkins? Sunflowers make an attractive, sturdy companion. But if you plant sunflowers on your lawn, be sure to gather them before they drop their seeds. A chemical in the hulls will kill the grass.

Pick a better pumpkin. Plant big pumpkins for jack-o'-lanterns. Medium-size varieties, on the other hand, are better tasting in pies and pumpkin bread. The miniature ones make colorful fall centerpieces.

Trick birds with tough berries. As soon as you see green strawberries on your plants, paint small rocks red and place them where birds might be looking for a snack. When the birds try to bite the "fruit," they'll quickly realize these berries aren't good enough to eat. By the time your strawberry crop ripens, they'll be gone, and you'll keep all those berries for yourself.

How to pick healthy strawberry plants. The first step to luscious strawberries is a healthy plant that can take whatever challenges your local weather and soil can dish out. So look for strawberry varieties that grow well in your area. Your local extension service or a good nearby plant nursery can help. To make sure you get plants that aren't struggling with hidden diseases, buy only plants that are certified virus-free.

Try a trick from the pros. Join the strawberry farmers who beat weeds and get better strawberries by treating their plants as annuals. Starting in summer or early fall, put the plants in the ground and give them a plastic mulch. Water regularly for the best results. After harvest, remove all the strawberry plants to make way for next year's planting.

Some strawberries worth the wait. June-bearing varieties of strawberry may not give you strawberries until the second year, but their flavor and quality are worth waiting for. Day-neutral varieties can give you berries the first year, but they may not be as tasty as the June-bearing berries. Why not split your strawberry patch right down the middle and plant both? When June comes, pull the blossoms from both kinds of strawberries for the first few weeks, but let the day-neutral fruits develop after that. While you're snacking on the day-neutral berries, be sure to keep pulling those June-bearing blossoms. If you do, you'll have more spectacular June-bearing strawberries to look forward to the next year.

Ideal depth for strawberry plants. Strawberry plants have three parts — roots, crown, and leaves. If you plant too shallow, the roots won't have enough cover to keep them from drying out. If you plant too deep, the crown, which is a short stem between the leaves and the roots, can get smothered. The best way is to cover the roots completely, but cover only half of the crown.

Find a favorable locale. To help avoid problems with pests and diseases, never plant strawberry plants where potatoes, tomatoes, or sod were recently grown.

Point strawberries in the right direction. To help strawberries dry out more quickly and avoid fungal problems, orient your rows so they run in the direction of the prevailing wind for your area.

Keep strawberry plants high and dry. If better drainage might help your strawberry plants, try growing them on raised rows 6 or 8 inches high. For best results, keep rows about 25 inches wide and space the plants 18 inches apart.

Give your strawberries a straw coat. If you live north of mild winter areas, plan on mulching your strawberries for the winter season. The good news is you won't have a hard time remembering what to mulch them with. Many experts recommend covering strawberries with several inches of straw.

Expand your horizons with herbs

How to grow the most basil. Instead of putting all your basil plants in the ground at once, do what professional basil farmers do. Stagger your basil plantings over several weeks or months. Just like the professionals, you'll have a fresh supply of basil leaves all season long.

Easy way to prevent basil wilt disease. When shopping for seeds of sweet basil, be sure to check whether they have been tested for fusarium wilt. If this fungal disease gets in your soil, you won't just lose your basil plants. You might have to wait as long as 12 years before you can grow basil or mint there again. So play it safe and buy only sweet basil seed that has been tested and declared disease-free.

Great news for basil lovers. While your fellow gardeners are worrying about fusarium wilt lurking in their sweet basil plants, you can grow the first sweet basil to resist this devastating fungal disease. Check with your favorite garden supplier for Nufar basil. You'll enjoy its mild, anise flavor, and you won't miss worrying about fusarium one bit.

Give basil a pinch. Keep your basil pinched back for bushier plants and to prevent flowering.

Grow your own bay leaves. Bay laurel trees are very difficult to grow from seed, so consider getting a cutting or simply buying a baby tree. If you live in a mild winter region, you might be able to plant your bay in well-drained soil. But in most zones, growing it in a large container is best. You can keep it indoors in cool weather and move it outside when the weather feels more tropical. Keep it protected from wind and water it whenever the soil is dry.

Keep bay tree scale-free. If you discover scale on your bay tree, try scrubbing it off gently with a soft cloth dipped in rubbing alcohol.

Dealing with ginseng and goldenseal. Growing these herbs isn't for the casual gardener. After planting these herbs, you may have to wait as long as five years before you can harvest your first root.

Wonder herb for health and garden. Eating garlic can do wonders for your health. Some researchers say it can attack atherosclerosis, clobber cholesterol, bring down blood pressure, banish bacteria, and crush blood clots. Plus, when you grow it in your garden, it keeps aphids away. In fall, when temperatures are cool, plant cloves 4 to 8 inches apart in fertile, slightly moist, well-drained soil. Harvest garlic before the temperature gets too warm. Usually that means May in the South and July in the North. Eight to 10 days before harvest, stop watering and let the soil dry thoroughly before digging up the bulbs.

Keep pests away with bay

Your bay tree can help you repel pests. Keep moths from setting up shop in your drawers by sprinkling bay leaves in them. You'll get protection for your clothes without the annoying mothball smell. While that bay scent may seem refreshing to you, ants don't care for it one bit. So sprinkle bay leaves on your windowsills to help keep those busy ants outside.

Bigger is better with garlic. Plant your biggest garlic cloves first if you want the best bulbs. Line up cloves at 6-inch intervals in rows 12 to 18 inches apart. Place each

> ! Use bay leaves to season your food while cooking but remove them before taking food to the table. Bay leaves are sharp and can cut your mouth or throat if you eat them.

individual clove 2 inches deep with its flat end down. Then cover them all with an inch of soil.

Cholesterol busters from your garden. Garlic, fenugreek, hawthorn, and onion are cholesterol busters you can grow right in your yard or garden. They might even help you slash your cholesterol without drugs. Dried hawthorn berries and leaves can be used to make a cholesterol-lowering tea. Just remember it takes a while to work and can be toxic if taken in large doses. Play it safe and check with your doctor before trying hawthorn or any herbal remedy.

Take "thyme" for a fragrant walk. Plant creeping thyme in the cracks between the stones of your garden path or sidewalk. Not only will it keep the weeds from taking over, you'll enjoy the pleasant smell that rises as you crush the tiny leaves underfoot.

Secret for harvesting chamomile. Harvest German chamomile flowers when the petals begin to bend backward and the center starts to go brown.

Be choosy with chamomile. When you ask for chamomile at your local garden center, be specific about which chamomile you want. German chamomile (*Matricaria recutita*) is an annual that grows to 18 inches, while Roman chamomile (*Anthemis nobilis* or *Chamaemelum nobile*) is a low-growing perennial sometimes used as a ground cover. If you plan to make chamomile tea, keep in mind that German chamomile has a sweeter taste than the Roman kind. German chamomile also grows better in clay soils.

Sit back and enjoy a cup of tea. You don't have to drink the same old tea day after day. Start an herbal tea garden for a fragrant array of fresh choices. Many tea gardens include chamomile (*Matricaria recutita*), peppermint (*Mentha piperita*), spearmint (*Mentha spicata*), pineapple mint (*Mentha suaveolens variegata*), and lemon balm (*Melissa officinalis*). To make herbal tea, add one cup of boiling water to a tablespoon of fresh leaves, or a teaspoon of dried leaves. Let steep for 10 minutes and strain.

Having trouble sleeping? Try a cup of chamomile tea. If you're allergic to ragweed or other types of pollen, sip lemon balm tea or catnip tea instead.

Harvest leaves before lunch. For many herbs, the best time of day to harvest leaves is morning — and here's why. Essential oils are the secret behind the incredible scents and flavors in herbal leaves. Those leaves are brimming with the most oil just after the dew dries from them. So for the best flavor and fragrance, harvest the leaves then.

Can't miss tip for harvesting roots. In autumn, keep an eye on the foliage of herbs, such as chicory. When the foliage fades, you can harvest the roots.

When to harvest for best flavor. When you're harvesting herbs to use in the kitchen, you always want to get the most essential oils from the seeds and flowers. To do that, harvest herb flowers for drying just before the flowers open fully. When harvesting herb seeds, wait until they change from green to brown. This applies to most culinary herbs, but don't forget that anise seed should be harvested when the seed heads turn either yellow or brown.

Freezing good alternative to drying. You harvested more fresh herbs than you can use right now, so your first thought is to dry them. But some herbs simply don't dry

Think twice before growing chamomile

If you're allergic to ragweed, asters, or chrysanthemums, you're more likely to be allergic to chamomile. People who are allergic to chamomile may experience itching, develop a skin rash, or have severe breathing problems — in rare cases. Fortunately, very few people are allergic to the herb. Between 1887 and 1992, only 50 allergic reactions to chamomile were reported worldwide. Generally, chamomile is safe, but keep these precautions in mind. Don't use chamomile while taking prescription drugs because it can interfere with the absorption of some medicines. And don't overdo it — large quantities of chamomile can cause vomiting.

well. For better results with chervil, chives, cilantro, or lemon balm, freeze them instead. Here's how to do it. After you've cleaned the herbs, tie them up in bundles. Dip each bundle in boiling water for a few seconds and then drop them in ice water to cool. To finish up, just pack them in plastic bags or containers and put them in the freezer.

Store parsley in water for quick use. You've just harvested some parsley, and you plan to use it in the next day or so. Instead of freezing it for long-term storage, keep the stems in a water-filled container in your refrigerator.

Enjoy best chive harvest ever. Get more chive flavor and more chive leaves with these harvest tips. Before you harvest from a chive plant for the first time, let the herb grow to at least 4 inches high. But when you're ready to take the scissors to it, trim it down to just 1 or 2 inches. This triggers your chive to sprout new leaves. If you just trim the tops, that won't happen. Also, be sure to harvest the leaves regularly. If you forget for too long, the flowers will bloom, which means poor flavor for the rest of your harvests.

Dry a smattering of seasonings. To dry a small batch of kitchen herbs, like sage, basil, parsley, chives, and rosemary, try this low-hassle hint. Spread them on a covered plate and put it in a dark, dry place for a few days. When the herbs crumble easily, store them in airtight jars in a dark place.

Dry herbs on window screens. Don't throw out those old window screens. Give them a good cleaning, and use them to dry newly harvested herbs instead. To set up "Herb Drying Central," just find a dark, dry place that is well-ventilated and free of pests. Next, place the screens so air can circulate above and below them. Then bring on those herbs. Dill seed, coriander seed, fennel, lemon balm leaves, summer savory, winter savory, and sage are just some of the herbs you can spread out to dry on these cost-free drying screens.

No-hassle way to dry seeds. To dry herb seeds without making a mess, hang the herb upside down in a paper bag and put the sack in a dark, dry place. The seeds will fall into the bottom of the bag.

Try your oven. To speed-dry herbs in your oven, place the leaves on a cookie sheet. Slide the pan into an oven set on low heat, no more than 180 degrees, and leave the oven door open. Drying should take about two to four hours, but this varies widely so be sure to check the herbs often.

Clever way to cook with basil. Drying isn't the only option for preserving freshly harvested basil. Try this great idea for basil you plan to use in cooking. Drop your basil into a blender with some water. Run the blender and pour the mixture into an ice cube tray. Let freeze. Store your basil cubes in plastic bags in the freezer. The next time you're making spaghetti sauce or soup throw a fragrant cube into the simmering pot.

Time garlic harvest perfectly. To know exactly when to harvest garlic, plant more than you need and keep a close eye on the leaves. Those leaves are your early warning system. When the lower leaves turn brown or yellow, harvest time is near. To find out whether it's really time to harvest, dig up one or two whole plants — roots, shoots, and all. Cut open the bulb. If the cloves inside have separated, start harvesting your other garlic plants, too.

Spice up meals with home-grown herbs

Check out these heart-healthy ways to perk up flavor without using salt. Be creative and try different combinations.

- Fish — basil, dill, garlic, parsley, fennel, or sage.
- Chicken — dill, garlic, or rosemary.
- Lean meats — bay leaves, caraway, chives, garlic, parsley, sage, or thyme.
- Soups — basil, bay leaves, chives, dill, garlic, oregano, parsley, or thyme.
- Stews — basil, bay leaves, or sage.
- Sauces — basil, chives, garlic, parsley, rosemary, or thyme.
- Vegetables — chives, garlic, or parsley.

Unbeatable herbs for shade. Many herbs will thrive in a shady area. For a spot that has partial or light shade, plant valerian, borage, chervil, lemon balm, pennyroyal, sweet cicely, comfrey, or violet.

Landscape with silver herbs. Looking for the right silvery accent to gild your garden's look? Herbs can help. Try lamb's ear (*Stachys byzantina*), dusty miller (*Senecio cineraria*), or silver sage (*Salvia argentea*) for that gentle brushstroke of silver to help make your garden picture perfect.

Tempt hummingbirds to visit your herbs. Herbs can attract hummingbirds to your yard. Try hyssop, anise hyssop, comfrey, rosemary, and catmint in your garden and see if you don't gain a hummingbird or two. Also, experiment with varieties of bee balm and sage to find out which ones your local hummers like best.

Super idea for marshy soil. If part of your yard or garden stays too damp for plants that don't like "wet feet," herbs could still be the answer. Try angelica, lovage, or a member of the mint family, such as spearmint or peppermint. Unlike most other herbs, these do better in wet soil.

Confine these herbs to hanging baskets. Peppermint, spearmint, and creeping rosemary do well in hanging baskets. But don't stop there. Hang them near your kitchen for easy snipping. Just be sure to water them often.

Bask in a lemony fragrance. For the fresh scent of lemons without the lemon tree, grow lemon-scented herbs. Gardeners recommend lemon verbena (*Aloysia triphylla*) for its fragrance. Lemon balm (*Melissa officinalis*) also has a lovely citrus aroma. For a delicious touch of lemon, add leaves from either one to tea. You can also grow lemon grass (*Cymbopogon citratus*) or the lemon-scented varieties of thyme, basil, catnip, or mint to add a delightful scent of lemon to your home or backyard.

Line edges with fragrant hedges. Some herbs are ideal for trimming into fragrant hedges. Lavender, rosemary, and santolina are good choices.

Plant an herb garden in a wheel. Would you like a charming way to plant a small herb garden — or even create a small theme garden? Nose around at yard sales or flea markets for an old wagon wheel. Find a good spot for growing the herbs and lay the wheel on its side. Fill the spaces between the spokes with fertile soil and plant a different herb in each one. Not only will you enjoy the herbs, you'll also love the way this charming piece accents your garden.

Great way to organize your herb garden. What might look like an old wooden ladder that's ready for retirement is actually an ideal herb garden organizer. Just lay it on the ground and fill the spaces with soil. When you're done, you'll have a line of small raised beds. All you have to do is plant different herbs in each section.

Say goodbye to fruit flies. Grow basil in window boxes and in pots near your doors to keep fruit flies from entering your house.

Turn weedy to wonderful with sweet woodruff. This hardy perennial is one tough customer. If you have a shaded, weedy area of your yard that has poor soil, try sweet woodruff as a ground cover. Not only can it do well in less-than-ideal conditions like these, it will also choke out weeds.

Keep dill and fennel apart. Do you love dill's delicious taste — or favor the flavor of fennel? Then be sure to plant them a good distance apart. If you plant these herbs side by side, they cross-pollinate and create odd-tasting seeds. To avoid these quirky flavors, make sure these two herbs only admire one another from afar.

Outsmart "pushy" herbs. To keep aggressive herbs, like mint, tarragon, or marjoram, from taking over your garden, bury a stovepipe and plant the herb inside.

Surprising way to perk up flavor. Your herbs are so loaded with healthy leaves, you just have to harvest a few. But when you use them, you taste barely a wisp of flavor. Even your seeds taste bland. What went wrong? Oddly enough, your herbs may be suffering from too much of a good thing — fertilizer. Try using less fertilizer and see if you get more flavor from your next harvest.

Why you might need cuttings. Some herbs don't produce viable seeds, while others grown from seed don't do very well. For example, oregano from seed may not produce enough aromatic oil to add any flavor to cooking. To save both time and frustration, grow the following herbs from cuttings — lavender, pineapple sage, English thyme, lemon thyme, oregano, peppermint, and French tarragon.

Nip the cats out of catnip. You can grow cat-free catnip with one of these three strategies. If chicken wire is easy to come by, get enough to make a cage around your catnip plants. If that isn't practical, grow your catnip in hanging baskets. Just make sure to put them well out of reach. Perhaps the most fun option is to grow lemon catnip. This lemon-scented variety lacks the full cat-drawing power of regular catnips. Some cats might like it, but most cats will ignore it completely. What's more, it makes a pleasant tea.

Even though it's a kitchen herb, marjoram can pull its weight in aromatherapy, too. It could help lower high blood pressure, relieve anxiety, and bring on restful sleep.

Action plan for healthy thyme. To prevent older thyme plants from developing an open center, divide them or replace them every three to five years.

Be rid of bee balm mildew. If your bee balm plants are plagued by powdery mildew every year, why not try a mildew-resistant variety? Marshall's Delight is a pink-flowered bee balm that might end your mildew problems once and for all.

Nab superb parsley flavor. When you see flower buds on your parsley, rush to remove the flower stalks before it's too late. If you let those blossoms bloom, your parsley leaves will taste bitter.

Save your valerian from cat-astrophe. Catnip isn't the only plant that needs protection from cats. The herb valerian seems to be a cat favorite, too. When you plant valerian, surround it with a chicken wire cage. Otherwise, it could suffer the same sad fate as unguarded catnip.

Repel mosquitos with plants. You may love the fragrance of basil growing in your garden, but mosquitos have a different take. They dislike the smell and will stay clear of your garden or patio where it's growing. And the tansy plant, with its pretty flowers, also smells bad to mosquitos. So plant it, as well, to keep your yard a pest-free zone.

Best way to start scented geraniums. Are you thinking about growing rose-scented geraniums or one of the many other fragrant geraniums? Strangely, many scented geraniums started from seed often have a different aroma than the plant that produced the seed. So instead of sowing seeds of trouble, start your new scented geranium from a cutting. You'll be glad you did.

Follow the rule when sowing seeds. Here's a general rule-of-green-thumb to use when deciding how deeply to plant an herb seed. Take a look at the diameter of the seed. Dig a hole twice that deep for the seed.

Shelter shallow roots. Many herbs have shallow roots, the kind that can easily be affected by soil heaving during spring thaws and freezes. To protect the herbs and their roots, lay a loose, 4-inch mulch around them after the ground freezes. Don't remove the mulch until you see your plants sport signs of spring growth.

Treat some herbs as immovable objects. Sprinkle chervil and fennel seeds directly on the soil. These herbs do not transplant easily and are best sown where they will grow.

Mulch herbs for stronger plants. When summer comes, you can protect your herbs and clean up that pile of grass clippings at the same time. Mulch your herb garden with grass clippings to help control weeds and keep the soil moist. Lay your mulch at least 3 inches deep for best results. If your grass clippings are already spoken for, try bark chips or compost.

Give potted chives a pick-me-up. Chives that dwell in containers — both indoors and out — need a little help every now and then. About every six weeks, give them a dose of liquid fertilizer at one-half the strength recommended on the label. If needed, you can treat them to a half dose of fertilizer as often as once a month.

Grow peppermint in a pot. If planted in the ground, this invasive herb will take over your garden. It's also important to keep it separated from other mints because it cross-breeds readily.

Some people find that sniffing the scent of peppermint oil helps them stay awake. According to research, peppermint oil seems to work best when you're most sleepy.

Attract ladybugs with parsley. Plant parsley, dill, and fennel in your garden, and you'll get more than just good-tasting herbs. These herbs also attract ladybugs — just what you need to help take care of aphid problems. Even better, you'll still be able to harvest and use these herbs after the ladybugs have done their work.

Grow your own calorie-free sweetener. Stevia is a South American herb you may be able to grow as an annual. Plant it in good soil after the last frost. Water frequently and feed it occasionally with a low-nitrogen fertilizer. Harvest the leaves before flowers bloom. The leaves can be dried and used as a sweetener for tea and other beverages.

Feel better with herbal teas

Hyssop (*hyssopus officinalis*) tea has been recommended as a decongestant for centuries. Drink it to loosen phlegm or gargle with it to soothe a sore throat. For tea, steep a teaspoon or two of dried hyssop leaves and flowers in boiling water for 10 minutes. For an upset stomach, drink up to four cups of peppermint tea between meals. To make it, pour a cup of boiling water over a tablespoon of peppermint leaves. Steep for five minutes. But be careful — peppermint makes heartburn and digestive troubles worse for some people. Herbs can interfere with some medications, so check with your doctor before trying any herbal remedy.

Refresh the air with fragrant hyssop. If you like a refreshing, minty, camphor-like smell, you may enjoy growing the herb hyssop. Pick a site with light, well-drained alkaline soil and plenty of exposure to sunlight. Sow seeds in the spring. Harvest the leaves of this perennial anytime, but be sure to pick the flowering tops just as they begin to blossom.

Grow lavender that can take the heat. Think you can't grow lavender because your summers are too hot? While it's true English lavender doesn't do well in hot climates, many other varieties do fine. Try French lavender (*Lavandula dentata*) or Spanish lavender (*Lavandula stoechas*). Just be sure the plant gets full sun and good drainage.

Choose oregano with lots of flavor. For a finer flavor in cooking, look beyond common oregano (*Origanum vulgare*). Grow Greek oregano (*Origanum heracleoticum*) for a more savory taste.

Mexican tarragon beats the heat. You'd like to grow some fresh French tarragon in your kitchen garden, but it can't take the heat of your climate. Try Mexican tarragon (*Tagetes lucida*). It's hardy as far north as zone 8 and can be substituted for French tarragon in cooking. Mexican tarragon is also called mint marigold or Mexican mint marigold.

Taste the difference with perennial cilantro. Instead of regular, old, annual cilantro, why not plant a perennial herb that grows well indoors and brims with better flavor? *Polygonum odoratum* is sometimes called Vietnamese cilantro or Vietnamese coriander. It likes warm weather, lots of water, and partial shade. Harvest the leaves and use them whenever you need cilantro.

Cucumber taste without the cucumber. The fresh, young leaves of salad burnet (*Poterium sanguisorba*) can add a hint of cucumber flavor to salads or other dishes, even if there's nary a cucumber in site. What's more, it looks attractive in hanging baskets or containers. Start it from seed or divide an existing plant.

Prolific chive thrives inside. Persuading herbs to grow indoors can be difficult, but growing the Grolau variety of chive is easy. These indoor chives feature dark leaves and good flavor. Let them grow to about 8 inches high and then trim regularly for an ongoing supply of fresh chives.

Create a successful window box. If you have room for an indoor window box, see if this setup helps your herbs grow better. Put herbs in pots and bury them up to the rim in your window box. Be sure to use pots with drainage holes in the bottom. For maximum sunlight, place the window box on a windowsill or right next to it. You might find that your herbs like their "box seats."

Give these herbs a taste of Jack Frost. Although frost kills many warm-season herbs, a few herbs actually need to "chill out" a little. If the first frost of autumn is a light one, keep chives, mints, and tarragon outside that night. When you bring them indoors the next day, they'll be in a resting state that leads to strong and healthy new growth.

Debug indoor herbs often. Aphids, spider mites, and white flies seem to have a talent for finding their way to indoor herbs. Check your plants for these pests on a regular basis.

Winter care tips for rosemary. Rosemary thrives as a perennial in mild winter areas, but it probably won't survive temperatures below 25 degrees Fahrenheit. So when the thermometer dips below freezing, bring your rosemary inside. To keep a fussy rosemary healthy indoors, remember these three things. First, put rosemary in a south-facing window so it can get plenty of sunlight. Second, put the plant where it can enjoy temperatures in the low 60s. Third, water the plant soon after it becomes fully dry.

Ease outdoor herbs into indoor light. Your sun-drenched, outdoor herbs will have a happier indoor life if you prepare them for less light. First, move them into partial shade for two weeks. Next, move them into deeper shade for a week or two. After that, they'll be prepared to come inside, as long as they get all the indoor light you can give them.

Beauty and first aid from one herb. Echinacea, or purple coneflower, is a real treasure in your garden. It beautifies your landscape with daisy blossoms that attract monarch butterflies. And the leaves can save you money on medicines year round. In summer, get relief from insect bites and stings, as well as minor cuts and scratches, by rubbing them with crushed echinacea leaves. In winter, make a tea to ease the sniffing, sneezing, sore throat, and achiness of a cold.

Headache relief just a leaf away. If you suffer from migraine headaches, plant feverfew in your herb garden. Some people get pain relief from chewing three fresh leaves a day. If you have plant allergies, are pregnant or nursing, or are taking a blood thinning medication, don't use feverfew without talking with your doctor.

Get something extra from fresh herbs. Your herb garden offers you an extra bonus if you're trying to improve your health. Add flavorful basil, rosemary, and parsley from your garden to your cooking. Not only will you taste extra zing in your food, you'll also get a hefty amount of disease-fighting antioxidants. Herbal experts say fresh herbs are much more potent than the dried variety, so get your herbs fresh from the garden. They really can help you stay healthy.

Try dandelions for good health. Don't think of dandelions as just a nuisance in your lawn. Herbalists have used them for centuries to treat illnesses ranging from acne to gallstones. The leaves are a great source of potassium, which helps you stay both mentally and physically healthy. So leave a dandelion patch in a corner of your lawn, but be sure it's free of pesticides before you cook up a batch.

Grow heart-healthy herbs. Working in your garden is good for your heart. And the antioxidant herbs you grow there — oregano, dill, rosemary, and parsley — can help your heart by fighting high cholesterol and lowering blood pressure. If you want to fight clogged arteries, grow garlic. And to help cut back on salt, which could contribute to high blood pressure, grow chives, sage, basil, and other flavorful herbs to spice up your food. Gardening also helps your heart by reducing stress. And when the work is done, relax even more with the scent of lavender blossoms while you sip a soothing cup of homegrown chamomile tea.

> Gardening has healing powers for people with Alzheimer's disease. It stimulates use of all the senses, puts them in touch with the outer world, and slows the loss of short-term memory.

Arthritis remedy from a flower. Arnica, one of the best medicinal herbs, has been used for centuries to treat arthritis pain. These yellow, daisy-like flowers grow in much of the United States, blooming in midsummer. To make an ointment to rub on painful joints, crush and blend flower petals with vegetable oil. Arnica can, however, cause a skin rash on some people and is poisonous if swallowed.

Everything's coming up roses

Coax more blossoms out of climbers. If you train climbing roses horizontally along a fence rail, the canes will sprout more bloom-producing branches. All those extra blossoms can turn a plain fence into a stunning border for your yard or garden.

Mulch roses with newspaper. Soak newspaper sections in a tub or pail of water. Then place them in 16-page layers under your bushes. Top with pine bark or other compost. This will hold in moisture and keep the roots cool, prevent weeds from growing, and encourage earthworms and other beneficial organisms to hang around.

Try a foul brew for fine roses. Throw an alfalfa tea party for your roses. For a teapot, grab a large outdoor garbage can. Toss in 10 to 16 cups of alfalfa pellets or alfalfa meal, and fill with water. Put the lid on the trash can. When you come back several days later, you'll have a swampy, nasty-smelling brew that's like liquid gold to roses. Give each rosebush a gallon from time to time during the growing season. You may be put off by the odor, but you'll be thrilled by the results.

Adjust the color of your roses. Do you crave more intense color in your roses? Epsom salt should do the trick. Feed your rosebush one teaspoon per foot of height or sprinkle half a cup around a mature rosebush.

Boost the blooms in your rose bed. In May and June, give your roses a little extra push to keep blooming. Sprinkle one teaspoon of Epsom salt per foot of height beneath each shrub.

Rundown of rose classes	
Hybrid Tea	Most popular class of rose. These fragrant repeat bloomers, often used in floral arrangements, usually bloom one to a stem.
Floribunda	Hardy class with shorter stems but more blossoms than hybrid teas. Great for landscaping.
Grandiflora	Cross between hybrid tea and floribunda. Flowers resemble hybrid tea, but bloom in clusters like floribunda. These tall roses make good background or border plants.
Polyantha	Low-growing, hardy class of repeat bloomers with clusters of flowers. Useful for hedges.
Miniatures	Simply tiny roses. These hardy plants with small stems, leaves, and flowers are ideal for containers.
Climbers	Long-caned class that can be trained on trellises.
Old Garden Roses	All rose classes that existed before the first hybrid tea in 1867 — such as Noisette, Bourbon, moss, gallica, and damask

Extend life of cut flowers. To make your freshly cut roses last longer, add a little antiseptic mouthwash to the water. This trick keeps other cut flowers fresh, too.

Roses find their place in the sun. Plant roses in a spot that gets at least five or six hours of sun each day. And give them a good soaking at the roots a couple of times a week when the weather is dry. Avoid light sprinklings over the bush. Not only does the water not reach the roots, wet foliage encourages fungus growth.

Serve roses a "spot of tea." Have you ever wondered why the British have such beautiful rose gardens? Maybe it has something to do with their love of tea. Roses love this refreshing brew for its tannic acid. So don't spend hours slaving away in the hot summer sun. Just sprinkle some tea leaves under your rose bushes and give them some water. You'll have roses that are bigger and more beautiful than ever — even in midsummer when typically they begin to slow down. And you can pour yourself a tall glass of iced tea, sit back, and enjoy the blossoms.

Feed flowers with fruit. Roses love banana peels, so cut some up and mix them in the soil at planting time. They rot quickly, releasing minerals roses need — calcium, sulfur, magnesium, and phosphates. You can also make a banana peel tonic for use after the plants are established. Just soak chopped pieces in a closed jar of water for two weeks. Pour the remaining mush under the rose bush. If that's too much trouble, chop the peels and scratch them into the soil below the plant.

Prune tree roses the proper way. Money may not grow on trees, but roses do. When a regular rose plant is grafted onto a trunk, it becomes a tree rose. To prune a tree rose, cut dead and diseased branches from the top of the tree and remove any suckers that develop on the trunk or base.

Foolproof way to time spring pruning. If you're not sure when to start pruning your roses, watch the forsythia in your area. When those yellow flowers start blooming, get out your pruning shears.

Bind climbers with invisible ties. Attach your climbing roses to a trellis or fence with mint-flavored dental floss. After all, it's strong and weather resistant — and the green color will blend with the green vines and leaves.

Use tongs for painless pruning. Before you prune your roses, grab the barbecue tongs off your grill. By holding rose branches with the tongs, you can remove them without getting your hands in thorny trouble.

Water well with a ring around the rose. Water your roses with a soaker hose, and you'll avoid the damp foliage that can lead to powdery mildew, black spot, and other fungal diseases. You can even get an inexpensive, small soaker hose loop to attach to the end of a regular garden hose. Lay it around the base of your rosebush, and give your roses a nice, long drink.

Give roses a good-morning shower. If you water your rosebush from above, do it in the morning. That way, the leaves have time to dry during the heat of the day. Wet leaves can lead to fungal diseases, like powdery mildew.

Avoid "shear" madness. Pruning your roses with anvil shears is a little like dropping an anvil on your rose stems. Anvil shears can crush the stems, leaving them vulnerable to insects and diseases. Instead, use curved bypass shears for pruning small growth on roses. You'll like the results much better.

Prune roses with the perfect tools. When pruning roses, the three tools to use are curved bypass shears, lopping shears, and a pruning saw. Use the lopping shears for rose canes that are large and thick. If the lopping shears won't cut it, the pruning saw should do the job.

Protect skin from thorns. Wear long, flexible gloves — goatskin are a good choice — that cover your forearms when pruning roses. They'll protect your arms and hands from thorns but allow you to maneuver your clippers with ease.

Spray away diseases. Try this homemade spray to protect roses from fungal diseases, like powdery mildew and black spot. Mix two or three tablespoons of baking soda with a gallon of water and a few drops of dishwashing liquid. Spray your bushes once or twice a week. It's a safe, effective alternative to chemicals and poisons.

Paste away pests. Stick it to those pesky cane borers. After you finish pruning a rosebush, place a drop of white glue on top of each cut stem. When the borers come, the stems will be sealed.

> ! If you have Japanese beetles in your rosebushes, avoid using Japanese beetle traps. Instead of solving your problem, these traps actually attract more beetles.

Beat beetles with a well-timed trim. Tired of watching Japanese beetles devour your lovely floribunda and grandiflora roses all summer? Try this. After you've enjoyed that wonderful first flowering of late spring, give those roses a good trim. You might miss them for a few months, but they'll start blooming again by September, when the beetles are gone. What's more, this tactic also works against black spot disease, which strikes around midsummer. But don't try this trick on climbers or other roses that bloom on old wood. It would just prevent later blooms.

Rinse out aphids with mouthwash. Mix equal parts antiseptic mouthwash and water to make a spray that banishes aphids and other pests from your rosebushes. Just be sure to spray those bushes regularly.

Guard roses with garlic. Plant garlic near your roses to help keep them free of pests and fungal diseases. You can also keep enemies away with a garlic spray. Just crush garlic cloves and soak them in water. Strain the mixture, and spray it on your roses about twice a month.

"Bee" aware of harmless pest. If you notice neat, semicircular holes in your rose leaves, don't worry. Leaf cutter bees make these distinctive holes, but they don't damage your rose plants like other pests.

Save roses from a whipping. Howling winter winds can whip long rose canes around wildly — and that's not safe for the gardener or the plant. But you can prevent it. When autumn comes, cut the longest canes down to a safer length. Avoid any other pruning until spring.

Let climbers recline for winter. If you live where winters are harsh enough to damage your climbing roses, shelter them from winds and freezes. Ease them off their fences or trellises and lay them flat on the ground. Tie the canes down, if necessary. In places where climbers need even more protection, wrap the canes in burlap or bury them in a blanket of soil.

Keep roses cozy until spring. If your roses need winter protection, try one of these strategies. To "mound," dig up soil from another part of the garden and pile it around the bush until it covers the bases of all the rose canes. Some gardeners build the mounds even higher to cover more of the bush — or even all of it. You can also buy plastic rose cones to put over each bush, but you may have to do a lot of pruning before they'll fit.

Take a winter tip from Minnesota. When just a little protection against winter blasts isn't enough, defend your roses with the "Minnesota tip." Dig a trench on one side of the bush and loosen the roots on the other side. Tip the rosebush into the trench and bury it under a shallow layer of soil. Add up to 18 inches of mulch for extra cold-busting insulation.

Split a spud to root a rose. An Irish potato makes a good rooting medium for a rose cutting. Just make a slit in the potato and insert the stem of the rose. Plant the potato in rich soil with the rose stem sticking up above ground.

Rethink yellow roses in damp areas. In humid or rainy climates, yellow roses might not be your best bet. That's because they are the most susceptible to black spot. If you already have yellow roses, spray them regularly to avoid this disease. In the market for a yellow rose? Don't give up hope. Just select varieties resistant to black spot — and don't settle for anything less.

Bare-root versus container roses. Waiting for containers of roses to arrive at your nursery in May or June may seem a better idea than planting those dead-looking bare-root roses in January

Browse rose catalogs for free

You can tour the latest offerings in roses with these free color catalogs.

Jackson & Perkins. With 130 years of experience in the rose business, they are still developing new varieties and winning awards. To order a catalog, go online to www.jacksonand-perkins.com or call 800-292-4769.

Nor'East Miniature Roses. Nor'East specializes in miniature roses, which they grow in their greenhouses in Massachusetts. For a catalog of all the latest varieties, visit their Web site at www.noreast-miniroses.com or write to:

Nor'East Miniature Roses, Inc.
P.O. Box 307
Rowley, MA 01969

See how roses rate with experts

To help you decide which roses to try, find out what members of the American Rose Society (ARS) think. The ARS rates rose varieties on a scale of 1 to 10. Varieties with higher ratings are more likely to grow well in most places. In the ARS publication *Handbook for Selecting Roses*, you'll find an extensive list of roses with their colors and ratings. ARS members get this list for free, but non-members can buy it for $3.50. To order the list or learn more about the ARS, write to:

American Rose Society
P.O. Box 30000
Shreveport, LA 71130-0030

You can also call 318-938-5402 or visit their information-packed Web site at www.ars.org.

or February. But the fact is, not only are the potted roses more expensive, their chances of surviving aren't very good. A successful move from potting soil and greenhouse shelter to the harsher garden environment when they are in the midst of a growth period is difficult.

Choose low grade for high quality. Roses come in three distinct grades — No. 1, No. 1 1/2, and No. 2. The lower the grade, the larger and more robust the plant is likely to be.

Smart solution for shady gardens. Most roses turn up their noses at shade, but hybrid musks can handle partial shade. While roses generally need at least six hours of direct sun, hybrid musks only need about four. Look for varieties in this class if your garden is too shady for other kinds of roses.

Turn old ladder into new trellis. Your old wooden ladder might be too rickety for you to climb, but it could be just perfect for climbing roses. With a little training, your roses can transform this piece of junk into a charming trellis.

Grow an ounce of prevention. Enjoy healthy roses with less work by growing disease-resistant varieties.

Hybrid tea roses that may resist black spot and other diseases include Chrysler Imperial, Electron, Miss All-American Beauty, Mister Lincoln, Olympiad, Pink Peace, and Tropicana. Queen Elizabeth, Sunsprite, Love, Europeana, and First Edition are just some of the disease-resistant floribundas and grandifloras. Many other rose classes feature disease-resistant varieties, too.

Nose around for rose tips. To find out which roses you can grow in your area, talk with other local gardeners, ask your county extension agent, or check with an experienced and reputable local nursery.

Can roses grow at 20 below? Roses might not grow in a blizzard or subzero temperatures, but they can grow in cold climates. Unlikely as it may seem, you can grow roses even if you live in Canada or chilly regions of the United States. Rugosa roses and roses from the Explorer series are good bets.

Branch out to help cuttings take root. Make your own rooting solution for rose cuttings. Gather several small, thin willow branches with bark on them. In a large cooking pot, bring a quart or two of water to a boil. While you're waiting, chop the willow branches into 1-inch twigs. When the water boils, turn off the heat and add your willow bits. Let cool in the pot overnight, then strain the liquid. Soak your rose cuttings overnight in the willow water. Now you're ready to plant.

Make the most of the coast. Living near a beach may be wonderful, but growing roses there can be woeful. Make coastal rose growing easier by planting a rugosa rose. This tough brand of rose can handle sandy soil and salty air. Find out which varieties are best suited to your area and give one a try.

Cover the ground with roses. Roses can make an enchanting ground cover. Experts recommend the Sea Foam and Max Graf varieties.

Grab a green rose. Roses come in a wide variety of colors. You can even find a green rose, *R. chinensis viridiflora*. However, neither a true blue nor true black rose is available yet. Rose experts are constantly working toward these colors, so stay tuned.

Block intruders with a rosy barrier. A thorny rose hedge can help keep animals and other unwanted visitors out of your yard. Consider rugosa roses for attractive hedges that don't require much care. If your climate isn't right for rugosa, try a thorny rose variety called Mermaid.

The "hip" way to attract wildlife. If you love seeing birds, deer, and squirrels in your yard, plant rugosa roses. Hungry foragers love the fruit of the rose hips, and the seeds buried inside provide them with protein and oils.

Caring for cacti and other succulents

Learn the "hole" truth about pots. Finding the right pot for your cactus is like winning a free game of miniature golf — you need a hole in one. You want a pot with a drainage hole at the bottom so water can run out. Cover the hole with a coffee filter to keep the soil in the pot while letting the water escape.

Throw some sand into the mix. Never use plain potting soil for your cactus. It holds too much water, which causes the plant's roots to rot. Instead, buy a bag of cactus soil. Or make your own by mixing potting soil with sand.

Keep cacti happy in cinderblocks. Cinderblocks can do more than hold up old, junky cars. They also make perfect planters for cacti. That's because they hold in heat. To save money on cactus soil, put a few aluminum cans in the hole before filling it. You'll need less soil to fill the hole, but it will still be plenty for your cactus.

Handle with care. This might seem obvious, but it is definitely worth remembering. Whenever you pot or otherwise handle a cactus, make sure you wear heavy-duty gardening gloves.

Good news for your hands. Next time you repot your cactus, subscribe to this handy tip. Fold several sheets of newspaper into a thick strip and wrap it around your prickly plant. Then simply lift the cactus from its current pot and place it in a new one.

Try tongs to avoid splinters. Here's another safe way to handle a cactus when repotting. Use kitchen tongs to lift the plant out of the pot. To make the whole experience gentler on the cactus, you can wrap the tongs in paper towels first. Rubber bands or twist ties will hold the paper towels in place.

Give your cactus a bigger home. Late winter or early spring is a good time to repot your cactus. First, check if your plant is getting too big for its britches. Tip the cactus out of the pot and look at the roots. If the roots take up almost all the space, transfer the cactus to a slightly larger pot. For best results, use a specialist cactus compost.

Shower cacti with light. Cacti and succulents certainly don't need to be pampered. They generally need little water and no fertilizer. Just make sure they get plenty of light, and they should be fine.

Protect plants from sunburn. Succulents love sunlight, but it's possible to get too much of a good thing. Plants accustomed to a greenhouse or indoor environment should be moved gradually into a sunny spot. Too much direct sun too quickly can burn them and cause damage.

Encourage a summer growth spurt. While most cacti don't need any fertilizer, you might want to give those in containers an occasional boost. Use a low-nitrogen, high-phosphorus fertilizer, like tomato food. A light, monthly feeding during the summer is all your plants should need.

Wait before you water. For most cacti and succulents, let the soil dry out completely between waterings. Remember, you're more likely to kill a cactus by overwatering than underwatering.

Get to the root of water problem. They say to believe half of what you see. That's good advice for succulent plants. If a succulent looks like it's not getting enough water, it might actually have too much. That's because its roots could be rotting in wet soil, losing their ability to supply water to the plant. Adding more water will only make the problem worse, and the plant will eventually die. Instead of overwatering the plant, tip it out of its pot and check the roots.

Keep your cactus clean. Like pets, cacti can use some grooming. Use a soft brush, like a toothbrush or makeup brush, to clean and dust your cactus. For that hard-to-reach grit between the spines, try tweezers.

Dress your cactus to keep it warm. When you think of cacti, you think of the Southwest. But you can also grow them up North. They just need a little more help. To lower humidity and keep them warmer, lay a top-dressing of coarse sand over the soil.

> To remove a cactus needle from your finger, try a piece of sticky tape. Just touch it lightly to the sore spot. When you pull off the tape, the needle should come with it.

Protect your cactus from frost. Start by covering its tips with Styrofoam cups. You can also tie burlap, blankets, sheets, or newspaper around the plant. Another practical — and festive — tip is to string big-bulbed Christmas lights on your larger plants to help keep them warm.

Double your cactus pleasure. You don't have to be a mad scientist to turn a prickly pear into a prickly pair. All it takes is this simple propagating technique. Just cut a pad or group of pads — the stem is divided into joints or pads — from your cactus, and let it lie in the sun for several days. Once the cut heals, plant it about 3 or 4 inches in the ground. That's it.

The key to successful rooting. It's easy to propagate cacti from leaf cuttings — unless you plant the cuttings upside down. Then they won't take root. If you cut more than one piece from the same cactus, make sure you can tell which is the top and which is the bottom.

Develop a taste for cactus. Cacti can be a valuable part of your home decor, but they can also be a tasty part of your next meal. That's right. You can actually eat some types of cactus. Throw the leaves on the grill, scramble them with eggs, or add them to soups and salads. You can even make cactus jelly. Just make sure you pick an edible cactus. Then scrub the leaves well and remove any spines before you start cooking.

Get ready to rock. Succulents and cacti make great additions to rock gardens. As long as you have a sunny, fast-draining spot for them, they should thrive. If you live in a mild climate, your options are greater, but you can also find succulents — like sedums and hens-and-chicks — that do well in cold-winter areas.

Plot a cover-up. Looking for an easy-to-maintain ground cover? Look no further than succulents. Some good choices include trailing ice plant, stonecrop and other kinds of sedum, and echeveria. They do their job while making yours easy.

Root out pests with mothballs. The fumes of these small balls don't just discourage moths. They also keep the dreaded root mealy bug away from your cacti and succulents. Add some mothballs to your potting mix, and you'll avoid future root mealy bug problems. Use this method only with clay pots because mothballs can damage plastic ones.

Inspire Christmas cactus to bloom. Like the poinsettia, the Christmas cactus needs darkness to develop its showy flowers. To encourage blooms, water as little as possible in the summer. In the fall, move the cactus into a dark closet or hide it under dark plastic from 6:00 p.m. to 8:00 a.m. Keep it watered and well-fed. Three to four weeks before Christmas, bring it out of the dark. Just on time, this winter beauty will add a touch of color to your holiday decor.

Move it and lose it. You've found the perfect spot for your blooming Christmas cactus. Good. Leave it right there. Moving or turning the plant will cause it to drop its buds and stop flowering.

Evade jade fungus. Jade plants, like most succulents, can be harmed by too much water. When watering your plant, be careful not to splash water on its leaves. Avoid misting the leaves, as well. Your jade plant could develop fungus or other problems.

Revive aloe with distilled water. Like people with high blood pressure, aloe plants don't need salt. Sometimes regular tap water provides too much. Signs of excess salt include brown tips or white marks on the stem. Fix this problem by watering your aloe plant with distilled water instead. To make distilled water, just boil tap water for 30 minutes.

How to grow hearty houseplants

Secret to prettier hyacinths. These plants are quick to flower, sometimes so hasty their stalks reach only a few inches high. To force the stem to stretch, wait until the buds begin to develop, then cover them with a paper cone or an inverted pot. Keep under wraps until the stalks reach their full length. Once uncovered, the pale stalks will quickly turn green and burst forth with fragrant flowers.

Spur stubborn violets to flower. Does your African violet refuse to bloom? You may need more fertilizer, or the fertilizer you are using may not be balanced for violets. On the other hand, too much fertilizer can blunt your plant's ability to take up nutrients. This will stunt flowers, so cut back if you are overfeeding. Finally, violets will not bloom if they do not get eight hours of darkness a day. Make sure to turn off grow lights at night.

Divert your cat from prized plants. Instead of fighting your cats for ownership of the houseplants, plant a special shallow planter with cat favorites. Leave a tray of sprouted catnip, oat, or rye grass where your cats can easily reach it, and they may leave your less-tasty houseplants alone.

Sticky solution to cat problem. To keep your feline friends out of your houseplants, spread double-sided carpet tape across the rim of your pot. Cats don't like the sticky surface and will go back to their litter box. If that doesn't work, try covering the dirt with pine cones, small rocks, low-growing plants, or anything unpleasant to dig through. As a last resort, spray the soil with a pet repellent, like Bitter Apple. Cats hate the taste on their paws and will soon leave your plants alone.

Keep plants well-groomed. Prune your houseplant so its best qualities show. If you like a plant for its leaves, pinch off any flowers so they don't compete with leaves for nourishment. If you grow a plant for its flowers, keep leaves at a manageable number. An African violet, for example, doesn't need more than four or five rings of leaves. Remove oldest leaves first.

Dust leaves in double time. Your knickknacks aren't the only thing that need dusting. Plants need clean leaves to breathe easier and absorb sunlight. To clean them, simply hold a soft, damp rag in each hand and gingerly clasp each leaf near its base. Gently pull your hands over the sandwiched leaf to clean both sides at one time.

Add shine with a peel. Don't throw away that banana peel before running its soft inside over the leaves of your waxy houseplants. This gently rubs away all the dust and gives your plants a glossy sheen.

Polish leaves with simple tools. Unlike humans, houseplants won't benefit from a milk bath, and vegetable oil or "leaf shine" products just clog up their pores. To make leaves shine naturally, use warm water and an old, cotton T-shirt on shiny leaves and an old makeup brush for furry leaves.

Save water ... shower with a plant. Every so often, treat your plants to a gentle, warm shower. The fine spray will invigorate them and clean the leaves of dust and insects. Before you begin, protect the soil by covering it with aluminum foil. Place the plant toward the back of the tub or stall where water won't hit it full force. Keep the water lukewarm and let your plant enjoy the soft spray. Remember to turn some of the leaves up to rinse their bottoms. Let the plant dry in the shower overnight, but don't forget to take the foil off so the roots can breathe.

Bathe your dirty plants. If summer finds you puttering outdoors instead of pampering your indoor plants, they could collect enough dust to cut off their oxygen. To clean small plants, cover the soil with a piece of cloth. Then fill a bucket with lukewarm water and add a few drops of dishwashing soap. With your hand holding the cloth in place, flip the plant over and gently swish it around. Now rinse it in clear water. Thanks to your minimal efforts, your clean, shiny plant has a new lease on life.

Detoxify the air with houseplants. Plants beautify your home and reduce indoor pollution. Scientific studies prove that tropical houseplants, like the peace lily, philodendron, spider plant, golden pothos, and dracaenas, absorb pollutants and clean the air. Even experts at NASA agree that it works. So fill your home with plants. Just be sure to trim off the leaves at the base of the plant so the soil has full exposure to your indoor air. Bacteria in the soil also help remove harmful gases.

> ! Many houseplants are poisonous. Philodendron, dumbcane, Swiss cheese plant, Jerusalem cherry, ivy, and the peace lily can cause swelling or burning of your tongue and throat. Oleander can be deadly.

Treat your plants to an outdoor vacation. At the end of a long, cold winter, your potted plants may be as eager to see the sun as you are. After all danger of frost is gone, move them outside for a few hours each day. Steadily increase their daily moment in the sun until they are out all the time. Once outside, plants need to be watered far more frequently — often once a day.

Make outdoor plants indoor favorites. If you hate to lose your favorite sun-lovers to the coming frost, bring them in from the cold. Pot up garden plants and spray them with water to clean off any dirt. Check carefully for pests. Leave the plants outdoors in a shady corner for a few days before easing them into your home. Keep these guests separate from your regular houseplants until they adapt.

Wise up to winter houseplant care. Bears aren't the only ones who hibernate in the winter — plants take a well-deserved rest, too. As days get shorter, wait for the soil to dry out completely before watering, and stop feeding all but your winter-blooming plants. Move shade-loving plants closer to a south-facing window so they can collect as many winter rays as possible. By spring, they will be well-rested and ready to grow and flourish.

Light up your plant's world. Plants can suffer from the winter blues, just like humans. Usually a little extra light will perk them up. Instead of buying an expensive professional grow light, supplement your natural daylight with a simple, flexible arm lamp, like an architect or gooseneck lamp. Screw in a 100-watt lightbulb and keep it pointed at the plant up to 16 hours a day. With all the extra light, your plant should be ready for spring before you are.

Lighten up lanky growth. Leggy plants can be rather unattractive with long stems and small leaves that seem to leap into space. If this describes your plant, it's probably pleading for more light. Trim off any gangly leaves and move your spindly friend to a south-facing window — or direct a grow light onto it for 12 hours a day. Its new growth should be more compact.

Measure light with shadowy method. Hold your hand up to a window and watch your shadow. If you can distinctly see the outline of your hand, you need plants that tolerate high light. If you can't see a shadow at all, you have low light. A fuzzy shadow is just right for plants that need medium light.

Add life to a dark room. You can spruce up even the shadiest of corners with a living plant. In fact, some of the most interesting and low-maintenance houseplants prefer low light. The popular peace lily, corn plant, cast-iron plant, Chinese evergreen, candelabra cacti, aloe plant, snake plant, and rubber plant all thrive where light is not bright.

> ! If your ficus suddenly drops all its leaves, check your gas lines. This plant is very sensitive to gas leaks and can warn you of impending danger.

Solve the mystery of growing orchids. Orchids are the crown jewel of many serious indoor gardeners. To get repeat blooms from your tropical beauties, make sure you vary the temperature in your home. Many orchids won't bloom unless there is a 15- to 20-degree difference between night and day. Depending on their type, keep the house between 60 and 65 degrees at night and 75 to 85 degrees during the day.

Simple way to increase humidity. Orchids thrive in tropical rain forests where humidity is very high. To create a similar environment in your home, set your pot in a shallow pan full of pretty pebbles. Be creative — metal trays, clay saucers, even deep glass bowls will work. Keep the container filled with about an inch of water. As it evaporates, the moisture will create an envelope of humidity around your blooming beauty. Just be careful water doesn't touch the pot, or the roots may rot.

3 signs it's time to supersize. Does your plant wilt between waterings? Does its soil pull away from the sides of the pot? If so, it may be time to repot. Soak the plant well, then lift it out and check the root ball. Long roots that coil around the base of a plant are a sure sign that it needs a bigger home.

Promote plant to bigger pot. When you repot, upgrade to a container that is only one size larger than your plant's current pot. With too much room, your plant will stop visibly growing while it fills the pot with roots. As you pull the root ball out of its tight confines, gently untangle the roots and cut off any dead ones. Fill the pot halfway with fresh potting soil and spread the healthy roots through it. Then add soil up to the base of the plant, tamp it down, and water thoroughly.

Quick tip for picking pottery. Tap a terra-cotta pot before you buy it. Hold it upside down, with your finger in the drain hole, and tap its rim with your knuckle. A solid, uncracked container will have a distinct ring to it, while a pot with air bubbles or other flaws will sound a bit muffled.

Age pot for antique look. To quickly give a new terra-cotta pot that lived-in look, coat the outside with yogurt. This will attract lichens and mosses, making your pot an instant antique — and giving it ageless appeal.

Quench terra-cotta pot's thirst. Make sure you completely submerge a terra-cotta pot in water before planting in it. Otherwise, the dry clay will soak all the water out of your potting mix.

Find free pots next door. Can't get your hands on enough pots? Find a free source just around the corner. Patrol the neighborhood just before recycling pickup. Recycling services rarely pick up clay pots, so you can just collect them off the curb.

Old records make great flowerpots. Scratched up records make great flowerpots! Preheat your oven to 200

degrees. On a cookie sheet, flip over a large, oven-safe bowl and balance the record on top. Stick it in the oven for five minutes — less if it starts drooping. Quickly pull it out and flip the bowl over, easing the now flexible record inside. Arrange the folds in a pleasing manner and let it cool. Fill your unique flowerpot with soil and a favorite bloom, and you have the perfect house-warming gift. If you're unhappy with the design of your new flowerpot, just reheat it and change the shape.

Grow herbs in a strawberry pot. This planter is perfect for growing a variety of herbs. And to make watering the pot easy, punch holes in an empty, two-liter soft drink bottle. Fill the planter with a few inches of light potting mix, and insert the bottle so its neck sits above the soil line. Plant your herbs in the pockets as you fill the pot with dirt. Be careful not to plant invasive herbs, like mint, because they will quickly take over. Fill the bottle with water, and it will release moisture slowly to the herbs. And best of all, when the weather turns cold, you can bring the pot inside and enjoy fresh herbs all winter.

Weigh down a tipsy pot. A blooming bush or a small, fruiting tree tends to tip over easily when it gets top-heavy. Instead of repotting, stick its pot inside a larger, more decorative container or basket, and fill the space between the two containers with gravel.

Dissolve salty residue with vinegar. A clay pot that looks weathered with white dust is actually saturated with salt. To clean it, water your plant well. Once the root ball is wet, lift it out of the pot and set it aside. Next, soak the pot in three cups of hot water with a cup of vinegar thrown in for good measure. After an hour, scrub off the residue with a sturdy brush, then repot your plant.

Train your plants to climb. Some houseplants are just as happy climbing as they are dangling. Make a simple pole to give them support. Wrap some chicken wire into a tube and secure it with twist-ties. Wedge the tube in your flowerpot, and stuff it with sphagnum moss. Attach your plant's tendrils to the pole with paper clips. Mist the moss pole often to keep it moist. Roots will eventually grow into the moss.

Guard plants with garlic. Does your potted plant seem to attract every pest out there? Stick a clove of garlic in its soil. Most bugs don't care for it and will stay away. Keep an eye on your clove, though. If you let it sprout, it could take root.

Soothe sunburned shrubbery. Age spots afflict plants as well as humans. Like your skin, their leaves are sensitive to excess light and can turn blotchy, pale, or brown in spots. If leaves look washed-out or burned, move your plant to a sheltered corner and let it recuperate in peace.

Multiply houseplants from mistakes. If your pet accidentally breaks a stem off your prized plant, don't throw it away. In most cases, you can start a new plant from just a small cutting. Trim the stem to within half an inch of the leaf. Dip it in a rooting hormone and set it in a small pot with damp peat and perlite. Cover the cutting with a clear plastic bag and secure it with a rubber band. Keep your plantlet moist and out of direct sun until it sprouts its own root system. Then transplant it into a permanent pot.

Lucky break for rabbit's foot fern. Soft, furry roots creeping around a clay pot make the rabbit's foot fern a great conversation piece. If you have one straining to break free, cut it up to share the joy with family and friends. It's simple. Carefully break off a few "feet" that already have fronds growing out of them. Plant them up to the leaf stem in a shallow tray with an equal mixture of perlite and vermiculite. Cover your cuttings with plastic. Within a month, they should grow their own roots and be ready for a new pot.

Grow your own pineapple. Nothing compares to fresh pineapple — except perhaps its price! So try growing your own. Cut the crown off and whittle it down until you can see light rings — these are root buds. Let the crown heal for a week in a dry place out of full sun. Then plant it in clean potting mix, set it near a sunny window, and water sparingly. In the winter of its second year, put the whole plant in a plastic bag with a couple of ripe apples to encourage it to bloom and form fruit. By summer, you'll harvest your own homegrown pineapple.

Bottles and prickles don't mix. Any small houseplant will thrive in the ideal environment of a terrarium. But this enclosed glass planter is no place for cacti and succulents, which will rot in all the humidity.

Prepare the perfect terrarium. Before you plant your terrarium, lay the proper foundation. Pour your planting materials into the bottle with a funnel or an empty paper towel roll. Start with an inch of gravel for drainage. Cover it with a thin layer of charcoal to keep bacteria under control. Finally, add a 2- to 3-inch layer of sterile soil. A balanced mix of potting soil, peat moss, and sand works best. For an interesting effect, push the soil around to form mountains and valleys.

Raid kitchen for terrarium aids. Household utensils make great terrarium tools. Use kitchen tongs to gently lower a plant into your bottle. You can also add new soil with a kitchen funnel and dig holes for planting with a spoon or chopsticks.

Withhold water from glass garden. A terrarium is the perfect choice for a scatter-brained gardener because it needs so little care. In fact, the most common mistake a terrarium owner makes is to soak the plants with too much water. A properly sealed terrarium may never need watering. Only water if condensation no longer forms on the glass or if your terrarium has an opening in the top. At most, add about two tablespoons of water a month.

Deliver a drizzle, not a downpour. To water a terrarium, tip the container slightly and let water trickle down the glass sides. This is far gentler on the tender plants than pouring water directly on them.

Wrap up out-of-town watering. Create a quick and easy greenhouse for your houseplants before you leave town on a short trip. First, soak each potted plant in water. Then push some canes, wooden skewers, chopsticks, or even plastic forks around the edge of the pot so they stick up over the leaves. Wrap the whole pot in a plastic bag, taking care not to squash any of the leaves, and seal the bag with a twist tie. While you're gone, humidity and condensation should keep your plant alive.

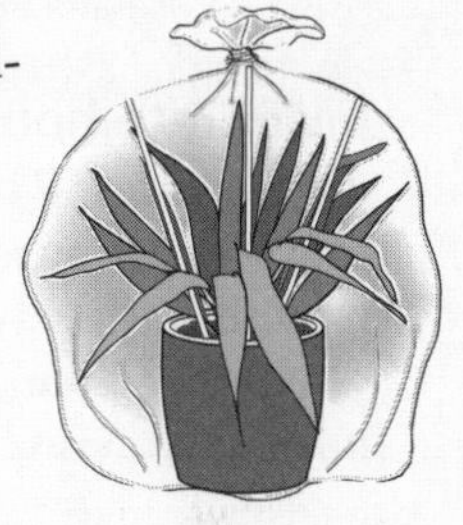

Save green with homemade greenhouse. Don't have the money to build a greenhouse for your plants while you're away? Make your own with cheap plastic and newspaper. Line your bathtub with a sheet of plastic, and stack several layers of newspaper on it. Set your houseplants on the paper and spray them down until an inch of water collects in the tub. Close the shower curtain, turn on the light, and enjoy your vacation. The damp newspaper will keep your plants' roots moist and the air humid until you return.

Pack a water bottle for your plants. Here's an easy way to water your plants while you're away. Fill a plastic bottle with water, then stuff a piece of an old cotton T-shirt into the opening. Flip the bottle upside down and plant it neck-deep in the soil of your houseplant. The cotton wick will provide a steady drip, keeping your plants' roots evenly moist until you return.

Swap sun for shade. If you're headed out of town for a short vacation, move the plants that usually enjoy a sunny window to a shadier corner of the house. That way, they won't need as much water.

Conserve moisture while you're away. Going away on a trip? Remember to bring your houseplants back inside if they've been summering on the patio. In a shaded and cool house, they should require less water.

Invigorate houseplants with tea. If your fern gets droopy, brew a batch of tepid, weak tea and serve it instead of water. In no time, you'll have lush, green fronds to replace the sickly growth. Sprinkle the fern with tea once a week until your plant is back to health. Then return to your normal watering regiment, with tea as an occasional treat.

Jump-start plants with gelatin. Are your houseplants droopy or dying? Perk them up with a simple gelatin tonic. Dissolve one envelope of unflavored gelatin in a cup of hot water. Add three cups of cold water, and feed this mixture to your plants once a month. The nitrogen boost will help them flourish.

Try tap test before watering. You can tell if a plant needs water just by tapping the side of its pot. A clay pot makes a dull thud when the soil is damp, but sounds hollow when it's dry. For a plastic pot, try the lift test. Pick it up and weigh it in your hand. If it feels light, it's time to give your plant a good soak.

Skip the cold shower. Your plants are about as fond of cold showers as you are on a typical winter morning. Wait for water to reach room temperature before watering your plants. Water that is too cold or too hot can send them into shock.

Listen to plants' watering needs. Houseplants may not speak, but they can still tell you when they're drowning. Mushy stems and falling green leaves usually indicate overwatering. Signs of too little water include wilting and brown leaf tips. Yellow leaves can be tricky. Bright yellow leaves sprouting close to the base of a plant mean "More water, please," while pulpy, dull yellow leaves scream, "Enough."

Get creative with plants

Woo guests with a birdbath. It's nice to provide water for your fine-feathered friends, but here's another reason to put a birdbath in your yard. It can add a touch of romance to your next outdoor gathering. Clean the birdbath, fill it with fresh water, and float some candles and flowers.

Be careful with candles. Fresh, pine-scented garlands and elaborate centerpieces are as much a part of Christmas as ornaments and stacks of gifts. But if an arrangement you brought home from the florist has candles in it, be careful not to light them. Greenery, especially pine boughs, are highly flammable. It's better to enjoy them unlit than to remember this joyful season as the "year of the fire."

Bring home a hearty Christmas tree. Check your Christmas tree for freshness before you strap it on your car's roof. A fresh tree looks bright green and has a strong fragrance. The needles bend — but don't break — when you press them between your fingers. Bounce the tree up and down on the pavement. If a lot of needles fall off, the tree is too dry. Look at the trunk. A fresh tree will have sap along the cut.

Think safety while holiday decorating. Garlands and Christmas trees grace many homes from November to January. While beautiful, they keep firemen up at night. To protect your tree from flames, make a fresh cut at its base before screwing it into the tree stand, and refill the reservoir daily with water. Keep greens in a cool spot away from radiators, heat vents, even TVs. The mantel is a natural place for a bough of mixed greens, but use a screen to protect the rapidly drying branches from sparks. Even strings of lights can cause a fire if wrapped around a dry garland.

Best way to water your Christmas tree. You can keep your Christmas tree safer by feeding it a homemade fire-retardant solution. In a two-gallon bucket, mix two cups of corn syrup, one-quarter cup of liquid chlorine bleach, two pinches of Epsom salt, a teaspoon of chelated iron, and a half teaspoon of Borax. Add hot water to the rim of the bucket. Soak the base of your tree in this solution for a day or two. Then add the remainder to the tree stand as needed.

Prevent a holiday tragedy. For a safer holiday season, make your fresh Christmas tree fire retardant. Mix together five tablespoons of borax, four tablespoons of Epsom salt, and two quarts of warm water. Spray the mixture on your tree and let it air dry.

Train ivy to form an elegant topiary. Stop admiring expensive topiaries and make your own. Plant a mature, long-legged, miniature ivy plant in a large pot and gently separate the stems. Invert a tomato cage and anchor it in the ivy pot, being careful not to crush any ivy stems. Wrap the creeping strands through the cage until most of it is hidden by green leaves. Mount a decorative finial at the top, and keep the finished topiary well-clipped to maintain its elegant silhouette.

Fill the air with ferns. To lighten the effect of a hanging basket, mix maidenhair or asparagus ferns with more substantial plants. Both ferns have a beautiful lacy look that takes the edge off stiff arrangements. If you can't get your hands on one of these classics, just about any open, feathery plant will do.

Secret to amazing container gardens. To get the look of a nursery-designed container planting without spending the money, mix long, trailing plants with flowering annuals in a half barrel. Ivy, lemon licorice, thyme, and morning glory vines all come in a wide variety of colors and mix well with almost any combination of flowers. Plant these on the outer edges of the barrel and keep them trimmed so they look their best.

Get creative with planters. Watering cans, discarded toilets, old washtubs, rusty strainers, toy trucks and wagons, driftwood, tea kettles, tires, even an inverted umbrella can make original and whimsical planters for your garden. The next time you're out and about, look around with a fresh eye. You might find some junk just waiting to be turned into plant treasures.

Never retire old boots. If you've got a pair of old boots hanging around, fill them with some gravel and a lot of dirt and plant pansies or other flowers in them. Just don't forget to add a few drainage holes. Sitting on a front stoop or in your garden, they'll bring a smile to your face and remind you of hours spent outside.

Add color to boring planters. Don't throw out half-empty paint cans. Instead, use the paint to create one-of-a-kind planters that will add a whimsical touch to your porch. Clay pots, tin cans, and even a five-gallon bucket can be painted with stripes, polka-dots, zigzags, or whatever and filled with plants. For a coordinated look, limit your palette to just two or three colors, and use different painting techniques to give them interest.

Salvage a broken pot. Don't let that broken terra cotta pot break your heart. You can still turn it into a gorgeous garden decoration. Just lay the pot on its side, broken part down, and bury part of it in your soil. Plant some annuals or herbs in the mouth of the pot, and marvel at the effect. It will look as if the flowers are pouring out of the container.

Make a stunning display. Take an old wooden shelf and cut out three to five holes large enough to hold a flower pot. Paint the shelf to match your trim and mount it outside. Choose a variety of plants or all the same. Just remember to keep these small planters watered.

Dry flowers like a pro. You can use two common household products to create your own beautiful dried flowers. Mix one part borax with two parts cornmeal. Put a layer of this mixture in an airtight container. Place the flower you want to dry on top of it, and sprinkle more of the mixture over the flower. Be careful not to crush or bend it out of shape. Seal the container and leave at room temperature for seven to 10 days. Remove the flower and brush off the excess powder with a soft paintbrush or makeup brush.

Easy-to-make flower press. Cut two pieces of plywood about 10 inches by 12 inches, or whatever size you like. Drill holes in all four corners and attach the pieces together with screws and wing nuts. Next, find some cardboard and cut it slightly smaller than your press. Trim the corners so it doesn't interfere with the screws. Open the press and stack several layers of cardboard on the bottom. Arrange your flowers on smooth paper towels, newspaper, or blotting paper. Cover with more paper and cardboard, close the press, and tighten the screws. Check on your flowers in two weeks. They should be dry.

Wow friends with designer leaf prints. Design your own wrapping paper, cards, and table linens with leaves of various sizes and a little paint. Start with heavy paper or pre-washed cloth. Using a small paint brush, apply tempera paint, or fabric paint if you're working with cloth, to the veined side of a leaf. Lay the leaf, paint-side down, on the surface you are decorating. Cover it with wax paper, and gently roll over it with a rolling pin. Remove the wax paper and peel the leaf back carefully, starting at its tip. Repeat with other leaves, laying them randomly in a pleasing pattern. To "set" the fabric paint, iron the design on the wrong side for several minutes. Just be sure the paint has dried for at least a day.

Create leaf designs with sunshine. From your favorite shirt to your living room drapes, the sun bleaches everything. With nothing more than cheap construction paper and a few leaves or fern fronds, you can turn this bleaching effect to your advantage and make sun prints. On a sunny day, go outside and arrange some leaves in a pleasing pattern on the paper. Hold the arrangement in place with small rocks or a piece of glass and forget about it for five hours. The sun will bleach the paper around the leaves, creating a distinct leaf design. Use this attractive paper to make cards and gift wrap.

Make personalized stepping stones. Use plastic, disposable containers, like frozen food containers, about 12 inches in diameter. Put a thin layer of petroleum jelly on the inside of each container. Mix up a bag of concrete in your wheelbarrow according to package directions. Using a plastic cup for a ladle, fill the containers about 2 inches deep. Stir the concrete gently to get rid of air bubbles and smooth over the top. After an hour or so, add decorative touches, like leaves, stones, or twigs. Let the concrete set up for a couple of days before removing your stepping stones from the containers.

Quick and easy birdbath. Waste no time getting a birdbath installed in your garden. Simply turn an old terra cotta pot upside down and place the saucer on top. Fill with water and enjoy watching the neighborhood birds.

Lower the ceiling with plants. Fill the cavernous space under high ceilings with a living wall of plants. Hang a trailing plant from a pulley near the roof beams. Add one on top of a high bookshelf, then put an ornamental plant below it on a credenza. Finally, group a collection of houseplants of various heights on the ground. This wall of green will visually connect the ceiling with your living space and transform it instantly into a cozy room.

Buy roses that will last. To choose the freshest roses for a bouquet, follow this advice from the experts. Gently press a bud. If it's tightly curled and unblemished, it will probably last a week or more once you get it home. Squishy buds, drooping heads, or dropping petals warn that the flowers are not fresh. Brown blotches on the outside petals mean the flowers were damaged while being transported. Finally, a rose that had its thorns removed probably won't last long in a vase because bacteria will attack the open wounds.

Perfect poinsettias – year after year! Don't toss them out and buy new ones next Christmas. Keep your holiday cheer alive and growing. In May, chop your poinsettia within 8 inches of its base. Water, feed, and prune it to maintain a compact shape through the summer. To get red bracts by Christmas, fake shorter days starting in October. Move your plant into a darkened room every evening, or gently cover it from 5:00 p.m. to 8:00 a.m. Don't forget! One well-lit night can delay the blooms indefinitely. With bright sun during the day, and dark nights, your poinsettia should bloom brightly in eight to 10 weeks.

Grace your table with a poinsettia. Poinsettias are just about the only thing in bloom around the holidays, but if a whole plant is too large for your table, decorate with single "flowers" called bracts. Simply cut them from the plant close to the top of the stem and sear the cut end with a match. This will stop the flow of white sap and keep the red bracts looking fresh for several days. Don't set the stems in water without sealing the cut end first, or the bract will wilt.

Clip stems to keep bouquet bright. When you bring flowers home from the market, trim off a half inch of each stem with a sharp knife. Then plunge the stems in room-temperature water. Make sure you cut on the diagonal and keep the ends under water at all times. This prevents air bubbles from getting stuck at the end of the stem and blocking the water traveling up.

Expert advice for handling lilies. With a simple pinch, you can easily remove the golden stamens of a lily before you pick it. Do this before the pollen gets all over the flower, your fingers, and your clothes. Removing the stamens will also help the lily last longer, since it wilts soon after pollination.

Train stems to stand tall. Black-eyed Susans and daisies will droop once they are cut. To keep them perky indoors, fill a vase with warm water — 105 degrees is ideal. Cut small holes in a piece of cardboard big enough to balance on top of your vase. Thread each stem carefully through a hole until the flower sits on the cardboard. Dangle the stems in the water. Keep the flowers in a dark, cool place for several hours. They will adapt to their new home and stand up straight.

Trim leaves to prolong flowers. To savor your bouquet for as long as possible, get your clippers out and cut off any leaves that are under water. These soggy leaves will rot and encourage bacteria to grow, which can mean a short life for your beautiful arrangement.

Keep cut flowers beautiful. Add two tablespoons each of sugar and vinegar to a quart of water. Pour the mixture in a vase and put in your flowers. The sugar will feed your blooms, and the vinegar will keep them fresh a long time.

Perk up flowers with soda. To give cut flowers more pep, add some lemon-lime soda to the vase. The small amount of citric acid will lower the pH of the water, making it easier for the stems to absorb. As an added bonus, the sugar will give your blooms a boost.

Straighten tulips with a penny. If you want your tulips to stand straight and tall, drop a few copper pennies in the vase. Though florists aren't sure how this works, the penny seems to keep them from twisting and turning in search of light.

Creative fillers for a clear vase. A clear glass vase is one of the most versatile containers for a flower arrangement. You can create different looks by using unique fillers to anchor your flowers as well as disguise the stems. Marbles, pebbles, sand, pine cones, fruit, nuts, shells, even Christmas ornaments make visually appealing anchors for your flowers. Just be sure your fillers don't steal the thunder from the real show stopper — the flowers themselves.

Cheap and easy flower "frog." To hold flowers in place, trim off the sharp edges of a small piece of chicken wire and crumple it loosely so it fits in the top of your container. Stick your stems between the wires, and your beautiful creation will stay put.

Resist the urge to reuse foam. Green floral foam makes flower arranging a snap. Just don't reuse it a second time. If you stick a fresh flower in an old hole, it can end up in an air bubble and die of thirst. For this same reason, don't push a flower too far into fresh foam and then pull it back out. Just start a new hole.

Dealing with florist foam. Before you arrange flowers in florist foam, make sure it's saturated with water. Don't put it under a running tap. This could leave dry spots in the center of the block. Instead, fill a bucket with lukewarm water and drop the foam on top. It will float at first, but as it absorbs water, it will sink. Take it out as soon as the foam is level with the water. Let it drain. If you let the foam soak too long, it will fall apart.

Cut corners for easy watering. For flowers that last and last, keep your floral foam damp. To make it easier to water your arrangement later, cut a wedge out of your foam before you position it in the vase. Once the flowers are in place, pour water into the wedge. That way, water will soak into the foam instead of just running off the sides of the vase.

Plan ahead when decorating. Cut floral foam down to size before you wet it. If you can't use it all at once, store the extra piece in a plastic bag for your next arrangement. Once the foam dries out, it's almost impossible to wet it again.

Simple trick for perfect arrangements. For a flower arrangement that cascades over the edge of your vase like the beautiful Dutch still lifes of the 18th century — leave about an inch of floral foam jutting up over the rim of your container. Make sure it's solidly wedged in. Now you can arrange flowers so they fall naturally around the front and sides of the vase instead of just sticking up straight as an arrow.

Pinch tape to increase space. To make sure your foam is wedged securely in your vase, use floral tape to anchor it in place. Build a grid by stretching strips of tape from one side of the vase's lip to the other. Once it's securely attached to the vase, squeeze each strip of tape where it crosses over the foam. This will narrow the tape, allowing more space for your flowers.

Basic principle of design. Think about space before arranging flowers in a vase. If the flowers will grace a large, open area, a lush, overflowing arrangement in an urn or a tall vase will get rave reviews. If the area is small and cozy, a wildflower bouquet or a single bud in a little vase would look better. Remember, a large arrangement can quickly take over a small table, and a few spindly flowers will get lost in a banquet hall.

Fit your flowers to your table. Nothing stops the flow of conversation like a wall of flowers between your dinner guests. Keep your centerpiece low, about 9 inches or less, so your friends can throw witty remarks across the table. The opposite is true for a buffet table. Arrange your flowers in a pedestal vase so they don't hang in the food.

Treat flowers as an art form. Variety is the spice of life and the lifeblood of a stunning floral display. That's why it's important to choose leaves and flowers of different shapes and textures. Thin, long leaves and stems make up the skeleton of your arrangement. Rounded flowers, like roses and carnations, are called filler flowers, and they are the meat of the arrangement. And airy filler material, like baby's breath and ferns, pull it all together and add lightness.

Anchor vase with sand. Most flower arrangements are top-heavy. To keep a vase from toppling, funnel a layer of sand or small stones into it before starting your arrangement.

Protect furniture from water spills. Never set a bouquet of flowers or a potted plant directly on wooden furniture. Water spills can damage the surface. Instead, set vases and flower pots on decorative trays, mismatched saucers, or shallow bowls filled with pebbles.

Help flowers live a long life. Prolong the life of your blooms by keeping them shaded and cool. Instead of placing them near a television, heat vent, or radiator, set them in a cool spot away from windows and drafts. Keep flowers out of direct sunlight, too, or they will wilt.

Spritz on everlasting shine. Dried flowers tend to fall apart and grow dusty, but hair spray can keep your arrangement looking fresh. Give them a quick spray before you put them in a vase. Hairspray will seal in their color and help them keep their shape so your flowers look fresh longer.

Remove pollen stains with tape. If some of the brown or yellow pollen from a lily bloom gets on your clothing, remove it carefully with the sticky side of a piece of tape. Try not to touch the pollen with your fingers, as the oil from your skin could set it, making a permanent stain.

Force trees to bloom in winter. Many trees and shrubs form flowers in the fall. After eight weeks of cold weather, you can force them to flower inside. Cut several long branches of apple, cherry, quince, spirea, or forsythia that are heavy with buds. Make a 2-inch slit in the bottom of each stem and set it in warm water. Keep the branches in a cool, humid area, out of direct sun. Be patient. The branches will take several weeks to bloom.

Pruning wisdom

Free advice from the experts. Gardening experts who are among the best in the world are happy to share their great growing secrets with you. Experts with the U.S. Department of Agriculture (USDA) have been studying and solving horticultural problems for over 150 years. Now, they are sharing their knowledge with you. The USDA has an amazing, fact-filled Web site ready to answer your gardening questions. Just visit them online at www.usda.gov/news/garden.htm.

Ask a local pro. Your state extension service gives you instant access to gardening advice specific to your area, and an array of experts who can answer your questions. Check the blue pages in your telephone book for the extension office in your area, or contact the nearest state university and ask about their extension service program. You can also find these offices quickly on the Internet by checking the nationwide directory at www.reeusda.gov.

Take a trip to the museum. The Smithsonian is more than a museum. It's a rich resource for gardeners. The Horticultural Services Division of the Smithsonian Institution has put out a series of pamphlets on specific types of plants, including violets, bromeliads, and ornamental grasses, just to name a few. You can get these fact sheets online by visiting their Web site at www.gardens.si.edu/horticulture/. Or you can call the Horticultural Services Division at (202) 357-1926, or write to them at Horticultural Services Division, Arts and Industries Building, 900 Jefferson Drive SW, Washington, DC, 20560-0420.

Pinch to prompt plant growth. Pinching your plants is imperative for the most bloom and growth. If you leave dead blooms on your plants, they will put their energy into setting seed rather than growing. Instead, encourage them to bush out and flower again by pinching off faded blooms. Your plants will thank you with vigorous growth and a new set of blossoms.

Quick trick for amazing flower displays. You know pinch pruning prompts a plant to bush out with side growth. Did you know you can use this technique to create incredible displays of blooms? Pinching out shoots delays flowering. If you stop pinching them during their blooming season, the shoots will all set buds and flower at the same time — about one to two months after you stop pinching.

Grow show-quality blooms. You don't need expensive fertilizers to grow award-winning flowers. You just need to disbud. In disbudding, you pinch off buds before they bloom. Remove all the buds on a stem, leaving just one at the tip. This forces the plant to devote all its energy into growing a single, spectacular flower. Rub out other buds as soon as you see them. If you wait too long, removing them will leave unsightly scars.

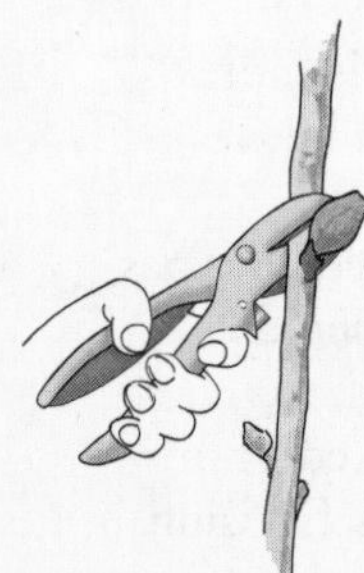

Slanting cut slashes disease risk. Make your pruning cuts at a gentle angle about one-quarter inch above a bud. An angled cut lets water slide off the wound, whereas a cut made straight across allows water to collect on top. Since water may carry fungi and other disease-causing organisms, you want it to roll off fresh wounds.

Expand plant with well-placed cuts. When you make pruning cuts, new shoots will grow in the same direction as the closest bud. Always cut back to a spot just above a bud that faces outward, away from the plant's center. This way, stems will grow outward, opening the plant up to air and light. Pruning to an inward-facing bud would cause shoots to grow toward the center, causing a congested tangle in the plant's heart.

Clip at the strong points. Woody plants heal fastest at the joints on their stem where a bud, leaf, fork, or branch collar sits. Clip stems just above these spots, and your plant will recover faster from pruning.

Know when to cut straight. You can't cut all stems at an angle. Some plants produce buds side-by-side. In these cases, making a sloping cut at one bud would damage the other. Compromise — make a pruning cut straight across just above the two buds. Although generally not recommended, a straight cut is the only way to prune these stems without harming the buds.

Prune shoots while young. Younger stems and twigs are not only easier to clip, they also heal faster than thicker, older branches. So don't put off pruning. Snip unwanted shoots on woody plants while they are young for the easiest cut and the least damage.

Right tools make trimming easier. Use pruning shears on soft stems and thin, woody stems. Loppers are the tool of choice for thicker, tougher stems. Special pruning saws, on the other hand, come to the rescue for big branches too thick for loppers.

Dull tools do harm. Use only sharp pruning tools. Dull ones crush and tear stems rather than cut cleanly, so your pruning may hurt the plant more than it helps.

Best way to hold pruning shears. Check your grip before clipping valuable plants. Hold pruning shears with the thin, narrow blade toward the part of the plant you are keeping, and the thick, heavy blade toward the branch you are pruning off. The branch you remove will take the brunt of any messy, crushing damage done by the lower blade, while the thin blade will leave a clean cut on the part of the plant that stays.

Wash tools to stop disease. Clean the blades of your pruning tools after each use either with denatured alcohol or a mild solution of one part bleach to nine parts water. This is especially important after trimming diseased plants. Be sure to wash the bleach mixture off the metal blades with soapy water. It may be a hassle, but cleaning your tools can help stop the spread of plant diseases and save you heartache later.

Splint bent stems with straws. Did you accidentally bend a stem while pruning a delicate plant? Splint it with a plastic straw. Cut the straw so it stands just a little taller than the bend in the stem. Slit the straw up one side and wrap it around the injured branch. Give the plant tender loving care, and remove the straw when the damage has healed.

Special care for clipping roses. Climbing and rambling roses need different treatment. Both bloom on last year's wood, but ramblers usually bloom only once a season, whereas climbers may bloom throughout. Remove dead or damaged branches on both in early spring. After the first bloom, prune old, unproductive wood and give the plants shape. Avoid hard pruning climbing roses since they don't grow as fast as their rambling relatives. Rambling roses can withstand tougher treatment. You can prune old canes down to the ground after the plant blooms, but have a lighter touch with new growth.

Inspire rosebush to grow sturdy stem. Anytime you clip a rose, whether pruning or simply gathering flowers, cut back to a stem with at least five leaves. This prompts the rose to put out a new stem sturdy enough to bear more blooms. If you prune to a point with fewer leaves, the plant will produce small, weak shoots.

Entice roses to bloom. For the most bang out of your blooming roses, deadhead them before they go to seed. You can even spur repeat bloomers to go ahead and set new buds. Cut stems that have finished flowering back to a bud with a full leaf, up to one-third of the way down the cane. This pruning prompts the rose to bloom again.

Give floppy flowers a strong backbone. Use chicken wire to support leggy flowers, like peonies and chrysanthemums. Cut a piece of chicken wire about the size of the flower bed, and stake it a foot above the ground. The plants will grow up through the wire, and their thick foliage will hide this homemade support from view.

Take the mystery out of pruning clematis. Clematis comes in three main varieties, each with its own pruning needs. Those that flower only once in the spring bloom on old wood. Deadhead the flowers and cut back dead, congested, or overly long stems as soon as the plant has finished blooming.

Simple advice for summer bloomers. Summer-blooming clematis flower on new growth. Go ahead and prune these stems between late fall and early spring, well before the plant sets new growth. Remove the old growth, as far back as 12 inches above the ground.

Clip clematis for three seasons of blooms. Some clematis bloom twice, once in early summer on old growth and again later in the summer or early fall on new growth. With careful cutting, you can turn these two sessions into one long-lasting bloom. Prune lightly in late winter or early spring, thinning out stems. This leaves a healthy framework of old wood for the spring blooms and encourages the plant to grow new shoots for later blooms. You can prune again after the first flower to spur on more new growth. Deadhead flowers after the second bloom.

Prune perfect pyracanthas. Shape up your pyracanthas midspring by pruning off damaged wood and branches that grow outside the form. Clip fast-growing shoots down to two or three leaves. This encourages them to make the spurs that will later bear colorful berries. Prune these plants again in late summer, removing new growth that covers up the ripening berries.

Cut crape myrtles late. You might be tempted to prune crape myrtles early and save yourself from raking up all those fallen leaves. Don't give in. Wait and prune them after their leaves have fallen, around December. Cutting them back in fall makes them less tolerant of cold weather.

"Hard prune" plants for vigorous growth. Prune hard to get more growth out of a weak plant. The more you cut it back, the stronger it will return. On the other hand, a strong plant needs just a little light pruning to keep it healthy.

Balance lopsided plants. Bring a lopsided shrub or tree back in balance with wise pruning. Cut back the weakest shoots hard, but only prune the tips of the strong branches. Continue doing this each year until the weak stems have filled in enough to balance the plant.

Great idea for spectacular foliage. Hard-pruning some trees and shrubs each year triggers them to produce large or especially colorful leaves the next. First, make sure your plant responds well to hard pruning — not all of them do. Then give it a balanced fertilizer in the spring to help it put out all that showy new growth.

Feed plants after pruning. Pruning makes plants hungry, especially hard pruning. Feed pruned plants in spring with a general fertilizer and mulch around them with the compost of your choice. This dose of nutrients will help it put out fresh growth triggered by your pruning.

Cut grafts carefully. Avoid cutting below the graft union when pruning grafted plants. Keep an eye out for shoots that may later sprout below the graft, and remove them as soon as you see them. A heavy pruning can trigger the rootstock to send out new growth of its own.

Say farewell to suckers. Suckers can turn your careful graft back to its wild rootstock. That's because these stems pop up from the original plant, not its grafted parts. If left alone, suckers will drain nutrients from the grafted species and may take over the plant. Cutting them back only makes them return stronger than before. Instead, trace them down to their point of origin on the root and carefully pull them off.

Prune "hard" for amazing display

Hard prune any of these shrubs for the most magnificent foliage effects.

- Buddleja davidii
- Catalpa Bignonioides 'Aurea'
- Cotinus coggygria
- Cotinus obovatus
- Eucalyptus gunnii
- Sambucus Nigra
- Sambucus Racemosa

Clip to help transplants survive. Tired of transplants dying? Scale back their top growth to give them a better chance in your yard. A container-grown plant may have more leaves and stems than its roots can support after the shock of being transplanted. Prune off some of this growth after planting to help it gain a foothold in its new home.

Prune shrubs on schedule. Timing is essential for the most beautiful blooms on deciduous shrubs. Pay attention to when they blossom each year. Those that flower in spring bloom on old growth and should be pruned when they finish blooming. Bushes that blossom after midsummer flower on new growth. Wait and trim these back while they are dormant in winter or early spring. Timing your trimmings this way gives your shrubs a chance to recover before blooming again.

Make room for new growth. Unless a shrub has specific pruning needs, prune some of the oldest wood each year. This opens the plant's center to more air and light and encourages new growth.

Cut off whole canes. Some shrubs, like forsythia, grow long canes from their base instead of the usual branch framework. Rather than pruning off half of an old, woody cane, remove the entire piece at its base. This encourages new growth and keeps the center from getting congested with old wood.

First aid for ailing shrubs. Neglected shrubs need tender loving care. Hard prune them after their growing season with an aim to remove dead, choked, or unhealthy branches. This opens up the center to let in more light and air. You can rehabilitate these special patients all at once in a single year, but not all plants do well with hard pruning. If your plant doesn't, spread out this work over two or three years.

Stop foliage from changing color. Plants with variegated foliage sometimes sprout an all-green shoot. The green foliage has more chlorophyll, so it tends to grow faster. Eventually, it will out-compete the variegated growth, and the plant will become solid green. Remove these shoots as soon as you see them to save your multicolored beauty.

Clip dead limbs without doing more harm. Leaving dead wood on a plant invites disease. Check to see if the plant has formed a clear barrier between the dead and healthy wood. If so, cut ailing stems just above the dead line. If you cut them back into living growth, the plant will spend unnecessary energy forming scar tissue over the fresh wound. The exception — if you can't find a clear line between damaged and healthy wood, prune the branch back to good wood. This helps contain an active disease before it spreads farther.

Disguise dead spots. No need to live with dead patches in a tree or shrub. First, prune off dead wood. Slide a cane or stake through the opening into the plant's center, and attach it to a main branch or trunk. Tie nearby limbs loosely to the cane to cover up the hole.

Trim evergreen shrubs on a timetable. Prune evergreen hedges in spring or summer, once all severe cold weather has passed. You can trim them lightly after they flower to deadhead them, clear out old unproductive wood, and keep their pleasing shape.

Angle formal hedges for best effect. Formal hedges lend order and symmetry to a garden. Protect your investment by properly pruning them. Instead of shearing the sides straight down, clip them at a slight angle so the hedge is narrower at the top. This lets more light reach the lower branches and keeps them from dying back.

Best way to build hedge height. Be patient and keep at it. Tall hedges can take a long time and a lot of patience to grow. Don't be tempted to let a shrub get leggy just to build height. No one wants a scrawny, lanky hedge. Prune it regularly to encourage dense, healthy growth. The height will come with time.

Limit hedge height for safety. Tall hedges offer privacy, but pruning them can be difficult, particularly if they have an exact shape and need more maintenance. Limit their height to a size you can easily trim, and save yourself the backache of bringing out the ladder.

Fashion templates to guide trimmings. Eyeballing it may work on trees or informal hedges, but topiary and formal hedges need more exact trimming. Make a template to guide you. Outline the shape you want with wire, or cut it out of thin wood or cardboard. Place your template over the plant and clip away foliage outside the guidelines.

Level hedge tops with ease. Cut a foolproof straight line across the top of your hedges with two sticks and a string. Drive a tall stake into the ground at each end of your hedge, and tie a string between them at the height you want to clip the hedge. Make sure the string is taut. Use it as a guideline while pruning, and you'll have a straight line every time.

Mix shrubs for colorful show. Formal hedges are usually made up of just one kind of plant, but you don't have to stick with tradition. Mixed hedges also offer privacy, and by choosing shrubs with a variety of bloom and foliage colors, you'll create a living quilt in your own yard. Hedge plants come in a wide palette of colors. Try mixing greens, golds, reds, and variegated plants for an eye-popping show. Yew, holly, beech, and viburnum are just a few known for their leafy beauty.

Spread a sheet to keep pruning neat. Stop stooping to clean up hedge trimmings. Spread a sheet or tarp under shrubs and trees while you prune them to catch cuttings. When you finish, gather up the corners and carry your clippings to the trash or compost.

Bigger is not better. When choosing a tree to plant in your yard, buy a small, sturdy sapling rather than a larger, already-trained tree. A young sapling may need a little more training, but it's more likely to survive the transplant and grow into a strong, healthy tree.

Stake saplings for steady stem and roots. You may have to stake a nursery tree its first year after planting to help it develop a straight stem and stable root system. Use the shortest stake you can, at least shorter than the lowest branches on the tree, and tie it loosely to the trunk. The sapling's trunk should be able to sway slightly in the wind. This gentle movement helps it develop a strong root system. Check the tree regularly, especially during growing season, and remove the stake as soon as the sapling can support itself.

Take steps to protect a staked tree. Use a spacer and adjustable ties when staking young trees. Place a spacer or other gentle buffer between the tree and the stake to stop the two from rubbing together. Check the adjustable ties holding the tree and loosen them as it grows. If they become too tight, they can chafe the bark, and cut off the sap flow.

Support big trees with guy wires. Large trees with trunks more than 4 inches thick may need more than one stake. Sink several stakes, hang guy wires over sturdy forks in the tree, and attach them to the stakes. Mark the wires with bright tape, paint, or streamers to remind yourself and passersby to watch out. Remove the stakes and wires as soon as the tree can support itself, generally within a year or two of planting.

Stand stakes against the wind. Set stakes facing into the prevailing wind so plants blow away from the stake, not up against it. In windy areas, you may need to use more than one stake, or angle them into the wind.

Plant trees in native soil. Don't bother amending the dirt around newly planted trees unless you have very poor soil. Instead, break up the native dirt around the root ball so roots can easily spread out, and backfill with native soil. Amending creates a line between the artificially rich soil and the native dirt. As the tree grows, its roots will want to stay in the amended dirt and may have trouble growing beyond that small area into the regular soil. This could set the stage for a weak root system and an unstable tree.

Single out the strongest leader. Two heads are generally better than one, but a tree with two leaders — two main branches — won't stand for long. One branch may eventually snap off the trunk and split the tree. Nip this in the bud early on by clipping off the weak leader, leaving the strong one to grow unchallenged.

Training a new leading shoot. Replacing a broken or weak leader may take a little training if the new leader is not perfectly vertical. Choose the strongest and straightest shoot for the new leader, then tie it vertically to a piece of cane with soft ties. Remove the cane once the leader is sturdy enough to stand straight on its own.

Find a form that fits. When training a tree, choose a shape that works with its natural growth pattern. Trying to force a tree into a shape totally different from the way it would normally grow can leave it structurally unstable.

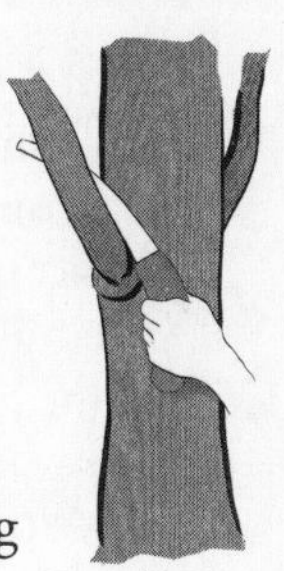

Cut branches cleanly for faster healing. Trimming a tree can be hard on its health if not done properly. Help your trees mend their wounds by clipping off branches cleanly. Make a smooth cut just outside the branch collar — the raised ring of bark at the base of a limb. The tree heals fastest here and will quickly form scar tissue over the wound. Don't cut into the branch collar, or you risk damaging the tree.

Wound paint can wound trees. Skip the wound sealer unless you are particularly worried about insects or disease infecting the pruning cut. Given time, trees seal off their own wounds. If you do use wound paint, let the cut dry for a while before applying it. Otherwise, you may seal moisture into the wound, a recipe for decay.

Prune trees in winter to see shape. Prune hardwood trees in the winter after they have shed their leaves, unless your tree has a different pruning schedule. It's easier to visualize the shape you want to create with the leaves gone. And for most trees, pruning in winter minimizes the risk for spreading disease, lessens the loss of sap, and cuts down on insect damage.

Pinch "candle" for fuller conifers. These trees and shrubs need special treatment to fill out. Instead of pruning them like their deciduous cousins, pinch off half of each candle, or new shoot, before its needles start to harden. But don't pinch off the whole candle, or you will stunt the growth of that branch.

Avoid cutting low conifer limbs. Don't prune off the lower branches on conifers unless they are damaged. They won't grow back, and the result will be a top-heavy tree. If you are worried about mowing or weed pulling under a conifer, mulch the area beneath it.

Ward off dwarf reversion. Dwarf conifers don't always stay small. Occasionally, a stem may start growing as a regular conifer branch. This wayward limb not only spoils the look, it may also take over the plant. Put a stop to the trouble by snipping off reverted stems at their point of origin, or right below the spot where the rebellious branch sprouted.

Weeping can weaken trees. Some trees, such as birch, maple, and willow, weep — or bleed sap — when cut. Losing a little sap is not usually harmful, but heavy weeping can weaken the tree. Try to prune these trees in winter when they are fully dormant, before their sap starts to rise.

Protect elms and oaks from disease. Avoid pruning elm and oak trees during the summer, especially in May and June. Beetles carry the fungi that cause Dutch elm disease and oak wilt. These bugs are most active in warm months, and open pruning wounds tend to attract them. Cut back elms and oaks while they are dormant during cold months, and you'll cut the risk for these diseases.

> ! Laburnums may be blooming beauties, but they're also deadly ones. Every part of this tree is poisonous. Protect yourself when pruning it by wearing gloves, long clothes, and other protective gear.

Time pruning to avoid silver leaf. Prune trees prone to silver leaf disease in the summer. That's when the fungus causing it is least active. Plum, cherry, and other fruit trees are susceptible to silver leaf, as are a variety of other plants. Ask your local extension service what plants in your area are at risk.

Sever roots for stronger plants. Pruning the roots could save an ailing shrub or tree. First, figure out where to cut the roots. Measure a tree trunk's diameter. For every 1 inch of trunk, move out 1 foot from the tree. Dig a shallow trench at the proper distance. Sever the thickest roots with a spade, but leave the fine roots intact. For a milder root pruning, you can skip the trench and simply sink your spade in a circle at the right distance around the trunk. To root prune a shrub, find the drip line where water drops from the plant to the ground. Sever the roots along this guideline.

As roots age, they become harder and less able to absorb nutrients. Pruning older roots allows new, more-fibrous ones to take their place, roots better at drinking up water and other nutrients.

Root prune rather than repot. Root pruning is a good alternative to repotting overgrown houseplants. Slip the plant out of its pot, grabbing it by the root ball rather than the stems. Gently pull out the roots to ease compaction, and shake out some of the old soil. Prune about a third of the smaller roots with a pair of sharp shears, but leave the larger, feeder roots untouched. Repot it in fresh soil, then cut back about one-third of the top growth. Never remove more than a third of the total roots on a plant.

Prune roots wisely. You may need to stake newly root-pruned plants until they can get reestablished in the ground. Some experts recommend root pruning in the fall before you transplant a tree or shrub to lessen the chance of the plant dying from shock. Only root prune trees and shrubs while dormant.

Fruit trees follow their own calendar. Prune established apple and pear trees in either late winter or early spring before they set new growth. Hold off on pruning stone fruits, such as plums, cherries, and peaches until summer.

Thin apples for fruitful harvest. Apple trees often set more fruit than they can fully ripen. For the juiciest crop year after year, thin apples to one fruit per cluster, then leave them to ripen. Letting the tree produce a heavy crop one year means a light crop — or none at all — the next.

Grow out, not up. Try training your climbers, fruit trees, and flowering shrubs to grow laterally along a wall or trellis. Branches that grow sideways produce more flowers and fruit than those growing straight up.

Give young plants early guidance. Spend time pruning and training plants when they are young, especially trees and shrubs. Give them shape early on, and they will need less pruning as they age.

Edge garden paths with stepovers. Stepovers make unique edgings for any garden. Start with a very young flowering tree, like an apple. Stake it, then tie a wire from that stake to another about 5 feet down the path. Bend the tree over and train it to grow along the wire between stakes. Prune it in summer and winter to keep its neat shape, and take care not to trip over it!

Not all climbers have arms ready to fan out. Encourage yours to branch out with hard pruning, either cutting back the entire plant or clipping chosen stems to within a few buds of their base.

Build fans for climbers. Fruit trees and climbing plants can take many forms, including the classic fan. You can build a fan on a trellis or a homemade wire support, but start training plants early. If you use wires, run them horizontally along a wall. Attach bamboo canes to them at angles to form a basic fan shape. Choose several long stems and tie them onto the canes or trellis in a fan. Prune out shoots that break the form by cutting them flush against the stem. You can prompt stems to grow faster and in a certain direction by clipping them back to a bud growing in the desired direction.

Give trained fruits the royal treatment. Fruit trees trained to grow against a wall or fence, called espaliering, need more care than their free-growing bushy relatives. Formally trained apples and pears need a summer pruning, in addition to their regular winter pruning, to keep their shape and ensure a fruitful crop. In the summer, snip off new side-shoots more than 6 inches long. Clip shoots sprouting on the trunk or main branches to a point just three leaves above the basal cluster — or lowest cluster of leaves. Other small shoots may sprout from existing side-shoots. Prune back these tiny invaders even farther, to one leaf or bud above the basal cluster.

Winning choices for a beautiful garden wall

Before you train a wall-climber, take a look at those the experts recommend. Here's a quick list of favorites from gardeners who know.

- Bougainvillea
- Ceanothus
- Clematis
- Cotoneaster
- Cytisus battandieri
- Euonymus
- Fremontodendron
- Honeysuckle
- Japonica
- Magnolia
- Plum
- Pyracantha
- Winter Jasmine

Simple fix for thirsty wall shrubs. Set plants 15 to 18 inches from a wall or fence. Otherwise, the barrier may block rain from reaching their roots, resulting in dry soil and thirsty plants.

Train your trellis vine. Strips of rags or old pantyhose work best to secure and guide a vine along a trellis. They are soft and gentle, unlike floral wire and bread bag ties. These are too sharp and can damage a growing plant.

Avoid trellis damage by tying. Train climbers properly. Tie vines and canes loosely to a trellis or fence rather than threading the stems through the structure. If you simply weave a stem in and out of trellis bars, it will tear the frame apart as it grows and push it away from supporting walls.

Use your fence as a ready-made trellis. Building a trellis takes time and money. Try training vines on your fence, instead. Some vines are eager climbers, while others need a little help. On wood fences, drive nails just deep enough to anchor twine. Run the string in a zigzag pattern up and down the fence, looping it around each nail. As your vines grow, train them onto the string supports.

Grow your own weeping tree. Train your own weeper to add grace to your landscape. You will have to train a naturally weeping tree to grow upright and get tall enough to form a cascade. Set a stake and tie it to the tree's leader. Let the tree grow to your chosen height, then pinch off the leading stem. This prompts the plant to branch out. Prune off stems lower down the trunk to keep the weeping growth at the top.

Put pruning castoffs to good use. Here's a handy use for all those clippings. Shove the stems of long shrub or tree cuttings down the middle of a row of young peas. "Plant" the cuttings close together so they fan out and form a natural trellis for the climbing peas. Once you've harvested, you can chip up and compost the whole bit, leaving nothing to waste.

A figure eight saves staked plants. Staking tomatoes is a little like staking a tree. You need to place a buffer between the plant and stake. Using soft strips of cloth, loop one end around the stake, cross it over in the center, then wrap it around the stem and back again. This forms a figure-eight between the stake and tomato plant and acts like a buffer.

Teach tomatoes how to grow. When growing tomatoes in cages, make sure the openings in the wire cages are large enough to reach through and pick tomatoes. And stake your cages to keep them from falling over. Just drive one or two long stakes into the ground and secure it to the cage with wire or twine.

Grow a hedge of tomatoes. For a whole row of tomatoes, make a hedgerow. Plant your tomatoes in a straight line, and set a tall stake on each side every few feet. Hang two long, tall fences of wire mesh, one on each side of your tomato row. Leave about 18 to 24 inches of space between the two fences for your plants to grow. Hang the fences a good 6 inches off the ground so you can weed under them, then attach them to the stakes. As your tomatoes grow, you can slide horizontal pieces of wood between the fences to give the plants extra support.

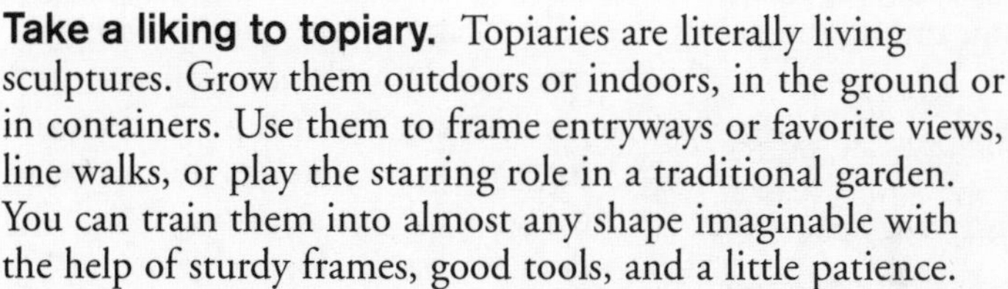

Take a liking to topiary. Topiaries are literally living sculptures. Grow them outdoors or indoors, in the ground or in containers. Use them to frame entryways or favorite views, line walks, or play the starring role in a traditional garden. You can train them into almost any shape imaginable with the help of sturdy frames, good tools, and a little patience.

Pick the perfect plant for your topiary. Not all plants make great topiaries. Choose shrubs, trees, or herbs that tend to grow dense, small leaves and are hardy enough to withstand regular pruning. Boxwood shrubs, yews, and ivy are good choices for topiaries.

Train a mop-head tree in three easy steps. Mop-head topiaries don't come cheap, but you can slash the cost by training your own. Choose an upward-growing potted plant with a strong stem. Prune off all the side growth except for a cluster of foliage at the top. As the mop-head fills in, shape it with light pruning. Occasionally, you may need to clip off new buds that pop up on the stem below the leafy top.

Braid stems for special effect. For this stem effect, you need either a single plant with three flexible stems or three plants growing close together. Clip off leaves growing low on the trunks, then braid them together just slightly near their base. You may need to stake the stems until they start to harden. As the plants grow, continue braiding upward. Eventually, the trunks will fuse together, making the braid permanent.

Turn herbs into art. Woody herbs make fragrant topiaries. Rosemary is a gardener's favorite, but bay, thyme, and others will work, too. Simply train them as you would other topiary plants. For instance, train an herb with a strong central leader, such as rosemary or bay, as a tree or shrub with a ball or mop-head top.

Get growing with cone topiaries. These simple shapes are among the easiest to create. Make a teepee out of bamboo or canes about the size you want your topiary, and tie the pieces together at the top. Set the teepee over your shrub, adjusting it so it doesn't wobble. Then clip the branches that stick out around the frame. This homemade guide will help you create the perfect cone-shaped topiary.

> ! Don't pinch off more than one-third of the leaves at a time when training your climbing topiary. Otherwise, the plant may go into shock. To remove all the leaves along a stem, prune gradually over several weeks.

Shape a spiral with ribbon and shears. Try this no-fuss way to shape a topiary spiral. Tie an extra wide piece of ribbon to the top of the plant you want to trim. Spiral it down around the plant and secure it at the bottom. Trim around the ribbon, cutting stems all the way back to the central trunk. When you remove your ribbon guideline, you'll have a shapely spiral topiary.

> Train outdoor topiary with young plants rather than established woody ones. They tend to have more flexible limbs and respond better to severe training.

Set your sights on climbing topiary. Train climbing vines over wire shapes for a unique look. Choose a climber with small leaves, like a potted ivy, and use a topiary frame at least one-and-a-half times the height of the pot. Press the frame into the pot's center and anchor it in the soil. Start by wrapping a stem around the wire base. Work your way up the frame, gently wrapping a stem around each wire and tying on stems that tend to stray. Cut off extra wire and pinch off unnecessary leaves. As the plant grows, continue training it around the form.

Keep topiary fresh with mist. Have a water mister handy and lightly mist your indoor topiary regularly. The leaves will look cleaner and healthier.

Emergency first aid for dry ivy topiary. Water topiary carefully. Too much, and the roots rot. Too little, and the roots die back. If your ivy topiary dries out, try reviving it with a deep soak. Fill a sink with a few inches of water. Set the base of the topiary in it and let the plant drink its fill.

Grow lions, and tigers, and bears – oh my! Large metal frames often house the fanciful shapes of outdoor topiary. Put the frame on the ground, and mark each spot where it touches the soil. Place a plant at each of those points, then set the frame over them. Train these plants up the metal form, tying rebellious limbs in place with soft ties. Clip the plants into shape as they fill out around the frame. Growing a large topiary like this may take several years, but the shapes you create will be worth the wait.

Make instant topiaries with moss. Tired of waiting years for your topiary to fill out? Create one almost instantly. Stuff a wire frame with moist sphagnum moss. Poke holes in the moss and plant the roots of a climber, like ivy, directly into it. In no time, the plant will spread across the frame, setting new roots in the sphagnum. For a large topiary, choose a heavy, sturdy frame that won't tip over. It won't be anchored to the ground by any roots, so it must be able to stand on its own. A moss topiary requires more watering than a soil-grown one since sphagnum dries out faster than other planting mediums.

Clip, clip, clip to make topiary grow. Regular trimming is key, whether training a new topiary or maintaining a grown one. Pruning new shoots on young shrubs helps them fill out densely and prevents leggy, sparse growth — the enemy of every green thumb. For established topiaries, try trimming new growth back to old growth. Trim it twice a year, once at the beginning of the growing season and again in late summer or after flowering.

Solutions to pesky plant problems

Evict pests for the winter. Clean up your garden in the fall to eliminate problems next spring and summer. Most insects overwinter among dead plant material and weeds. They're not active or laying eggs and just need a sheltered place to hide out until it gets warm. Molds, diseases, and harmful bacteria will stay dormant in the old diseased growth of last year and pop up again in the spring. So get rid of all the debris and dead stuff so they won't have a cozy place for the winter.

Stop insects with seaweed. Keep pests away from your plants with seaweed. A healthy garden is the best defense against insects and disease. Seaweed contains iron, zinc, barium, calcium, sulfur, and magnesium. These trace elements make it wonderful for promoting growth and giving plants the strength to fight off enemy attacks. Apply seaweed fertilizer either as a mulch or a spray and watch your garden grow strong.

Invite a toad to share your yard. Toads can eat more than 50 grubs, grasshoppers, and cutworms a night and, unlike birds, they don't eat plants, too. If a toad likes you and your garden, he'll stay for years. Toads eat at night and hide out during the day. They drink through their skin and need to get into water from time to time. Encourage toads with damp, shady spots in your garden.

Nab pests with an amazing bacteria. *Bacillus thuringiensis* (Bt) is a naturally occurring bacterial insect disease used as an insecticide ingredient. It's considered one of the safest and most effective pest defenses. Bt paralyzes insects' stomachs so they stop eating and starve to death. Used mostly to stop leaf-eating caterpillars and larvae, some Bt strains also target the larvae of mosquitos, black flies, and fungus gnats. The best part is, it only harms its specific target. Look for products with Bt in the organic section of garden specialty stores.

The latest way to pester pests

Floating row covers protect annual vegetable plants from a variety of pests. They are made from lightweight, spun, synthetic fabric that keeps out bugs, but lets light and water through. Make sure you get the right fabric — plain, clear plastic seals out air and water — and throw it over the entire crop. It's so light it literally "floats" over the plants. Anchor down the edges, leaving plenty of slack for the plants to grow. Row covers are particularly effective against chewing caterpillars that evolve from eggs laid by adult insects. They can't get in to lay eggs on the foliage.

Remove covers for pollination. When plants under floating row covers begin to flower, it's time to take off the covers so bees and other insects can get in to pollinate the blossoms. If you time it right, the egg-laying cycles of the cabbage worm, cabbage looper, leaf miner, and other moths should have passed. If not, you have several choices. You can put the covers back, rely on the mature plants' ability to resist the caterpillars that come from the eggs, or let good insects, like ladybugs and lacewings, take over.

Kill insects with nematodes. Use parasitic nematodes instead of pesticides to take care of many insect pests. These microscopic roundworms get inside grubs, beetles, and other insects and release bacteria that kill the host by blood poisoning. Insect parasitic nematodes only go after insects. They're not harmful to people, plants, or animals. Purchase nematodes from biological supply distributors. You'll mix them with water and spray them on. Be careful to get the right type for your particular pest problem and follow instructions closely.

Tobacco and coffee kill pests. Drop some chewing tobacco or coffee grounds into your watering can to get natural pest protection. Caffeine and nicotine are pesticides that some plants have developed to protect themselves. But don't overdo it. Caffeine will also kill your plants if you use too much. And nicotine in concentrated form is a deadly poison to humans and other animals. Both will also kill good bugs along with the bad ones. In addition, don't use tobacco teas on tomatoes or other nightshade plants. They can cause disease.

Only kill the bad bugs. Think twice before using pesticides, either natural or chemical, to take care of a bug problem. Wide-spectrum products kill beneficial insects right along with the ones that eat your plants. If it is necessary to spray, do it when the bugs are present and use insecticidal soaps, dormant oil sprays, or pyrethrins that kill on contact and have little residual effect. For preventive measures, encourage ladybugs and lacewings to take up residence. They eat the eggs of bad bugs.

Ladybugs love aphids. Sometimes aphids get so bad the only thing to do is destroy the infested plants. A better way is to let their natural enemies take care of them. The ladybug, or ladybird beetle, is the number one enemy of aphids. You can attract ladybugs to your garden with tansy, yarrow, marigolds, and daisies. And another thing — don't use chemicals that kill good insects as well as bad. Ladybugs also eat whiteflies and mites. Lacewings, wasps, and spiders also feed on aphids.

Add ladybugs to your garden. Ladybugs love to eat aphids and whiteflies. You can buy mated females from larger garden stores, catalogues, or Web sites. When they arrive, keep them in the refrigerator for a few days. It helps them calm down from the stress of traveling. Ladybugs are less inclined to fly at night, so release them in the evening. Spray a mist of weak sugar water — half water and half soda works well — on them to stick their wings shut. It will dissolve in a few days. Adult ladybugs will fly away if the pest population is low. Yet, if they lay eggs first, their offspring will still be there.

Halt home invasion by lady beetle. The multicolored Asian lady beetle eats aphids, just like domestic ladybugs. But she ranges in color from bright red-orange to pale yellow-orange and can also make a pest of herself — she likes to come inside your house for the winter. When the Asian lady beetle is excited, she emits a sticky, yellow substance that smells awful and gets all over your things. Don't use pesticides on these good bugs, but seal up cracks and windows where they might gain entry. If they get inside anyway, use a vacuum or a broom and dustpan to gently gather them up and take them back outside.

Discover the power of aphid lions. The green lacewing, also called the aphid lion, looks like a miniature alligator. It devours aphids, whiteflies, and other bad bugs — just like its more famous cousin, the ladybird beetle. But ladybugs will "fly away home" when they've eaten up all the pests. Lacewings are more apt to stay put and make your garden their home, since it's only their larvae that are predatory. Adults live on nectar and pollen and are attracted by flowers like yarrow, goldenrod, and asters.

Clobber bad bugs with lacewings. Green lacewings are good for your garden because they eat aphids, whiteflies, leaf miners, mealy bugs, thrips, and spider mites. If you don't have any, or if you want more, buy their eggs or larvae at larger garden stores or by mail. It's the larvae that eat the other bugs, so if you get adults you'll have to wait until their eggs hatch before you get any pest reduction. For best results, release another batch after five to seven days.

Unleash round-the-clock predator. Buy praying mantis eggs through the mail or at larger garden supply stores, and let them hatch in your garden. They're carnivorous so they don't eat plants, but they will eat most any kind of bug — and lots of them. Unfortunately, when they run out of bugs, they eat each other. Bigger than most insects, the praying mantis is easy to spot and interesting to watch. It's the only predator to feed at night on moths and also the only predator fast enough to catch mosquitos and flies.

Foil attacks with spined soldier bugs. Don't go to war with the spined soldier bug, a stink bug that feeds on the larval forms of many beetles and moths. It's pale brown, shield-shaped, about the size of your thumbnail, and feeds by sucking out its prey's internal juices with a long beak it keeps folded under its body. The helpful spined soldier bug is quite sensitive to pesticides, so if you see them around, let them kill your pests instead of spraying. Its prey includes the Mexican

A unique approach to controlling pests

Integrated Pest Management (IPM) is a way to deal with pests without overusing broad-spectrum pesticides. IPM recognizes that a healthy garden can tolerate a certain amount of pest infestation without showing ill effects. It seeks to manage pests to a tolerable level by using natural parasites, predators, and diseases; better yard and garden planning; use of resistant plant varieties and crop rotation; and sanitation, trapping, and other various cultural practices. IPM doesn't rule out the use of pesticides, but encourages their use only when necessary and only in the amount needed to take care of a specific problem.

bean beetle, diamondback moth, corn earworm, cabbage looper, Colorado potato beetle, and flea beetle.

Learn to like wasps. Several varieties of small, nonstinging, parasitic wasps feed on the eggs of other insects. Even the dreaded yellow jacket can bring over 225 flies an hour to a nest to feed its young. It also drags caterpillars home from your garden. Other wasps lay eggs among the larvae of leaf-eating caterpillars, aphids, flies, and beetles. When they hatch, it's the baby wasps that win. Attract good wasps to your garden by growing flowers from carrots, celery, parsley, and Queen Anne's lace.

Companion plants lure good bugs. Companion plants help attract beneficial insects — the predatory and parasitic bugs that keep pest populations in check — to your garden. Adult beneficial flies, midges, and parasitic wasps need nectar for energy to lay eggs. Ladybugs and green lacewings stay healthy on pollen when prey is scarce. The small flowers of dill, parsley, thyme, and other herbs provide food for tiny parasites that can drown in the nectar of larger flowers. Daisies, coneflowers, and yarrow are good pollen sources.

Repel bugs with plants. Most plants have certain odors and root secretions that repel certain insects, but some have more than others. Plants that are universally "unappealing" to insects include marigolds, chrysanthemums, chives, onions, garlic, basil, horseradish, mint, and nasturtiums. The more of these you have in your garden, the fewer pests you'll have.

Solve your blackfly problem. Nasturtium is often recommended for the garden because of the pests it repels, including whiteflies, woolly aphids, and ants. But it also attracts the pesky blackfly, an aphid relative that infests vegetables, such as broad beans and cucumbers, as well as chrysanthemums. Plant nasturtiums between the rows, and blackflies will swarm to them instead of the plants you want to save. Eventually, natural predators, parasites, and diseases will get rid of blackflies, and they won't even hang around the nasturtiums.

Tomato and asparagus are a dynamic duo. These two companions are a delicious combination on your salad plate — and in your garden. There's something about asparagus that tomato hornworms don't like, and asparagus beetles avoid tomato plants. Plant them together to rid both crops of their deadliest enemy.

Serve dill to hungry hornworms. If you can't keep tomato hornworms out of your tomato patch, try planting some dill nearby as a trap crop. Hornworms like dill better than tomatoes, and they'll go after that instead. Then they'll be out of your tomatoes and easier to pick off and drown in soapy water.

Plant plants that keep away ants. Keep annoying ants away from your house and garden with plants that have natural defense systems against insects. Ants particularly don't like three members of the mint family — peppermint, spearmint, and pennyroyal. Southernwood, a fragrant and shrubby relative of sage brush and wormwood, is another ant repellent. Also try onions, chives, sage, and catnip. Plant tansy next to your peonies. It rejects the little sugar ants that crawl all over peonies and kitchen cabinets. If the mints and tansy are too aggressive for you, grow them somewhere else and spread cuttings to shoo the ants.

Use spices to spike ant entrances. Ants help gardeners by eating other insects and cleaning up dead material. But there's nothing good about them when they're inside your house. Spread ground cloves or red pepper around doors, windows, and other places to keep the busy little buggers away from your home. Cinnamon, cream of tartar, and dried paprika are other items in your spice cabinet that ants don't like.

Chase away ants with candy canes. Ants don't like peppermint. Keep them away from plants, your house, and other buildings by grinding up peppermint candy and sprinkling it about. Convince them to abandon an anthill by leaving a peppermint stick or two near the entrance. Mix up an anti-ant spray with a teaspoon of peppermint extract in a quart of water. Add a few drops of lemon ammonia to give it an extra boost.

Send ants running with orange peel. Citrus fruits contain natural pesticides. To keep ants away, steep the peels from one orange in two cups of hot water for about 24 hours. Strain out the peels, add a few drops of liquid dishwashing detergent, and use it as a spray. Or just grind up a whole orange in the blender, add water, and pour it on the ant hill.

Ants won't cross chalk line. Make a barrier for ants around your garden or your house with a line of chalk or diatomaceous earth. They won't cross it. For area control of ants, aphids, thrips, earwigs, slugs, and snails, sprinkle more diatomaceous earth. It has microscopic razor edges that cut into an insect's protective covering, dry it out, and kill the bug by dehydration. You can find diatomaceous earth at garden supply stores.

Experiment with boiling water. Ants on your patio? Or do you need a quick way to get rid of anthills that suddenly erupt in your garden? Pour boiling water on them. It may seem a bit cruel, but it's a simple, nontoxic, and time-proven remedy. Add several drops of hot chili oil to make things even hotter. Or try this — brew a tea with the hottest peppers you can find, finely chopped in a food processor and mixed with the hot water. You may have to scald the ants more than once, but eventually the survivors will give up and go someplace else.

Eliminate ants and aphids with vinegar. Just when you decide a few ants are no big deal, you find out they raise aphids. You don't want aphid-farmers in your garden so you need an inexpensive, natural way to get rid of them. Just pick up a big jug of white vinegar at the store, pour it on the ant hill, and watch it bubble down to the heart of the nest. If you still see ants after a day or two, douse it again. It shouldn't take more than three doses for them and their aphid herd to be gone for good.

Oust ants with bait. Poison baits are a good, long-term control for ants. Worker ants carry the bait back to the mound and feed it to the rest of the colony. It works best when the queen gets a taste of the "poison apple" and no longer lays eggs to replace dead ants. Sometimes, the colony gets nervous and just changes locations, which may be enough to get them out of your yard. When using bait, get a product designed for the kind of ants you have and be patient. It takes two or three weeks to affect the whole colony.

Give fire ants grits for breakfast. Fire ants are a major problem in the southern United States, which is also where you're most likely to find a cheap, nontoxic solution for them on the pantry shelf. Grits, a breakfast staple in the South, is an often suggested bait for fire ants, who take the little white morsels home to share with their friends. When they eat grits and drink water, the grits swell up inside them, and they die. Sprinkle grits on and around ant mounds. You'll be amazed how fast they get picked up and taken inside.

Kill ants with boric acid. Use boric acid for a great homemade ant killer. Dissolve four teaspoons of the white powder and a cup of sugar in three cups of not-quite-boiling water. After the mixture cools, moisten cotton balls with it and leave them as bait. The ants take nibbles of it home to share with their brothers and sisters, and eventually it kills the whole colony. Boric acid is best known as a roach poison, and it can cause stomach problems for people and animals. Keep your ant killer under cover by using a plastic food container with holes cut in the sides.

Snag ants with petroleum jelly. Ants like the sweet nectar you put in your hummingbird feeder, but they don't like petroleum jelly. Keep them out of your feeder by smearing the string or wire holding it with petroleum jelly. You can also keep plants ant-free with a ring of petroleum jelly around the base of their stems. They won't try to cross the sticky stuff.

Trim branches to avoid carpenter ants. Carpenter ants work slowly, but they can cause major damage to your home if you let them get established. Keep them away by trimming shrubs and tree branches back 2 feet from your house and make sure there's no firewood or dead limbs stored close to the house.

Shoo away neighbor's cat. Other peoples' cats is an age-old problem for gardeners. Their cute kitty is your source of dirty, smelly waste and chewed-up plants. Instead of throwing a shoe, shoo away your neighbor's tabby by dropping orange rinds and coffee grounds around your garden. Cats don't like the smell of orange peels, and they tend to shy away from coffee grounds, which can be toxic for cats and dogs.

Peel away cat problems. Orange peels aren't the only fruit rinds cats don't like. Keep them away with any citrus smell — lemon and lime peels work, too. Or mix two cups of rubbing alcohol with a teaspoon of lemon grass oil and spray it if you want less mess.

Keep cats out with rue. Cats don't like the ancient medicinal herb rue — also called the Herb O'Grace. Sprinkle dried rue leaves here and there or plant it in or around your garden. You'll like its silvery, blue-green foliage and pretty, early-summer yellow flowers. Other anti-cat plants are marigolds and pennyroyal.

Play "Kitty, keep away." Do you get the feeling neighborhood cats think getting chased out of your garden is just a game? Sprinkle black pepper, cinnamon, or pipe tobacco around the playing field to discourage them from showing up to play.

Encourage cats to scat. When cats in your flower beds get to be more than you can take, convince them to find another place to hang out by mixing two tablespoons each of cayenne pepper and powdered mustard with five tablespoons of flour. Then add a cup of vinegar and five cups of water to make a potent spray for your garden. Use this mixture only on your plants. It can cause serious problems if cats get it in their eyes.

Give cats a chili reception. A half-teaspoon of chili powder and a half-teaspoon of cayenne pepper mixed with a teaspoon of dish soap and some water makes a good spray to keep cats out of your vegetable patch. Just be sure to apply it to the plant leaves only. If either the strong pepper or the potent powder is on the ground, cats can pick it up on their paws and then get it in their eyes while washing themselves.

Use tomato cages to keep out cats. If you're tired of raking up cat poop every spring, take your flat, collapsible tomato cages in the fall and lay them down in your garden. Cats like to have room to scratch around, and there's not enough space between the wires. You can also lay out bamboo poles or the thorny clippings from your rose bushes. Chicken wire works, too.

Deny cats a place to dig. Cats like to dig in soft, dry dirt before they go to the bathroom, which is why your garden often becomes their toilet. Be unwilling to give them a place to dig by using attractive river rock to fill up empty spaces and hold in moisture. Space larger rocks so there's not enough room to stretch out and dig.

Pamper feline with its own outhouse. If you want your outdoor cat to keep out rodents and, at the same time, keep out of your garden, consider making her a spot where she can dig and defecate without disturbing your prized plants. Cats like to dig in soft material, so a big sand pile or an area with loose dirt or small bark mulch ought to make her a luxurious restroom. Plant some miscanthus grass for her to chew on, or maybe a little catnip would keep her coming back.

Discourage cats with a water gun. Want an excuse to buy one of those great big water rifles the kids play with in the swimming pool? It's a great way to chase cats out of your garden. Cats don't like getting wet, so discourage trespassing with a blast of water. Put a little vinegar in the chamber for even better results.

Give cats the slip. Keep cats out of your birdhouse with a piece of stove pipe attached to the post it sits on. When kitty tries to climb up the post, she's stopped at the pipe because she can't sink her claws into its smooth surface. The pipe comes flat with grooves in the middle so you can wrap it around and fasten it together. A couple of nails keeps the sleeve from slipping. Put it high enough off the ground so cats can't jump above it. You can also use dryer pipe, galvanized sheet metal, or PVC pipe.

Surprise shower keeps cats away. Scare cats and dogs away from your yard and garden with a motion-activated water sprinkler. You'll have to get your movement and watering zones set up just right, but it won't take too many trips for pesky pets to learn to stay away. Don't forget it's there, or you might get soaked, too.

Chase dogs with garlic. Doggy-do messing up your garden? Mix up a little of this garlic brew, and Fido won't return to your yard. Put some cloves of garlic and a few of the hottest peppers you can find into a blender and puree. Add some water and pour the pungent solution wherever you don't want dogs hanging around. They'll turn tail when the first whiff of your sizzling sauce hits their delicate nostrils. Add a chopped-up onion and a tablespoon of Tabasco sauce for an even more pungent brew.

Scare off deer with soap. Deer are beautiful to watch — until you see them grazing in your garden. To keep them out of your yard, hang small bars of soap, the kind you find in hotels, from your trees. Drill a hole in the middle of the soap bar. Then use an "S" hook on a wire to hang them about 4 feet off the ground, four or five to a tree. The deer would rather eat in the woods than hang around where there's a scent of soap. You can also nail soap to stakes or fence posts.

Visit your barber to intimidate deer. Deer shy away from the smell of human hair, so the next time you get a haircut, ask if you can gather up the clippings from the floor. Take them home and scatter them about your garden. They'll also help keep rabbits away. Another way is to hang several handfuls of hair in a mesh bag or piece of old pantyhose about 3 feet off the ground. Hang a bag every 3 feet and refresh them once a month.

Strong odors keep deer on the run. Smells are important danger signals to deer. You can use certain odors, like rotten eggs, to keep them away from your garden and orchard. If you want to try something more exotic, visit a local zoo and buy coyote or mountain lion urine or tiger dung. Scatter it around your garden, and the deer will make a hasty retreat.

Shoo rabbits with pepper. Rabbits don't like hot pepper on their salad. Wet the leaves on your vegetable plants and sprinkle finely ground cayenne pepper on them to repel the cottontailed pests.

Milky spore kills grubs. Milky spore is one reason Japanese beetles and lawn grubs aren't much of a problem in Japan. This natural remedy contains bacteria that infect the grubs — actually the larvae of the beetle — with a deadly disease. So no more grubs, no more Japanese beetles. Grubs are the favorite food of moles, so you may get rid of them, too. Milky spore comes in a powder that you spread on your lawn. It multiplies over time, and it does not hurt other living things, including earthworms. One application can last up to 40 years if the winters aren't too cold.

Force out hungry moles. These small, burrowing animals have to eat all the time. Fortunately, they prefer insect pests, like cutworms, grubs, and slugs — not roots and bulbs. Even so, they can make a mess of your lawn. If you want them to vacate the premises, get rid of their food supply. With no grubs and slugs to munch on, the moles won't stay around, and you'll be free of two sets of pests.

Send moles packing. Some people say the only sure way to get rid of moles is to trap them, but you can use castor oil to send them packing without hurting them. In a blender, mix 3 ounces of castor oil and three tablespoons of liquid dishwashing detergent until you get a frothy mixture. Add eight tablespoons of water and blend until frothy again. Put a cup of the potion into a 15-gallon hose-end sprayer. Fill the rest with water and spray the mixture on your lawn and garden, thoroughly soaking the soil. Another method is to flood the mole's tunnel with castor oil and water. Either way, there's something about the oily mix that sends Mr. Mole looking for somewhere else to live.

Make your own mole trap. Catch moles alive with a pit trap made from a large can or wide-mouth jar. Find an active runway by stamping down a section of tunnel. If the mole reopens it, dig a hole deep enough to bury the container so the top is just below the bottom of the tunnel. Fill the approaches to the trap and cover the top with a board or a piece of cardboard and dirt from the hole. When the mole opens the tunnel again, he'll drop into your pit trap. Check the trap several times a day. When you've caught a mole, release him where he won't ruin your lawn.

Mulch after frost to discourage mice. Don't enhance the mouse population by putting down your winter mulch too soon. Wait until after a heavy frost so mice, meadow voles, and other rodents have found somewhere else to avoid the cold. If you don't, the little critters may simply burrow into your mulch and make your garden their cozy winter hideaway.

How to attract garter snakes – or not. Garter snakes eat slugs and mice and are generally considered beneficial to your garden. Sometimes called "garden snakes," they need water, long grass or low-growing foliage to hide in, and a place to bask in the sun. Encourage them to hang around your garden by providing these things. Or, if you don't want garter snakes — or any kind of snake — around, discourage them by getting rid of shelter and sunning spots.

Easy way to nail cutworms. Protect your new tomato transplants — or any other tender young shoot — from cutworms by pressing a ten-penny finishing nail into the soil next to it. Let the nail stick out about an inch. That makes the stem too wide for those hungry pests to wrap themselves around. It keeps slugs away, too.

Save seedlings with a toothpick. A simple toothpick is one of the cheapest ways you can find to protect brand-new seedlings from cutworms. Stick one or two next to the tender shoot when it first breaks through the ground. The hungry chewers in your garden can't bite through the wood and leave the young seedling alone.

Slug bait kills more than slugs. Whenever possible, look for nonchemical ways to get rid of the slugs that chew up your broccoli, strawberries, and other garden goodies. Most commercial slug baits use metaldehyde, which is good at killing the slimy creatures, but it will kill cats, dogs, and birds, too. It's also toxic to children and other humans and shouldn't be used once fruit starts to form on your plants.

Tempt slugs with beer. Beer attracts slugs, and slugs can't swim. So if you have some beer in your garden, slugs will leave the tomato plants, crawl into the beer, and drown. Bury a plastic butter tub or similar container to hold the beer. Only fill it about half full so they can't climb back out. It's the yeasty smell they like. To brew your own concoction, combine two cups warm water, two tablespoons flour, a half teaspoon brewer's yeast, and one teaspoon sugar.

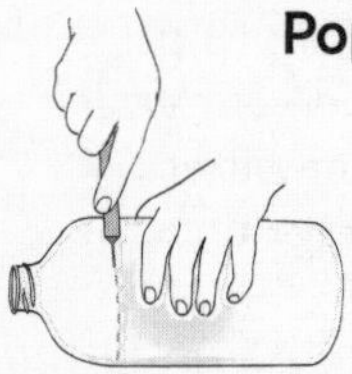

Pop bottle makes cheap slug trap. Make an inexpensive slug and snail trap from an empty two-liter soda pop bottle. Just cut off the top third of the bottle and stick it back into the bottom, neck first. Secure the edges with duct tape or staples, and drop in some slug bait or beer to attract the slimy critters. As they crawl in and die, their carcasses will invite even more slugs into your clever cage. When it's full, throw it away and make a new one.

Set up a slug sleeping bag. Leave a moist garbage bag in your garden for slugs and snails to crawl into overnight.

In the morning, tie off the bag and put it in the freezer for a few hours to kill them without a mess.

Sneak up on slugs. Slugs like it cool, dark, and damp. That's why they're easiest to find at night. Take a flashlight into your garden and catch them in the act. Pick them off your tender leaves and drop them into a jar of soapy water. It's best to have a screw-on cap for the jar. They've been known to crawl out when the lid is not tight.

No need to touch slippery slugs. Don't like picking up slugs? Try wearing rubber gloves or using large tweezers when you pick them off your vegetable leaves.

Send slugs packing with herbs. Slugs love to chew on potatoes, tomatoes, beans, and lettuce, but they hate the taste of highly scented foliage, like lavender, rosemary, and sage. So plant some of these aromatic herbs among your vegetables to keep those destructive mollusks away.

Secret weapon in slug battle. "No man's land" in war is an area filled with mines, barbed wire, and artillery fire that makes a barrier to keep out the enemy. You can use sand, gravel, dry dirt, lime, or eggshells to create a "no slug's land" around your garden. Slugs and snails need a moist surface to move around on, and they can't manufacture enough mucus to get across dusty, scratchy areas.

Slug slugs with a cup of coffee. When your morning coffee gets cold, throw it on your garden. Caffeine deters slugs and snails, killing the small ones and scaring off the larger ones. It attacks the central nervous system of all kinds of insects, but works really well with slugs and snails because it is water-soluble and seeps in through the mucus membranes these slimy creatures get around on.

Soapy solution gets rid of bugs. Dump your old dishwater into a watering can and pour it on your plants for a cheap cure for slugs and soft-bodied insects, like aphids, mealybugs, thrips, and red spider mites in your garden. Some bugs just don't like the taste of the sudsy solution, and it's actually toxic to others. Mix a tablespoon or two of liquid soap or mild dishwashing soap with a quart of water for the same result. Other sprays become more potent when you add a few drops of soap. It helps them stick to plants and pests better.

"Clean up" bugs with insecticidal soap. Plain old dishwashing soap will do a job on many bugs, but insecticidal soaps are even better at killing aphids, thrips, mites, and other soft-bodied insects. It washes away their protective coating, but the soap must come in full contact with the pest to work. As with other soaps and most nonchemical sprays, insecticidal soap doesn't work after it dries. So soak your bugs good and be ready to spray again if you don't get them all the first time.

Chase away pests with garlic. Try a garlic spray to get rid of aphids, slugs, cutworms, caterpillars, cabbage worms, wireworms, ants, and whiteflies. There are lots of recipes for the smelly concoction, but most all of them involve adding soap to garlic that has been chopped or crushed and then steeped in water for a period of time. For a more potent brew, add onion and cayenne pepper. Be sure and strain out the particles before putting it into your sprayer.

Kill pests with tobacco tea. Make your own tobacco tea for a nicotine spray that's great for killing aphids, caterpillars, Japanese beetles, and similar pests. But be careful — it's also toxic to humans, animals, and beneficial insects. In addition, it kills tomato, eggplant, and other nightshade plants. Just soak cigarettes (without the filters), cigars, or chewing tobacco in water for about 24 hours, then strain and spray. For a weaker solution to avoid harm to ladybugs and bees, soak the tobacco for only 30 minutes. Nicotine breaks down quickly and has little long-range effect.

Repel insects with volatile oils. Eucalyptus and citronella are the most effective nonchemical insect repellents. You can use these oils to make your own repellent, or you can look for them on the ingredient lists of commercial products. Other natural herbs used to keep bugs away include rosemary, thyme, lavender, and lemongrass.

Apply pressure for best results. When spraying plants for pests, use a pressurized tank sprayer that has a wand with a bend on the end. That will help you get the underside of plant leaves, where most little bugs like to live and eat. Some never show up on the top of leaves, and squirt bottles and pump sprayers don't do a good job of getting underneath. This is especially important when you're using insecticidal soaps and other contact sprays that only work when they're applied directly on the insect.

Put bugs on the menu

One way to get rid of ants, grasshoppers, and grubs is to eat them. Ugh, you say? It's really not that unusual. In Mexico, edible grasshoppers are sold by the pound in village markets. Some Washington, D.C., restaurants have insects on the menu, and you can join San Francisco's Bay Area Bug Eating Society (BABES) via the Internet. An Ohio State University Fact Sheet suggests that if people would put up with more insects in their food, farmers could use fewer chemicals on their crops. After all, wouldn't you prefer nutritious bug parts over poisonous pesticide residue?

Sure-fire way to fend off pests. Keeping your garden healthy is the best way to avoid pest damage. Insects aren't as likely to come around when you eliminate weak plants, build healthy soil, and clean up trashy areas where they like to live.

Just like people, plants have natural defense systems that work better when they're strong and healthy. Bad bugs and diseases are more likely to pick on a weak plant.

Banish bugs without chemicals. Here's an amazing trick to banish pests from your garden forever — grow companion plants to keep unwanted insects away. Some plants have natural chemical defense systems that certain bugs can't stand. Garlic, mint, marigolds, and a wide range of herbs repel the little critters using their natural oils. It's a healthier, and less-expensive, alternative to harmful chemicals.

Attract aphids with the color yellow. This might be the answer to the white crawly things that are turning your beautiful green plants an ugly brown. Those little white spots with legs are probably aphids or whiteflies, who both like the color yellow even better than sucking the life from leaves. So take a yellow index card, smear it with petroleum jelly, and put it in the infested area. When the bugs make their way to the yellow card, they'll be stuck and die. You can also put soapy water in a yellow pan and drown the little buggers.

Wipe out aphids with milk. Don't stand idle while aphids kill your new plants by sucking the moisture out of their young, tender leaves. Wipe them out in a hurry with this simple solution and a spray bottle. Mix powdered milk with warm water, spray it on your plants' leaves, and let the mixture dry. As it dries, the milk will kill the aphids.

Show aphids the unwelcome mat. Aphids enjoy munching on vegetable, flower, tree, and shrub leaves. When there's a lot of them, they can cause quite a bit of damage. And once established, they're hard to get rid of. But never fear — you can keep them from coming around in the first place by mixing plants they don't like in with the rest of your garden. Aphid-repellent plants include mints, garlic, chives, anise, and nasturtiums. Take it a step further and grow marigolds and tansy. They attract beneficial insects, like ladybugs and lacewings, who love to feast on the little buggers.

Protect cucumbers with radishes. Cucumber beetles, both the striped and spotted kind, feed on tender seedlings, foliage, and roots of cucurbit crops — cucumbers, melons, and squash. Probably the worst thing they do is carry bacterial wilt from plant to plant. Adults overwinter under plant debris and become active when the weather warms up. Cucumber beetles don't like radishes, so put a couple of radish seeds in each cucurbit hill at planting time.

Cheesecloth keeps cuke beetles out. The most critical time for cucumber beetles is when your plants are just breaking through the ground. Later on, the plants get strong enough so the bugs don't bother them as much. To protect your tender shoots, use a trick reported back as far as 1841. Take cheesecloth or some other fabric thin enough to let light through, and spread it over the plants. Be sure to anchor down the ends so the beetles can't crawl under.

Beat beetles with big brown bats. Farmers love the big brown bat. A colony of 150 of these beetle-loving mammals will eat enough cucumber beetles in one summer to eliminate the eggs of 33 million of their larvae — the corn root worm, a major agricultural pest. The big brown bat will also keep future generations of most beetles and other night-flying insects out of your garden. Unfortunately, the natural habitat for bats is disappearing, and they sometimes roost in attics and garages. Why not build a bat house, or buy one at your local garden center, and enjoy the benefits without having to share living quarters.

Beetles shy away from shiny mulch. Reflective mulch under cucurbit crops, which include cucumbers, cantaloupes, pumpkins, and watermelons, keeps cucumber beetles away. Many researchers believe it's because it upsets their sense of space. Spread a square of aluminum foil at the base of your plants or buy aluminum-coated plastic mulch. The bouncing light on the bottom of leaves seems to disorient them, and they go someplace else.

When to plant to avoid bean beetles. The Mexican bean beetle looks a lot like a ladybird beetle — round with black spots on its back and about one-third inch long — except the bean beetle is more yellow. And the red-coated ladybug eats bugs that eat beans, but bean beetles just eat the beans. They're a major economic problem in soybean fields, as well as garden pests for snap, lima, pinto, navy, and kidney beans. Bean beetles do their most damage in July and August, so early and late plantings are a good way to avoid them. Other nonchemical solutions are hand picking and parasitic wasps.

Chase bugs with beans and potatoes. If potato bugs and bean bugs bug you, then plant the two crops next to each other in your garden. That's right, the Mexican bean beetle doesn't like to be around potatoes, and the Colorado potato beetle can't stand beans. Putting the plants side-by-side keeps both bugs away from the whole patch. For a

Funny-looking trap attracts deer flies

It was the most fun Russ Mizell ever had in 30 years of entomology research. The Florida University professor discovered you can trap deer flies with a 6-inch, upside-down, bright blue flowerpot or drink cup covered with sticky stuff. There's something about the shape, size, and color of the device that deer flies love. It has to jiggle and be moving, so stick it on a pole and troll for the blood-loving biters. It will work in your yard just like it does on forest trails. In some parks, rangers mount traps on a bicycle and pedal through every couple of days so hikers can enjoy the trails unmolested. It also works on horse flies and yellow flies.

bigger boost, put in a flowery border of nasturtiums to repel potato beetles and marigolds to chase away bean beetles.

Give natural enemies a chance. There's more than one reason not to use pesticides to stop Colorado potato beetles. Not only do they build up immunity to the chemicals, but predators of the potato bug will also die. Among these natural enemies are two kinds of stink bugs, the spined soldier bug and the two-spotted stink bug, who eat both eggs and larvae of the potato beetle. Ladybird beetles, or "ladybugs," feed on the eggs, and there's a parasitic fly and a fungus that attack the potato beetle itself.

Spray early to stop potato bugs. If you're going to spray for Colorado potato beetles, don't wait until you see adult bugs. They're hard to kill and become resistant to insecticides. The best time to get 'em is when they're small larvae, which eat just as many leaves as the fully-developed beetle. For a nonchemical spray, use *Bacillus thuringiensis* (Bt) variety san diego. The larvae eat the Bt bacteria, which makes them stop eating, and they starve to death. It takes a few days for them to disappear, so the earlier in the cycle you use Bt, the better it works.

Kill potato bugs with wood. "Sure-Fire Way to Kill Potato Bugs!" claimed a long-ago newspaper ad. When a reader sent in his money, he got two pieces of wood and the instructions, "Place bug between blocks and squeeze." In today's environment, that may not be such a scam. The Colorado potato beetle is notorious for its ability to resist insecticides. Often the best solution is to pick potato bugs and their larvae off the leaves by hand. Each one you drop into a can of soapy water — or crush between two blocks of wood — eliminates about 500 eggs apiece that it and its babies will lay.

Sticky trap catches flea beetles. Flea beetles have lots of cousins with names like toothed, striped, sweet potato, cabbage, eggplant, and desert. The thing they all have in common is the way they jump about like fleas when they're disturbed. Take advantage of that habit to get them out of your garden. Smear a board or box with Tanglefoot, Vaseline, or plain old axle grease. Attach a handle to this sticky trap and swing it around where the jittery jumpers are feeding. When they hit the board, they won't be going any further.

Keep flea beetles at bay. Here are a few things you can do to keep flea beetles from becoming anything more than a minor nuisance. Get rid of weeds around the edge of your garden. Weeds attract flea beetles, and they go from there to your vegetables. Clean up dead plant debris where they spend the winter. Wood ashes and mints, like spearmint, peppermint, and pennyroyal, are good flea beetle deterrents. Wood ash is especially effective around potatoes.

Make friends with big-eyed bugs. Before you spray for chinch bugs, make sure you're not making the problem worse by taking out big-eyed bugs. The two look alike, but big-eyed bugs kill chinch bugs and other pests. Keep this in mind — the chinch bug's head is narrower than the rest of its body. A big-eyed bug has a head at least as wide as its body and, of course, large, protruding eyes. Other good bugs include minute pirate bugs and ants. Too much insecticide can kill off so many predators that you actually end up with more chinch bugs. So only spray when you absolutely have to.

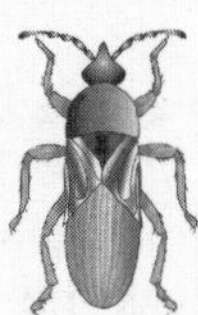

Identify problem to find solution. Islands of dead brown grass surrounded by halos of yellowing, dying grass are signs of chinch bugs, but some lawn diseases produce the same symptoms. Part the grass and look for the insects themselves to make sure it's chinch bugs and not disease or drought that's causing your problem.

Water "just right" to avoid chinch bugs. Cut down the risk of chinch bugs in your lawn by watching the way you water. Too much or not enough water can lead to problems. Chinch bugs like hot, dry conditions. Drought-stressed grass is hurt worse by the little pests. The saturation that comes from overwatering, however, deprives soil of the oxygen needed to support microbes that break down thatch, where chinch bugs like to live.

Encourage chinch bugs to relocate. Chinch bugs like to live in thatch and organic debris, so mow often to reduce thatch buildup and keep them from moving in. Mulching lawnmowers cut clippings into small pieces that decompose easily. If thatch gets too thick, you may want to rent equipment or hire a lawn service company to remove it. You can also aerate your lawn to reduce thatch by punching holes in it to increase air and water penetration.

Secrets of the chinch bug

The common chinch bug is found in an area between South Dakota, Virginia, central Georgia, and central Texas. It prefers grain crops but also likes turf grasses, like fescue, Kentucky bluegrass, rye, Bermuda, and zoysia. North of the common chinch bug's home, the hairy chinch bug goes after the same grasses. In the South, the southern chinch bug is a big problem for St. Augustine's and other warm-weather grasses. They all suck the juices out of grass stems while injecting a toxic saliva that wilts and discolors the plant. The grass first turns yellow and later dries up and turns brown.

Try a homemade chinch bug counter. More than 20 to 25 chinch bugs per square foot and visible damage to your lawn means it's time to resort to insecticide. Find out the density with a simple flotation trap made from a used coffee can. Cut out the top and bottom of the can, push it into the ground 3 or 4 inches, and fill it with water. Within 10 minutes, the chinch bugs will float to the top. If you have four or five bugs in a 6-inch cylinder or eight to 10 in 9 inches, it's time to spray.

Spot signs of spider mites. Plant damage is the best way to tell if you have spider mites. Spotting the little bitty bugs with your naked eye isn't easy. The first signs are tiny yellow or white pinpricks on the leaves where they have taken a bite to suck sap. When many of these are close together, the leaf takes on a yellow or bronzed look. As it gets worse, leaves may drop off, and the plant can die. Some spider mites spin fine silk webs that collect dust and make the leaves look dirty.

Expose spider mites with paper. Spider mites are spiders, not insects. If you could see them, you'd notice they have four pairs of legs. But they are so tiny it takes 50 or more of them to make a line an inch long. To find out if spider mites are on your plants, tap a leaf over a piece of white paper or cardboard and wait a moment. If the little specks of dirt start moving, chances are they're spider mites walking around on their eight legs.

Float away spider mites. Spider mites are likely to show up just about anywhere. One kind, the two-spotted spider mite, fancies 180 different plants, including field crops, garden vegetables, and houseplants. One of the best controls for spider mites is predatory insects — lacewings, ladybugs, and predatory mites. Knock small numbers off your plants with a stream of water. If chemicals are necessary, choose "soft" pesticides, like soaps and oils, first. Beyond that, you'll need to use a specific miticide, since regular pesticides won't usually kill spider mites.

Trap sap beetles with vinegar. Sap beetles — sometimes called picnic beetles — are tiny brown bugs that get into sweet corn, tomatoes, melons, strawberries, and raspberries. They are attracted by bruised, damaged, or overripe fruit, but they also like the smell of vinegar. To get rid of them, take a couple of disposable, aluminum pie pans, cut some holes in the sides of one and attach it upside down on top of the other. Fill this trap with vinegar, set it out, and wait for the curious little buggers to go in and drown. Try this with other kinds of beetles, too.

Watch out for cabbage loopers. If you're growing cabbage, broccoli, cauliflower, or any of their relatives, be prepared to deal with the cabbage looper. The parents of this destructive, little green inchworm are mottled gray moths that winter where it's warm and come north with the spring breezes. When you first spot the moths, install floating row covers to keep them from laying eggs on your plants. Later, you can spray *Bacillus thuringiensis* (Bt), a bacteria that makes the worms get sick and die. Bt doesn't harm natural enemies, like the tachinid fly and parasitic wasp that are the most effective controls of cabbage worms.

Fend off tarnished plant bugs. These destructive bugs suck sap from tender, young foliage and flower buds. They like fruit trees, vegetables, and strawberries and cause distorted leaves, buds that never open, and misshaped fruit. Your best bet for controlling tarnished plant bugs is to clean up leaf litter and weeds where they spend the winter. They start to feed and lay eggs in early spring and can produce up to five generations per season. Use white sticky traps to find out if they're around, and spray insecticidal soap every couple of weeks to get them before they mature.

Simple solution to mealybug problem. If you spot what looks like specks of cotton on your plants, you've probably got mealybugs. They cover themselves and their eggs with white, waxy filaments that look like fluffy cotton. They feed on plant juices, which turns leaves and stems yellow. The best way to take care of these little sapsuckers is to pick them off the plant or wipe them away with a swab dipped in rubbing alcohol. Look for them every day. They like the hidden, tighter areas of a plant and can be hard to find.

New twist on bug zappers

Watch for a wonderful new gadget that kills mosquito larvae when you drop it in the water and push a button. The Larvasonic uses sound waves that vibrate the larvae's air bladders, causing the little bloodsuckers to explode and die. Invented by a 15-year-old as a science project, the device is now being used by county and municipal health departments to prevent the spread of West Nile disease. Not surprisingly, a lower-priced consumer model is under development. Tests so far show that it works in about three seconds and only affects mosquitos.

Give fungus gnats the heave-ho. Fungus gnats aren't a problem outdoors, where natural predators and the weather keep them in check. But they can be a nuisance for indoor gardeners. Adult fungus gnats are small, black flies that lay eggs in moist soil, which hatch into little maggots that feed on fungi and organic matter. They will also eat tender roots and shoots. Prevention is the best way to deal with these pests, so don't overwater and let the soil dry out occasionally.

Think twice about bug zappers. Don't believe the claims that electronic bug zappers will rid your yard of mosquitos. They actually kill more good insects — the ones that eat the eggs and larvae of the bugs that bite you — than they do 'skeeters. They also attract insects to your yard that wouldn't normally be there. You'll do more good by getting rid of standing water and other places in your yard where mosquitos breed.

Put the bite on mosquitos. No matter what you do, mosquitos are usually buzzing around when you want to work outside. Not only are they annoying, these pests can transmit serious diseases, like West Nile virus and several kinds of encephalitis. Avoid them by staying inside around dusk and dawn — their peak activity times. Mosquitos will bite right through tight-fitting clothes, so wear loose-fitting, light-colored pants and long-sleeved shirts. Use personal insect repellents on exposed skin and treat your clothes with a repellent containing permethrin, which kills and repels insects on fabric, but not on skin.

Attack mosquitos before they attack you. The best way to control mosquitos is to eliminate the places they breed. Getting rid of large, swampy areas and sluggish streams usually takes a community-wide effort, but there's a lot you can do on your own. Remove standing water in puddles, pots, and drainage ditches. Change the water in birdbaths and wading pools every few days. Remove debris from rain gutters. Get rid of old cans, buckets, and tires that might hold stagnant water. Repair leaky outside faucets, pipes, and air-conditioning units.

DEET lasts longer but follow directions. You can get insect repellent that uses citronella, eucalyptus, or soybean oil, but DEET gives the longest-lasting protection. When you use a DEET-based repellent, follow label directions and pay attention to how much active ingredient it contains. Higher concentrations don't give better protection — it just lasts longer — so you're just as well off using a weaker solution and reapplying it if you're still outside after a few hours. If you see mosquitos landing on you but not biting, it's a sign that the repellent is wearing off.

Overpower bugs with bath oil. Avon's Skin-So-Soft bath oil is often recommended as an insect repellent. What's more, there is evidence it works for many people, even though no one knows why. To make it even more effective, some outdoor enthusiasts mix it with citronella oil, eucalyptus oil, or isopropyl alcohol. The bath oil also soothes itching caused by insect bites that occurred before you put it on.

Make a poultice with meat tenderizer to treat the itching and burning of wasp or bee stings. Or saturate a cotton ball with household ammonia and apply it to the sting.

Put the sting on wasps and bees. Get rid of wasps, bees, and yellow jackets with an easy homemade trap. Just use a two-liter bottle about half full of sugary water. The flying invaders will crawl in and drown. It works even better if you cut off the top and invert it back inside the base. Secure it to the top with tape. Punch holes in the sides and hang your trap about 4 feet off the ground for best results.

Banish pests with sulfur. A little sulfur protects roses and other plants from tiny insects and fungi, like black spot and powdery mildew. Dust foliage with garden sulfur when it's damp so the powder will stick better. A more natural application is to plant garlic, onions, or chives around your garden. These alliums leach sulfur into the soil, and it's taken up by other plants to provide the same protection.

Wipe out fungi with garlic. Garlic spray is a popular organic pesticide, but it also works well as a fungicide. The sulfur in garlic helps prevent downy mildew, cucumber rust, tomato blight, and other fungal diseases. To make a spray, puree several garlic cloves with a little water in a blender. Add the pungent mixture to a gallon of water.

Cut the odds on powdery mildew. This fungal disease can make a mess of your roses, strawberries, fruit trees, and their relatives, so take steps to stop it before it starts. Space and prune your plantings carefully. This will allow plenty of air movement to carry away the humidity that makes powdery mildew thrive. Destroy completely any dead or infected stalks and leaves, especially when cleaning out your beds for the winter. Otherwise, the spores will stay dormant and spread to new growth in the spring. One of the best things you can do to avoid this fungus is to plant mildew-resistant varieties.

Stop powdery mildew with baking soda. You can easily prevent this white, powdery-looking growth on ornamental and vine plants with baking soda. About once a week, mist both sides of the leaves with this solution — a tablespoon of baking soda for every gallon of water. Several drops of mild dishwashing soap or baby shampoo will help it stick better.

Put an end to black spot. Black spot only affects roses, but it ruins leaves much like powdery mildew does on other plants. Since both are fungus diseases that thrive in humidity, you can fight black spot with the same tactics you use for powdery mildew. Start by pruning away and getting rid of all infected debris over the winter — the spores lie dormant and spread to new growth when the weather warms up. Locate your roses so there is plenty of air movement to reduce humidity and plant varieties that are disease resistant.

> ! Some people can have severe allergic reactions to bee and wasp stings. If this happens, get medical help quickly. Symptoms include difficulty breathing, dizziness, and nausea.

Cure black spot with simple mixture. Black spot leaf disease is a big problem for rose gardeners, but you can cure it with a simple mixture of two common household ingredients — baking soda and soybean oil. Put a tablespoon or two of the soda and a tablespoon of oil into a gallon of water and spray it on your roses once a week. It's best to do your spraying in the morning to give it time to dry.

Use pasteurized soil to stop damping-off. This fungal disease kills new seedlings. It is activated by nutrients released from germinating seeds. Guard against damping-off by using pasteurized soil in seed flats to kill soil-borne fungi before they attack your tender baby plants.

Stop damping-off with cinnamon. Sprinkle cinnamon powder on the soil when you start plants from seed. It helps stop damping-off, a disease that kills tender, young seedlings. Damping-off is caused by fungi that live at the soil level. Fortunately, cinnamon is a natural fungicide.

Make life tough for fungi. Once seedlings have broken through the surface, increase their chances against the damping-off fungi by watering less often. Thoroughly saturate the soil and then wait to water again until the plants are almost ready to wilt. The longer you keep the surface soil dry, the less advantage there is for the fungi, which thrive in moist soil.

Fight sap with garden hose. Use your garden hose to fight the sap on cars parked under trees in the spring. But spray the trees, not your car. The sticky stuff is "honeydew" produced by aphids sucking sap from the fresh, juicy leaves of maple, birch, and other trees. Knock them off with a stream of water, and they can't climb back up on the leaves. Natural predators — ladybugs and green lacewings — are the best cure for aphids, but they usually don't appear until there's plenty to eat. So have some patience, and it may all clear up naturally.

Safeguard fruit trees from codling moths. Codling moths can ruin the fruit of an entire apple orchard or just one backyard apple, pear, or walnut tree. The moths emerge from cocoons in the spring and lay eggs that hatch into caterpillars, or "apple worms," that tunnel into the core of the fruit and out again to spin new cocoons. This cycle may be repeated several times a season. Holes surrounded by a brown spot on fruit and little cocoons under tree bark are signs of codling moths. Effective control includes trapping adult moths, spraying newly hatched eggs, and destroying larvae.

Brew a moth "cocktail." To make a long-used formula for trapping codling moths, combine a cup of cider vinegar, one-third cup dark molasses, one-eighth teaspoon ammonia, and enough water to make a quart-and-a-half total liquid. Put this mixture in a plastic milk jug and make small holes just below the shoulder on the side away from the handle. Cap the jug and hang it by the handle from a tree limb, using cloth strips to protect the tree. Put two or three of these traps in each apple tree to catch codling moths before they can mate and lay eggs.

Destroy worms to end egg laying. Fighting codling moths and their apple worm larvae is a continuing process. Don't give up because you have wormy fruit. If you do, it'll be worse later on. Those little caterpillars will spin a cocoon and emerge next spring or next month as egg-laying adults. They leave the fruit after just a few days, so pick damaged apples off the tree and off the ground every week. Then bury them 6 to 12 inches deep or put them in a black plastic bag in the sun for at least four weeks to make sure the larvae won't mature.

Outsmart codling moths with cardboard. Attach 4-inch strips of corrugated cardboard to a tree and help prevent future generations of codling moths. After ruining an apple or pear, a mature codling moth larva leaves the fruit and usually ends up on the ground. It climbs back up the tree, looking for a nook or cranny in the bark to make a cocoon and turn itself into an adult moth. The nice little tunnels in the cardboard are attractive alternatives. Once several have holed up, take the cardboard down and burn it.

Leave slime flux alone. That ugly, stinky, slimy stuff seeping from your favorite tree is called slime flux or wetwood. It happens when certain bacteria get into trees and promote fermentation in the sapwood. Pressure builds up and the slime is forced out through cracks or wounds in the tree. The best thing to do about it is nothing. Trees with slime flux usually continue living for years and, with good tree health practices, eventually stop oozing. Drain tubes not only don't stop the slimy flow, they actually help spread it and create an entry point for other infections.

Remove stressed trees to foil bark beetles. Several varieties of pine bark beetles can destroy a pine, spruce, or fir tree in just a matter of days if there are enough of them. They attack weak and dying trees in both forests and yards. Once they've killed the first tree, winged adults will fly to another tree and start over. Bark beetles mature in about a month, so widespread infestation, which can include healthy trees, doesn't take long. The best defense is a healthy tree. Remove dead, damaged, or unhealthy trees before these voracious little bugs can get started.

Watch for bark beetle signs. When bark beetles burrow in to lay eggs on a healthy tree, the tree produces pitch or sap to cover up and "pitch out" the bugs. Popcorn-like growths, called pitch tubes, will appear on the bark of the tree. Another sign of bark beetles is boring dust, which looks like fine sawdust and appears in bark crevices. If you notice pitch tubes or boring dust, contact a tree expert immediately. You might be able to treat the tree. You will probably have to remove it, however, to keep the beetle infestation from spreading to your other trees.

Keep tabs on tree damage. Heart rot is a serious disease of hardwood timber in the South, and it also affects shade trees. It's caused by fungi that destroy the dense core that supports the tree. You can't fix heart rot, so watch out for damage to outer layers that lets water, boring insects, and fungi get to the inside of your trees. Damage can come from broken limbs, lightning, improper pruning, or running into the tree with a tool or a truck. Make sure those little wounds heal properly, or you could lose the tree.

Telltale signs of heart rot. Heart rot affects the heartwood of a tree, but there are some outward signs that there's trouble inside. One is the appearance of a cavity in the trunk, usually near the ground. Others are too many woodpecker holes, carpenter ants coming and going from a hole in the tree, shelf-like mushrooms growing on the side of the trunk, sunken or flaking bark, and dark ooze dripping from the trunk after a rain.

Play it safe and remove weak trees. Some trees, especially large ones, form a bowl or depression where the main limbs spread out from the trunk. If rainwater sits there too long, it can start heart rot. Keep an eye on trees with that condition. Heart rot destroys the center of a tree — wood that is actually dead but provides much of its support. As the tree gets hollowed out, it becomes too weak to stand and should be cut down.

Garden tool know-how

Get a handle on tangled twine. Coffee cans double as handy twine dispensers. Drop the ball of yarn, twine, or string in the can, then cut an X-shaped hole in the center of the plastic lid. Close the lid, and thread the twine through the hole. This homemade dispenser is light enough to carry around the garden with you, and you'll never fight with another tangled skein.

Straighten up and work right. Gain some leverage in your everyday garden battles. Instead of bending, squatting, or kneeling to work in the garden, use long-handled or curved-handled tools. They're easy to grip and easier on your body.

Sharp tools reduce sore muscles. Just keeping your tools sharpened can save time and ease the workload on your joints and muscles. Use a file to keep shovels, hoes — and yourself — in peak condition.

Sit down on the job. Gardening should be enjoyable and relaxing. Bring a chair or stool into the garden to cut down on the usual, and uncomfortable, squatting and bending.

Carry tools in a bucket seat. Use a 5-gallon bucket to carry your small gardening tools. As a bonus, you can flip it over and sit on it as you weed, plant, or just take a breather.

Reflect on this handy bug tool. Make a homemade bug finder by gluing a mirror to an old mop or broom handle. No more crouching, bending, or playing a frustrating game of hide-and-seek with pests. Just stroll through your garden, glancing at your makeshift mirror on a stick to spot bugs lurking on the underside of leaves.

Dabble in homemade dibbles. Instead of spending money for a dibble — and bending over to use it — try making your own. Sharpen one end of an old broomstick handle or just use a walking stick with a brass tip. That way, you can simply walk through your garden and poke holes for your seeds.

Put your finger on dibble substitutes. Who needs a dibble? Poke holes for planting seeds with a stick or pencil instead. Or you could just use your finger.

Spot tools with this bright idea. Do you spend as much time searching for your tools as you do using them? Paint your tools a bright, easy-to-see color, and they'll stick out like a sore thumb amid the camouflage of your garden. Wrapping bright electrical tape around your tools' handles also helps.

Make your tools measure up. Turn your hoes, rakes, and shovels into handy rulers. Just paint or notch marks for inches and feet on the wooden handles of your tools. That way, you'll always have a measuring device when you need one.

"Re-cycle" foam bike pads. Slip spongy bicycle accessories, like handlebar grips or crash bar pads, over your tool handles. You'll get a larger, more comfortable handle to grip. You can also widen your handles by wrapping them with grip tape.

Dress like a handyman. Buy a canvas carpenter's apron with several pockets at your local hardware store. Wear it while gardening. It's a handy way to carry small tools or seed packets.

Baby monitor keeps you informed. You need to work outside, but there's a breaking news story you want to follow. Use a baby sleep monitor to help you do both. Just put the monitor next to your radio or television. Take the other part outside with you, and you can keep up with the news while you rake leaves or plant your garden.

Fork over old kitchen utensils. The dish ran away with the spoon — but where does that leave the fork? In your garden, where a simple kitchen fork comes in handy for aerating the soil and digging out weeds in tight spaces.

Branch out with barbecue tongs. Trimming roses and other thorny plants can be a real pain. Protect your fingers by holding the branch you want to remove with barbecue tongs.

Sharp way to avoid thorns. When pruning roses or other thorny plants, wear oven mitts rather than regular gardening gloves. Your hands will appreciate the extra protection.

Gobble up gas with kitchen tool. Keep a turkey baster with your gardening tools. It comes in handy for removing gasoline from your lawn mower at the end of the grass-cutting season.

Just the thing to dispense string. Turn your old teapot or watering can into a portable string dispenser. Put a ball of string or twine inside and pull the end through the spout. For added convenience, you can even tie a pair of scissors to the handle.

Neat way to wash produce. Next time you pick fruits and vegetables, put them in an old, plastic laundry basket or colander. Then use a hose to rinse off your produce outside. That way, your kitchen stays clean.

Support your local climbers. Use clothespins to give your peas, cucumbers, or other climbing vines a little support. Just thread some twine through the springs of the clothespins. Then clamp the clothespins to your trellis on each side of the sagging plant. This method lets you adjust the twine easily, without searching for knots buried somewhere in the plant.

Dig this homemade scooper. Make a cheap, yet sturdy, scooper out of an empty bleach bottle. Just rinse it out, and slice off the bottom diagonally. Then grip the handle and start digging.

Iron out potting problems. An old ironing board, especially the kind with adjustable heights, makes a great potting bench. You can even fold it up for easy storage.

New use for an old wagon. Your child or grandchild may no longer enjoy his little red wagon — but that doesn't mean you can't. An old wagon comes in handy for transporting gardening tools, heavy rocks, bags of soil or fertilizer, bulbs, and plants.

"Putt" your tools in a golf bag. Fore! An old golf bag makes a terrific caddy for your long-handled garden tools, like rakes and shovels. And your gloves and hand tools fit neatly in the side pockets.

Special delivery for your tools. Neither rain, nor sleet, nor snow, nor hail will harm your tools. Just keep them in an old mailbox in your garden. It's an ideal way to store gloves, a trowel, pruning shears, and other small tools.

Find comfort at your computer. Gardening can be tough on your knees, so here's a tip that's bound to click. Kneel on old computer mouse pads to cushion your joints. As a bonus, you'll also keep your pants clean.

Rest your knees on an old pillow. Just because your bed pillow has lost its fluffiness doesn't mean you should put it to sleep. Use it as a kneeling pad in your garden. To keep it clean and dry, put it in a plastic garbage bag and tape it closed.

Protect your eyes with a tennis ball. If you use a cane while gardening, cover the top of it with an old tennis ball. This makeshift cushion will protect your eyes when you bend or stoop.

Measure rainfall with coffee cans. After it rains, you may wonder if your garden got enough water or if you need to turn on the sprinkler. To solve the mystery, place empty coffee cans throughout your garden. When the rain stops, just measure the depth of the water in the cans. If you have at least an inch, there's no need for additional watering.

Simple trick to control unruly hose. Sometimes it seems as if your garden hose has a mind of its own — and it's determined not to coil peacefully. Make hose handling easier with this trick. Leave the water on as you coil your hose on the ground. You'll avoid the maddening kinks and twists of an empty hose.

Steer your hose into shape. Here's a cheap, easy way to tame your wild garden hose. Just nail an old tire rim to the side of your house. Your hose will curl up nicely around the rim, and it will unroll easily without tangling. You can even paint your new hose holder to match your house.

Turn a bucket into a hose holder. Use a sturdy, metal, 5-gallon bucket to store your garden hose. Mount the bottom of the bucket securely to the side of your house or shed, with the open end facing outward. Then wrap your hose around it. Inside the bucket, you can stash items like hose nozzles, fertilizer sprayers, and gardening gloves.

Seal with a twist. After you flush and drain your irrigation system, make sure to seal the ends of the pipes for the winter. To do this cheaply and easily, slip a plastic sandwich bag over the end and fasten it with a twist tie.

Plastic knives make great labels. Sometimes, gardening is no picnic. But white plastic picnic knives sure come in handy as row markers. With an indelible pen, write the name of the plant on the knife's flat blade. Then push the handle into the ground.

Give dirt the brushoff. Just as your current toothbrush fights cavities, your old toothbrush can fight garden grime. Use it to scrub your hands and fingernails after working in the garden.

Pay now, save later. Everyone loves a good bargain. But when it comes to gardening tools, you don't want to skimp. Buy the best-made tools you can afford. They'll save you money in the long run because you'll rarely have to repair or replace them.

Shield yourself from the sun. Gardeners should appreciate the power of the sun. Without it, your plants wouldn't grow. But you should also beware of it. Protect yourself from sunburn and skin cancer with important gardening "tools," like a wide-brimmed hat, gloves, and sunscreen.

Wear gloves that fit like a glove. When it comes to gloves, think like Goldilocks' three bears. Don't settle for gloves that are too loose or too tight. Make sure they're just right. Otherwise, you can end up with painful blisters.

Give old gloves new life. Don't ditch your cloth gardening gloves just because they have a few holes. Pull the old switcheroo — switch hands and wear the gloves backward. You'll get some extra use out of them that way.

Have no fear with sharpened shears. Always use freshly sharpened shears or clippers when pruning hedges. Dull blades can lead to split or broken branches — and open the door to diseases and pests.

Special tools for small hands. Think small when it comes to tools. If regular-size tools are too big or heavy for you, consider buying a set of children's tools. Just make sure they're smaller, sturdy versions of real tools — not cheap plastic toys.

Rent to save cents. A rototiller comes in handy, but how often do you really use it? Consider renting, rather than buying, expensive equipment that you'll only use a few times a year.

Scour tools with homemade paste. Rusty gardening tools? Get them back in tiptop shape with a little salt and lemon juice. Mix enough salt into a tablespoon of lemon juice to make a paste, apply to rusted areas with a dry cloth, and rub.

Give rusty tools a vinegar bath. Before you decide to throw away that rusty trowel or other gardening tool, try soaking it overnight in cider vinegar. Wipe away the residue with a cloth, and you may find it's as good as new.

Bust rust with petroleum jelly. Rusty tools can put you in quite a jam. Counter with some jelly — petroleum jelly.

Coating your tools with petroleum jelly will help guard against rust.

Create a sandbox for your tools. Mix 40 pounds of sand with a quart of motor oil. After using your tools, push them through this gritty, oily mixture a few times to clean and lubricate them for storage. It's an easy way to prolong the life of your tools and keep them rust-free.

Dispense oil the easy way. Oiling your tools doesn't have to be a messy job. Put some mineral oil in an old bottle of lotion or hand soap and simply squirt it on your tools. Wipe them down with fine steel wool, and they're good as new.

Use old oil to keep tools looking new. Kill two birds with one stone as you prepare your tools for the winter. Drain the oil from your power tools, then use the oil to rustproof your metal tools. Just dip a rag in the oil and wipe them down.

Add rust protection to your toolbox. Tired of the same sad story of the gardener and the rusty tools? Then check out this absorbing tale. Put a charcoal briquette or a piece of children's sidewalk chalk — the thick, colorful kind — in your toolbox during the winter to absorb moisture. This time, your story will have a happy ending.

Read the latest news about tool storage. Extra! Extra! Here's a hot scoop to beat rust. Wrap your gardening tools in newspaper during the winter. Just make sure to clean and oil them first.

Turn away rust. Help your wheelbarrow stand up to rust. Turn it on its side when you're not using it. That way, water won't collect in it and cause rust.

Chalk up a plan for tidy tools. Install a pegboard in your garage or toolshed. It comes in handy for hanging small tools neatly. Once you arrange the tools the way you want them, trace around each tool with chalk. Then you can tell at a glance which tool goes where.

Make use of a broken rake. Don't throw out your rake just because the handle broke. Attach the rake head to the wall of your toolshed and hang hand tools from the teeth. You can even use the handle as a stake for tall plants.

Simple way to cover sharp blades. Put your old garden hose to good use. Cut it into sections to fit over the blade of your hoe or the tines of your tiller during storage. This trick protects not only the blades of your tools but also any unsuspecting fingers that might come in contact with them.

Lawn mowers, start your engines. You really should drain the gas from your lawnmower before you store it for the winter. But if you forget to do that, at least remember to start it up once in a while so the gas doesn't become stale.

Cool your engine. You're understandably excited to be done mowing your yard. But take some time to let your hot riding mower cool down before driving it into your garage and shutting the door. Otherwise, you'll risk an explosion or fire.

Spray away sticky grass. Here's a simple way to keep grass from sticking to your lawn mower blades. Just coat the blades with nonstick cooking spray before you mow. In fact, cooking spray comes in handy for cleaning the rest of your lawn mower, too.

Derail dirt with cooking spray. Gardening is enough of a chore without the messy cleanup. Before you head for the garden, spray your shovels, hoes, or other tools with nonstick cooking spray. Soil won't stick to your tools, and cleanup will be a breeze.

Give tools a rubdown. Remember to keep your tools clean. Burlap and steel wool all come in handy for rubbing or scraping off the dirt.

Smooth splintery handles. Splinters can take all the fun out of gardening. Sand your tools' handles or wrap insulating tape around them when you notice them becoming rough.

Rub out splinters. Watch out for wooden handles on wheelbarrows and tools. As they age, they can get rough on your hands. Prevent splinters by sanding the handles and rubbing them with linseed oil.

Reconcile splits in tool handles. You hate throwing anything out. So don't toss your split tool handles. Rescue them by prying open the split and applying wood glue or epoxy. Clamp the area until it dries, then sand the handle so it's smooth. Just like new.

Hone your sharpening skills. Follow this easy tip for sharpening your tools. Shade the area that needs sharpening with a felt-tip pin. Then, with a whetstone, sharpen the blade evenly until you can no longer see the ink.

Zap sap from shears. Don't let sticky sap gum up your pruning shears. Before you start pruning, give your shears a spritz of vegetable oil spray. Plant sap will wipe right off when you're finished.

Get infection protection with bleach. It's easy to spread infections from one plant to another when you're cutting into them with pruning shears. To prevent the spread of disease, regularly clean your shears with a solution of 10 parts water to one part bleach.

Dip before you clip. Take precautions to stop the spread of disease in your garden. If you've just snipped off diseased leaves, stick your pruning shears in some rubbing alcohol before using them on your healthy plants.

Help for a leaky hose. You can plug it up temporarily with some chewed gum. For a more permanent repair, heat up the tip of an ice pick with a flame. Then gently touch the hot tip to a bit of the rubber around the hole. It will melt and seal it.

Iron out hose cracks. If your plastic hose has a small hole or crack, try this cool trick. Take a hot soldering iron and lightly touch it to the area. It should seal the leak.

Give your yard a makeover

Expand your horizons. Give a narrow yard a wider look. Landscape with plants that have broad, round leaves or spreading shapes.

Great reasons to plant a hedge. A hedge screen can hide ugly garbage cans, block noise from the street, or simply give you a little privacy. For year-round screening, go with evergreens. Find a variety of holly that grows in your area. Not only does it make a good screen, it can also be your personal source of trimmings for Christmas decorating. If hollies aren't the evergreen for you, find out which varieties of boxwood, yew, viburnum, or arborvitae grow well where you live. If you only want screening during warm weather, deciduous shrubs, such as Japanese barberry and privet, may work quite well.

Landscape for extra security. You can plan your landscaping to discourage burglars, intruders, and pranksters. To set up a natural security system around your ground floor windows, plant bushes or trees with thorny, thick branches, like hawthorn. Put down loose gravel or pebbles between the bushes. They will make a racket whenever someone steps on them. To build a natural fence around your yard, plant sharp, dense shrubs, like barberry.

Make icy lights for winter nights. The bad news is temperatures won't climb above freezing for days. But that's perfect weather for ice luminaria. For each one, you'll need small rocks, a votive candle, a 16-ounce plastic or cardboard container, and a gallon or half-gallon bucket or carton. Fill the small container with rocks and put it in the larger container. Pour water into the large container until it nears the smaller container's rim. Let freeze. Pour warm water in the small container and pull it free. Remove the ice block from its container, place it outside, and drop in a candle.

Good news for allergy sufferers. Does anyone in your family struggle with allergies during the growing season? Then choose plants with bright blossoms. These plants don't need much pollen because they attract insects to spread the pollen for them. Plants that depend on wind for pollination produce a lot more of the sneeze-starting powder. If you struggle with pollen allergies, shrubs like azalea, hibiscus, oleander, pyracantha, and yucca are good choices. You'll also be safe with cacti, chrysanthemums, crocus, daffodils, ferns, hyacinths, irises, lilies, orchids, and tulips. But banish privet hedge, Bermuda grass, bluegrass, artemisia, amaranth, and sorrel from your yard.

Dealing with tree allergies. Allergy sufferers can make their lives a lot easier by choosing the right trees when landscaping. Plan your design around trees such as fir, magnolia, palm, pear, redbud, and yew. And be sure to avoid elm, sycamore, oak, walnut, birch, ash, willow, and pecan.

Convert a toy into a trellis. Turn an old swing set into a new trellis for veggies — or remove the swings to make a squared garden arch for climbing roses or flowering vines.

Relax among fragrant vines. Twine fragrant, flowering plants on an arbor, trellis, or pergola, and you'll gain a serenely scented spot that tempts anyone to linger. Jasmines and honeysuckles are sweet selections. So are variegated kiwi vine, evergreen clematis, and mountain clematis. Rose lovers can plant New Dawn for fragrant pink roses or Wedding Day for aromatic white roses.

Quick way to cover an arbor. That slow-growing perennial vine is going to make your arbor or pergola look wonderful a few years from now, but you want something growing there sooner — even if it's just temporary. Speedy-growing annuals are just the vines to solve your problem. Black-eyed Susan vine and morning glory are just two of the annuals that can give you a season of flowers to ease the wait on that slow-growing perennial.

Pick perennials that climb fast. For surging perennial vines that sweep over arches, arbors, and pergolas, why not try mountain clematis or one of the honeysuckles? You could have flowers on the rise before you know it.

Attract birds with berries. Chokeberry, serviceberry, mulberry, and elderberry shrubs are like a magnet for your feathered friends. And the red berries of the dogwood tree are especially attractive to blue birds.

Natural shrubs best for birds. If you want to attract birds to your yard, don't trim your berry-bearing shrubs into formal shapes. Leave them natural, and they'll have more berries to attract your feathered friends.

Invite birds to take a bath. While sparkling, clear water will draw winged friends to your birdbath, they'll stay away if it's covered with green slime. Clean away the algae with bleach, and rinse with clear water. Thereafter, scrub the basin clean and change the water every week. To really catch the birds' attention, decorate the bottom of the birdbath with a few marbles or glass nuggets.

Keep dead wildflowers for wildlife. Don't clear away plants like thistle and milkweed in the fall. They contain flossy materials birds like to use in building their nests. To find out what particular materials birds in your area like, take apart a few old nests and see what they used to make them.

Serve birds from a natural feeder. When the sunflowers in your garden are fully ripe with seed and the petals have dried, cut the flower heads and hang a few face-up with twine from the branch of a tree. Birds will land and feed until the seeds are gone. To keep them returning, sprinkle more seeds on the empty flower heads.

Invite birds for an after-Christmas treat. You can encourage colorful birds to flock to your yard, even in January. After you've finished with your live Christmas tree, take off all the decorations except for cranberry and popcorn strings. Lay it on its side in an out-of-the-way corner of your yard, and let the birds remove the popcorn and cranberries for you.

Befriend birds with a clean feeder. Don't let diseases and parasites spread to your feathered friends from a dirty bird feeder. Occasionally give your feeder a good scrubbing, and then soak it in a solution of 1 quart chlorine bleach to 9 quarts warm water. Rinse well with clean water, and allow it to air dry thoroughly before filling with seed.

Serve birds a hearty dinner. Spread peanut butter on pine cones and hang them out for hungry birds this winter. Or smear cones with bacon grease and sprinkle with birdseed. You'll find a happy flock singing for a second helping.

! Locate your garden and other plants away from your black walnut tree. These trees produce a chemical called juglone, which is toxic to many plants.

Hang nesting supplies for feathered builders. Birds like a variety of materials you might ordinarily throw way — lint from your dryer, hair from a hairbrush, pieces of colorful yarn or cotton — for making their nests. Place these treasures in a mesh onion bag, and hang it from a shrub or tree branch.

Turn a soggy spot into a special garden. Does your yard have a place where the soil is acidic and takes forever to dry out? Congratulations, you have nearly ideal conditions for "bog gardening." Here's how you can convert that ugly, marshy spot into an enchanting garden. First, lay down stepping stones in the swampy area. Stand on these to plant astilbe, irises, sweet flag, lizard's tail, and other plants that don't mind "wet feet." Once you're done, keep a soaker hose ready so you can wet the soil if your bog starts to dry out.

Help soil stay marshy for bog garden. If you have acidic soil that doesn't stay damp, you can still have the attractive mystery of a bog garden. Check yard sales for a small, shallow, plastic children's pool. Choose your bog site and dig a hole deep enough for the pool — but save the soil you dig up. Drop the pool into the hole and shovel the soil back into it. The site should do a better job of retaining the moisture a bog garden requires.

Get free landscaping literature

The Natural Resources Conservation Service exists to help people conserve, improve, and sustain this country's natural resources — including those in your yard. The NRCS offers free, detailed brochures on subjects such as backyard ponds, tree planting, composting, terracing, and even creating a wildlife habitat in your yard. For more information, visit their Web site at www.nrcs.usda.gov or contact them at:

Natural Resources Conservation Service
Attn: Conservation Communications Staff
P.O. Box 2890
Washington, DC 20013

Toll-free number: 888-LANDCARE

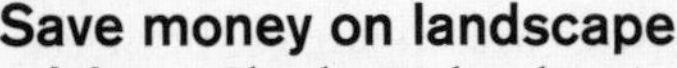

Save money on landscape advice. Check out local agricultural colleges for students of landscape design or horticulture. They might be willing to come to your home and design a garden scheme for you for free or a reduced cost.

Cut landscaping costs down to size. Major landscaping projects can have major costs to go with them. If you're landscaping a yard from scratch or taking on expensive renovations, see if the changes can be done in phases. Splitting the cost over several seasons or years can help you save money and stay within budget. It may even let you leave room for unexpected expenses. And you might be surprised at how much better your landscaping projects turn out.

Split big expenses. If you're looking at a large landscaping expense, ask neighbors and friends if they need the same supplies, service, or equipment rental that you do. You could find someone willing — and relieved — to split the cost.

Attract butterflies – not pests. Plant stinging nettles in a corner of your garden to both beautify and protect it. This plant attracts Royal Admiral butterflies. They come there to lay their eggs on the underside of the leaves, which provide the first meal for the caterpillars when they hatch. And for a powerful pesticide, soak stinging nettle stems and leaves in a bucket of water for 24 hours. Use the liquid, which now contains formic acid, to kill mites and aphids in your garden.

Attract butterflies with herbs. Just because you dedicate part of your garden to herbs doesn't mean you can't enjoy butterflies, too. Plant herbs like yarrow, sage, lavender, bee balm, valerian, and rosemary to help attract colorful butterflies.

Encourage bees and butterflies. If you plant marjoram and rosemary near your vegetable garden, you'll see more bees and butterflies and fewer garden pests. What's more, some folks say marjoram grows well with sweet peppers, too.

Create an urban wildlife garden. You don't have to have a big backyard in the country to provide a habitat for wildlife. Provide food, cover, and a nesting place for birds with small shrubs that produce berries. If you have room, add one or more birdhouses and feeders. Grow colorful flowers to attract butterflies and hummingbirds. And provide water in a small birdbath, or even a clay pot saucer.

Pick trees that love city life. Don't waste money and energy planting trees that won't stand up to pollution, heat from the pavement, and a small growing space. Buy trees that love city living. Ginkgo, sweet gum, and red oak do well. City life is tougher on flowering trees, but two that seem to thrive despite pollution are golden rain tree and saucer magnolia.

No room for a garden? You might be surprised how much you can grow on an apartment rooftop or balcony. Use wooden containers rather than clay. They are lighter weight and drain better. Containers made of lightweight, galvanized sheet metal might be even better. Place bushy vegetables, like bell pepper plants, or heat-tolerant ornamentals, like sedums, in front of trellises of flowering vines or climbing beans or tomatoes. Let ivies or other dangling plants hang over the edges of your planters.

Help for a high-rise garden. A container garden on a high-rise balcony needs more frequent watering because of extra sun and wind exposure. Drought tolerant plants, like salvia, Boston daisy, dwarf morning glory, and California poppy, as well as plants with waxy leaves, tend to do best. Add a screen to provide some shade during the hottest parts of summer days.

Make a small yard look bigger. A small yard will seem to expand like magic if you plant cool-colored plants at its far end and warm-colored plants at the front and entry. Warm colors include red, orange, and yellow, whereas blue, purple, and pastel pink are cool colors.

Focus attention with warm colors. Do you have something in your yard or garden you want people to notice? Plant yellows, reds, and oranges around it. These warm colors naturally draw people's eyes and get their attention.

Cool a garden hot spot. Blue creates a feeling of coolness. If part of your yard or garden sizzles in the sun, try growing plants with blue flowers or blue-tinted foliage in and around that spot. You might find your hot spot is not so hot.

Light up the night with white. White flowers and foliage are the last plants to fade into darkness at twilight, so they're ideal for yard and garden areas used during the evenings or around dawn. And just think how eye-catching they could be as edging for walkways, decks, and patios.

Energize your garden with color. Try one of these three color combinations to add liveliness to your landscape. Plant blue and orange close together — or yellow and purple — or try that old time-honored pairing of red and green.

Add pizzazz to shady areas. You can cheer up a shady spot without making a long-term commitment. Plant light-colored annuals this spring. If they grow poorly or you don't like them, you can try different annuals next year.

Make vanishing plants reappear. Dark-colored plants and flowers seem to disappear in shade, but that doesn't mean you should dig them up. Instead, plant bright, light-colored plants behind the dark ones for vivid contrast and eye-catching interest.

Keep eyesores in the background. You're growing a screen to hide those trash cans by the driveway but that could take awhile. What do you do until then? Plant bright red, yellow, or orange annuals on the other side of the driveway and back them up with taller plants in the same colors. The eye will be drawn right to your hot-colored plants — and away from your trash cans. Once you plant your hot bed of ornamentals, don't be surprised if you have to show some folks where the trash cans are.

Design a flower bed like a pro. Planning a new flower bed? Borrow this idea from landscape professionals. Instead of straight lines, try beds with curved shapes. Lay a garden hose on your lawn and experiment with gentle curves. When you're happy with the design, temporarily secure the hose while you use a spade to mark the edge of your new border. Then put the hose aside and start digging.

"Enlarge" your garden with mirrors. An old mirror can help you decorate and enlarge a small garden. Try using a mirror of any size as a garden accent. Once you reflect on the results, you might find yourself hunting for other shiny accessories to add.

Get the facts before you plant. Don't risk a size surprise when you're picking plants for your landscape. A cute little sprig of rosemary can turn into a shrub that's 4 feet high and 5 feet wide in just a few years. Before you buy any plant for your yard or garden, find out how high and how wide it can get. Then you can be sure to place it where it will grow well and look its best.

Learn the basics of landscaping. Unity is one of the first design guidelines landscaping students learn. When a yard has unity, everything looks complete and polished. Give your yard unity by picking two or three themes to repeat throughout the landscape. For example, you could use the same classy rock border around all your beds and islands, plant a favorite flowering tree in several places, and feature matching birdhouses in key locations. Pick out a few theme ideas you like, and see how well they can bring all the pieces of your landscaping puzzle together.

Unite garden with groups of three. One tried-and-true way to create unity in your yard or garden is the odd-numbered group technique. Pick your favorite bush or flower and plant it in groups of three throughout your yard. Groups of five or seven work well, too.

Help your yard keep its balance. If you're working on a new and improved look for your yard, remember to keep it "balanced." This means one side shouldn't attract more attention than the other. The formal way to balance your yard is to make sure the left half mirrors the right, almost exactly. A less-formal look allows you to have different plants and themes on each side, but they must still catch your eye equally.

Accent hardscape with softscape. Picture an unadorned gazebo on plain grass. Now imagine that same gazebo surrounded with flowering shrubs. What a difference! Gazebos, fences, decks, patios, and other man-made items are called hardscape. Anytime you accent hardscape with plants, known as softscape, you bring balance to your landscaping and add both charm and style to your yard.

Match plant size to yard size. Imagine a mighty giant oak in a tiny courtyard. In most cases, the sheer mass of the tree would overwhelm such a small setting. That's why landscapers recommend matching plant size to yard size. Short or compact plants with diminutive features complement a small yard. Larger plants with bolder features are better for bigger yards.

Make the most of a small yard. That small yard or garden may keep you from growing an acre of vegetables or a sprawling garden maze, but you can jazz it up by splitting it down. Instead of one big garden, make several beds — each with its own theme and purpose. Or think of your yard as an extra part of your house just waiting for you to divide it into useful space. Reserve a near corner for cooking out, a far corner for a cozy sitting nook, and a broader expanse for a children's play area. When you see what your small space can do, it won't seem very small at all.

Save space with containers. Instead of cluttering your porch with dozens of plants in individual pots, invest in a few large containers and group together plants that have the same light and water requirements. Not only will this save space, it will also save time — you won't need to move your hose from one pot to the next.

Grow a snow fence for your driveway. Does snow seem to blow onto your driveway every winter? Consider lining part of your driveway with a dwarf or low-growing hedge.

Take the heat off cooling bills. If you live where the summers are anything but mild, shade your outside air conditioning unit with shrubs. Plant the bushes far enough away to leave room for air circulation and repairmen. Shrubbery not only helps you save a little money on power bills, it also screens your air conditioning unit from view.

> ! If a hedge or fence along your driveway is over 3 feet tall, make sure it ends at least 15 feet away from the street. Otherwise, it can block a driver's view of oncoming traffic.

Lose the chain-link look. Wondering how you can turn a chain-link fence into something more attractive? You may have a hard time choosing from all your options. If juicy blackberries sound good to you, find out which varieties grow well where you live. You can train blackberry canes to run along the fence. Do you want something more ornamental — and perhaps even elegant? Climbing roses can be trained and tied to a fence. Classy English ivy can bring fast-growing, year-round greenery in most zones. Or, for heavenly scented flowers, hunt for a honeysuckle that grows well in your area.

Charming way to hide a fence. To soften the corners of a fence, add rounded flower beds. You can also design a long, curved bed to camouflage the fence's lines or add a small tree or tall plant. Just a few specimens reaching up above the fence line could be enough to replace that fenced-in feeling with reminders of spring forests and summer gardens.

Good fences don't always make good neighbors. Imagine coming back from vacation only to discover that your next-door neighbor put up a tall privacy fence — or removed a tree that had shaded both yards. Even if you like the change, you'd probably have liked it more if your neighbor had checked with you first. Before you add or remove any major planting or hardscape feature in your yard, play it safe and check with your neighbors. Not only will you avoid potential problems, you might pick up some useful information along the way.

Spotlight entryway with a specimen. Put a "specimen plant" near your front door, and you'll highlight your home's main entrance. A specimen plant is landscapers' lingo for any plant with eye-catching and attractive features. Enchanting flowers, bright berries, or an interesting shape can grab visitors' attention — and guide them straight to your front door.

Attract year-round attention. Spring-flowering plants near your front door might draw delighted attention in May, but what about December? For your front entrance, pick at least one plant with year-round interest. Such four-season workhorses could offer evergreen color, sprightly berries, or peeling bark in cool weather, followed by long-blooming flowers or unusual foliage during warm weather.

Put your foundation planting to work. Plants that grow along the front side of the house — from the door to the home's front corners — are your foundation plantings. You can design a foundation planting that showcases your front entrance and pleasantly breaks up the long, eye-wearing horizontal lines of your house. Here's how. At your home's outer front corners, put your tallest plants. Choose and place the remaining plants so they get smaller and smaller as your eye moves toward the front door. This foundation planting should make your house blend neatly into your yard, while guiding newcomers to your front door.

Spice up foundation with variety. Resist the temptation to plant the same variety of shrub along your front foundation. Instead, add extra zing by planting a deciduous bush with two evergreens. You'll get fall color and still keep a little green around all winter long.

Avoid overplanting to hide foundation. If your house is small and has eye-catching architecture, limit your front plantings to the entrance and the corners. Although you might see extra plantings between the front door and front corners of larger houses, experts say you probably don't need them. So skip the extra planting. You'll save yourself some work and avoid the classic mistake of overplanting.

Spruce up a gate. Try topiary to give your garden gate a charming look. Plant an evergreen shrub on each side of the gate and prune them into matching shapes.

Dig up utility details before digging. All it takes to cut your phone service or cable TV viewing is one unfortunate jab with a shovel. And you probably don't want to imagine what digging into a sewer or plumbing pipe might lead to. Before you do any digging for landscaping, contact your local utilities and find out where lines and pipes are located in your yard. The calls and information are free.

Scout out permits. Before you draw up plans or start work on fences, decks, patios, lighting, ponds, or other yard additions, check with your local government. You may need to comply with building codes, zoning rules, or other regulations. You might even need to apply for a permit. Contact local authorities to find out. If you are a member of a neighborhood association, read up on their bylaws and check with them, too.

> ! For some landscaping projects, you might need to use a contractor. Before hiring one, get references and check them. Also make sure the contractor is properly licensed and insured.

Choose long-lasting wood. Cedar and redwood can be attractive choices for outdoor structures, but don't buy just any cedar or redwood. Heartwood, sometimes called heart grade, is more resistant to decay than sapwood.

Pine for stronger lumber. Consider pine if you want to use strong lumber. It's stronger than either redwood or cedar. But choose wisely — pressure-treated pine is also resistant to decay.

Good reasons to reduce lawn size. A carpet of grass is expensive and requires lots of time and energy to maintain.

It wastes water — 30 percent of the water used on the East Coast and 60 percent on the West Coast goes to watering grass. The average lawn, per acre, gets 10 times as much chemical pesticide as farmland, killing 60 to 90 percent of the earthworms, which are important to soil health. Native plants, on the other hand, provide variety and beauty and save you money and energy. Since they are naturally adapted to the environment, they require less water, fertilizer, and attention.

Simple way to add garden space. Less lawn means more room to garden — especially in small yards, so consider minimizing or even scrapping your lawn completely to gain garden ground.

Be patient for soil test results. It's never too early to plan ahead — particularly before putting in a new lawn or renovating an old one. Start extra early if you want an inexpensive soil test from your local extension service. Be prepared to wait as long as seven weeks for those valuable soil test results. Allow a few more weeks so you can follow the recommendations from the soil test — the payoff could be your most luxurious lawn yet. For the best results, plan to send off your soil samples at least two months before your new lawn will be installed.

How to prepare for a new lawn

After all construction materials, trash, weeds, and grass are removed from the site, it's time for rough grading. This usually includes sloping land away from buildings, filling in low-lying areas, and making harsh slopes less steep. After last-minute cleanup, the soil can be fertilized, supplemented with topsoil, or tilled, as needed. At last, the final grading and leveling can occur, and the site is ready for a new lawn.

Smooth the way to a new lawn. Before planting a new lawn, the entire planting surface must be smooth. You can even out small dips and humps yourself. The right tool for this will most likely depend on the size and difficulty of the job. Use a rake, rent a landscape drum, or search for a castoff section of chain link fence that can be dragged or towed across the soil.

Enjoy Christmas lights on warm nights. Get bonus mileage out of miniature outdoor Christmas lights. Use them for decorative outdoor lighting in warm weather. Wrap a string or two around your backyard deck railing. Copy vacation resorts and wind lights around step railings for safety and a celebratory touch. Top off a half-empty trellis with a string of lights. You can put the lights almost anywhere as long as they can be plugged in and won't create a safety hazard. Walk out your back door and look for places where Christmas lights might add gentle brightness to your spring and summer evenings.

Expert grading advice

Whether you're laying a brand new lawn or renovating an old one, the site must be graded correctly before the final planting. To guide water away from foundations, the land should slope away from the base of the house and other buildings. Many experts recommend a slope of 1 or 2 percent — which is about a 6-inch to 12-inch drop for every 50 feet of distance away from the building. Also, for easy mowing, the entire surface should be smooth and free of small dips and humps.

Go lightly with landscape lighting. After all the time you've spent creating an inviting yard and garden, you don't want to stop enjoying it after the sun goes down. Add landscape lighting to dress up your landscape for the evening. For best results, avoid bright lights and direct light. Soft, low-level lighting and indirect lighting are more attractive.

Make outdoor lights seem brighter. If outdoor electrical lighting is a little dim in your yard, make the most of it by putting a piece of reflective aluminum foil behind the lamp.

Save energy with low-voltage lighting. For paths, walks, or edging, try an energy efficient low-voltage lighting kit. A small one is easy to install because you don't need any special electrical knowledge — not even to connect the lights to the electrical cable. Although it may take some elbow grease to dig a shallow trench for the cable, you can place the stake-mounted lights just by pushing them into the ground. The system even plugs into any regular outdoor outlet that has GFCI (ground-fault circuit-interrupter protection). Ask your local garden store staff for an easy-to-install system and follow the instructions that come with it.

Plant a tree to enhance property value. Greenery in front of your house not only beautifies it for your enjoyment, it increases your property's value. And while flowers may increase curb appeal and attract a buyer when you're ready to sell, hardier shrubs and trees are more likely to raise the selling price.

Easy way to increase your home's value. Your property value may grow right along with the trees you plant. One study found that prospective buyers were willing to pay 15 percent more for a house with two red oaks, each just 2 inches in diameter.

Curves more interesting than straight lines. Curvy garden paths lead the eye onward and outward, even if your yard doesn't go very far. Make your walkways change direction, and you'll expand the look and feel of your garden.

Blaze a tentative trail. Use your garden hose or a long rope to lay out a garden path or trail you'd like to create in your yard. Once you see how it looks, you can adjust it again and again until you have a final plan for your path.

Surround your patio with flowering trees. Dress up a bare patio with a crabapple or dogwood and you'll shower it with flowers in the spring. Crabapples and dogwoods are great patio trees. They are attractive year-round and won't grow too large. Just remember to stick with disease-resistant varieties.

Picture changes in your garden. Take your camera when you visit other gardens to capture ideas to try in your own. And when your garden is established, take photographs every month — more often when a lot of changes are taking place. Keep these pictures dated and in a scrapbook with notes about your garden. You can see where you need a bit of color or one flower is hiding another. Later when plants have stopped blooming or have died back, you can still see where new plants are needed and what needs moving.

What to plant in windy areas. Do you need plants that can grow in a windy place — like out by your mailbox or on a terrace? Daylilies and geraniums won't give up at the first gust. Lavender is wind hardy, too. If your windy environment is near the coast, you may have luck with artemisia, sea holly, plantain lily, bearberry, cotoneaster, or silver lace vine.

Good choices where water is scarce. Whether you want drought-tolerant landscaping or just live in an arid climate, these are good trees to try — common hackberry, Russian olive, goldenraintree, Chinese pistache, and Japanese pagoda tree.

What to grow near the shore. If landscaping near a salty environment has you stumped, give these trees a try — sycamore maple, American holly, live oak, and horse chestnut. These, along with some kinds of pine, are seasoned seashore successes. Round out your landscaping with these shrubs — red chokeberry, saltbush, summersweet, Rose-of-Sharon, inkberry holly, bayberry, Japanese yew, and arrowwood.

Plant shallow under trees. If you'd like to plant flowers under a tree, build a low rock border and fill it with 6 inches of rich soil. Plant impatiens, hostas, and other shade-tolerant plants that have fairly shallow roots. This way, you won't disturb the roots of the tree or create problems by burying too much of the trunk.

Design an impressive shade garden. Got a shady patch where your sun-loving flowers won't grow — or have you despaired of growing anything in a yard packed with shade. Turn dim into delightful by creating a shade or woodland garden. Plant ferns for lush greenery and grow colorful shrubs, like azaleas and mountain laurel. Add interesting foliage from woodland favorites, like pulmonaria or caladium. Astilbe, bergenia, and hydrangeas are a few more of the many attractive plants that thrive beautifully in forested shade.

Get ideas from nearby forests. To add a natural touch to your woodland garden, choose plant varieties native to your region and group them into clumps. If possible, include mosses, ferns, or ground covers.

Add trails to your woods. If your shady woodland garden is large enough, divide it into different areas or "garden rooms." Connect those natural rooms together with a wilderness-style trail that meanders lazily through them.

Create a shady garden room. Under a ceiling formed by branches of tall trees, plant walls of smaller trees and shrubs. Decorate as you wish — with natural logs and stones or formal seats, statues, and fountains. Before you plant, observe how much light filters through and choose plants to suit the amount of shade. You can thin out a few branches to allow more light in if it's too shady.

Beautify banks and reduce erosion. Water speeding down a slope or bank in your yard causes soil erosion. Fortunately, some attractive plants can slow down the water and the erosion. For a beautiful display of flowers, find out which varieties of daylilies do well in your area and plant them throughout the bank. If you'd rather have a cascade of roses, check whether the Sea Foam rose can grow where you live.

Consider easy-care shrubs for slopes. A great way to stop erosion on steep banks is to plant low-maintenance shrubs. One charming choice is seaberry or sea buckthorn. This hardy, thorny shrub may sport cheery orange berries well into winter if you plant both genders. Cotoneaster and juniper are good slope shrubs, too. Both these shrubs come in many varieties, so you probably won't have a hard time finding one that can grow where you need it.

Turn a slope into a charming garden. You can convert a sloping yard into an eye-catching rock garden. Stagger groupings of partially buried large and medium rocks so water can't wash down the hill in a straight path. Fill in gaps with smaller stones and plants suitable for your area.

Bump off a tough little stump. You cut down a small tree, but before you knew it, new growth appeared. To get rid of it once and for all, you must kill the roots. For the stump of a tree no more than 2 inches in diameter, cut a deep cross with a saw or hatchet and fill the open space with baking soda. Leave it for 20 minutes and pour vinegar into the space. This will destroy even a tough stump, like mesquite.

Stump removal got you stumped? Here's an easy — and cheap — solution to your dilemma. When you finish cooking on your grill, dump the remaining hot coals in the center of the stump. Each time you do this, a little more of the stump will burn away until it disappears. Take the money you'd pay to have it ground out and fill your freezer with steaks for future cookouts.

Start a dyer's garden. Just like your ancestors, you can make fabric dye out of the roots, stems, and leaves of common garden plants. Coreopsis and goldenrod will give you yellow dye. Madder roots will dye cloth red. Blackberries will stain cloth purple. Acorns and marigolds will dye it brown. Indigo will give you a deep blue, and lily of the valley and rhododendron produce a lovely green dye. Grow plenty of each plant, since you will need a lot of raw material to make a strong dye bath.

Great plants for a rock garden. Wondering what to plant in your rock garden? Try lavender with its inviting scent or pick your favorite variety of thyme. Add some basket-of-gold, Arabis procurrens, primroses, tulips, moss pink, cottage pink, or Sedum kamtschaticum. Small shrubs, such as dwarf junipers, sun rose, scotch heather, and dwarf Japanese holly look good in a rockery, too.

Ease into evening with special garden. Imagine a garden with moonlit flowers, silvery foliage, and fragrant scents. This "moon garden" could become your favorite place to relax after a busy day. To start your very own moon garden, select plants with light-colored flowers and leaves so they'll show up well in moonlight or gentle evening lighting. Evening primrose, white roses, and alyssum are good flower choices, while dusty miller serves up a shimmer of silvery foliage. For sweetly fragrant plants, pick popular classics like moonflower vine or flowering tobacco.

Delight in herbal knot gardens. By the 16th century, herbs were right at home in formal estate gardens. In fact,

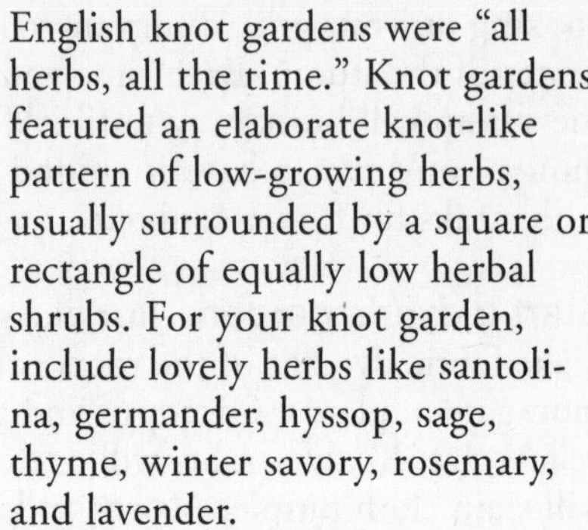
English knot gardens were "all herbs, all the time." Knot gardens featured an elaborate knot-like pattern of low-growing herbs, usually surrounded by a square or rectangle of equally low herbal shrubs. For your knot garden, include lovely herbs like santolina, germander, hyssop, sage, thyme, winter savory, rosemary, and lavender.

Design a garden to complement your home. Not sure what style to choose for your yard or garden? Consider this. Many experts say houses with elegant or formal historic styles are ideal for formal gardens, while modern houses pair more easily with informal gardens.

Look before leaping into formal gardening. Can you picture a European estate garden with its finely manicured plants, elegant accents, and exquisitely ordered patterns? This is the prime example of a formal garden, where neatness reigns and flaws are forbidden. If you dream of a formal garden, even a small one, check your schedule before you start planting. Upholding the perfect order of a formal garden demands frequent weeding, pruning, and attentive care. If tending

Design a healing herb garden

Medicinal herb gardens are a centuries-old favorite. Here are some ideas to help you start your own healing garden.

- Grow immunity-boosting garlic for its anti-infection power.
- Plant hyssop and thyme for teas that may help congestion.
- If you don't have ragweed or other pollen allergies, grow chamomile for a scented tea that can soothe an upset stomach, a sore throat, or jangled nerves.
- Raise lemon balm or catnip to make relaxing teas that can help you sleep.
- Plant feverfew and chew on the leaves to help prevent migraines.
- For a soothing whiff of aromatherapy, grow lavender.

Just be sure to check with your doctor before trying any herbal remedy.

a less-formal yard or garden already fills your time, consider a different kind of garden or recruit some extra help. Or try a little brainstorming to see if your garden plan, or your schedule, can be adjusted.

Think vertically for more space. It's easy to increase planting space in a small garden. Here's how — grow climbing plants on a trellis, put up wind chimes, or mix in plants that trail from hanging baskets. Give it some thought and keep an eye out for chances to add more "upward mobility" to your garden.

Get a new trellis for Christmas. After the holidays, offer to pick up discarded, live Christmas trees from your neighbors. They'll appreciate the help, and you'll get free material for a decorative, new trellis. Two trees are all you need for a single trellis. Prune them down to their trunks, but save the branches to use as mulch. Plant the trees upright near your peas, pole beans, or any other plant that needs a trellis. Run a few lines of string between the trees, and your trellis is ready.

Put pesky bamboo to good use. If a patch of bamboo is taking over your yard, why not harvest some of it to build a trellis or fence? Select stalks that are 3 to 5 years old. They're the ones that have traded their earlier bright green color for a more golden tint. Use only the strong lower and middle parts of the stalk. The upper sections may be too weak. Make your top cut just above a node, which is solid all the way through. You'll have a natural top, so rain can't rot the stalk.

Recycle an umbrella into a trellis. Make a unique and lovely trellis for your morning glories or other climbing plants. Remove the fabric from an old or worn umbrella and bury the handle in the ground.

Create a free-standing bamboo trellis. Need an easy, free-standing trellis? Get three or four tall bamboo stakes about the same height, strong twine that won't rot, and scissors. Position the stakes in a teepee or pyramid shape with the bottom ends splayed apart and the top ends crisscrossing one another. Wind the twine around the stakes where they cross. After several loops, wind vertically so the string also passes above and below the crisscrossed area. When the stakes are firmly secured, tie off the twine and clip it with scissors. If wind or pets are a concern, tie down your new trellis until your plants can anchor it.

Make a masonry wall magnificent. A bare garden wall in stone, brick, or concrete is just a gardener's blank slate. For a classy look, adorn it with English ivy — which comes with its own wall-climbing equipment. Creeping fig also brings its own climbing gear, so it's another good choice. Find a trellis to tuck snugly against the wall, and you can try flowering climbers, like wisteria, jasmine, and roses. For a different approach, place a potted trailing rosemary on top of your garden wall so it can send its foliage cascading down.

Test drive a water garden. You'd like to try water gardening, but you don't want to put much time, effort, and money into something you might not keep. Why not try a container water garden? You'll find out what it's like to tend a water garden, without the commitment and expense of a full-size pond.

Turn a bathtub into a garden accent. An old, free-standing bathtub is a fine container for a water garden — especially if you can find one cheap at a yard sale or flea market. For a rustic touch, turn a watering trough or whiskey barrel into a water garden container just by adding a liner. What's more, if you give up water gardening or decide you want a pond, any of these containers can be recycled into planters.

Fend off algae with plants. Considering a water garden? If you don't want your water garden to become an algae garden, you need at least two kinds of plants — submerged plants and surface plants. Submerged plants, which stay below the water surface, steal nutrients that algae need to grow. If fish swim in your water garden, submerged plants or "oxygenators" help them get enough oxygen. But don't forget about surface plants. By blocking out sunlight, they help keep algae from growing, too. Surface dwellers can either float freely or grow upward from underwater pots.

Keep water gardens under cover. Cover at least 50 percent of your water garden's surface with floating plants — like water lilies — that cast a shadow. These plants slow algae growth by limiting the amount of sunlight reaching the water.

Protect water garden from trees. Whether your water garden is container bound or free, don't place it near trees. Falling leaves are tough on water gardens. If you don't fish them out, they can harm your fish and plants. Even water gardens equipped with pumps and filters can have problems because leaves clog up the works. Keep your water garden in the clear by putting it in a clearing or other tree-free spot.

> ! Some water garden plants are so invasive they're prohibited in certain states. Before buying plants for your water garden, check with your county extension office to find out which plants are restricted.

Simple trick keeps water garden clean. Water gardens may need dirt, but they should never be dirty. After all, that's why you use underwater "oxygenator" plants — to help keep the water clear. Before putting pots of oxygenator plants in the water, cover the soil with pea gravel so dirt won't float freely throughout your water garden.

Water gardens easier than ever. Think you can't have a formal water garden because of the difficulty of laying and setting concrete. Think again. Water gardens used to require concrete, but now you can use strong liners made of fiberglass, plastic, or rubber to hold your pond. Liners can either be pre-shaped and rigid, or they can be flexible to match the shape you choose to dig.

Easy way to foil sneaky algae. Your pond surface is algae-free, but you've spotted something that looks like long strands of green cotton under the water. What is it? That's blanketweed, an underwater algae. Grab a stick or a pitchfork and wind up that blanketweed strand like you're winding spaghetti around a fork. Lift it out of the pond and get rid of it. Keep doing this until all the strands of blanketweed are gone.

Cut back on mowing. Got an area of your yard that's tough to mow — or you just don't want to mow? Plant a stand of wildflowers. Once you get them established, they'll require very little care.

Go wild with a wildflower meadow. You can have your own meadow of wildflowers if your yard has an open, sunny spot. Try sun-worshipers like black-eyed Susan, Queen Anne's lace, butterfly weed, New England aster, and yarrow.

Ditch weeds in wildflower garden. Herbicides that kill weeds can also kill flowers. That's why you should wipe out weeds before planting a wildflower garden. Preventing weeds after planting will be trickier but here's how to start. Avoid cultivating the soil deeply when you prepare it for planting. Use a rake and don't go deeper than a half inch. That way you won't turn up weed seeds and cause them to sprout.

Pass up roadside wildflowers. Resist the temptation to transplant wildflowers from roadsides and other places where they grow in the wild. Many species are protected, so collecting them may be illegal. Buy from plant nurseries or mail order sources instead.

Find a home for wildflowers. Take a second look at that shady spot in your yard. It might have the right conditions for a woodland wildflower garden. Woodland wildflowers won't grow in the darkest shade, but light or dappled shade suits them fine. They also like soil that sees its fair share of moisture. If that dirt also has a good helping of organic left-overs, wildflowers will probably take to it, especially if they get some organic mulch after they're planted.

Brighten a bog with wildflowers. It is easy to add color to a bog or swamp garden with wildflowers. Just use water-lovers, like marsh marigold, Joe Pye weed, sedges, and water plantain.

Feed birds from a fish tank. An old aquarium makes a good bird feeder. Just turn it on its side and place it where it's fully supported. Scatter seed inside for birds to feed on, protected from wind and rain, while you enjoy watching them from any direction.

Stick bird treats to a tree. Wrap strips of tape, sticky side out, around the trunk or branches of a tree. Press bird-seed against the tape. They should stick tight until the birds find the feast.

> *Grow a wildflower garden in your yard, and you may get a colorful bonus — butterflies.*

Organic gardening good for birds. Don't use chemicals on your lawn or in your garden if you want a healthy bird population. The worms and insects that thrive there provide them with good food, while they, in turn, keep down the pests that might do damage to your plants. It's not just insects that die when poisons are used. The pesticides in insects also endanger the birds that eat them.

Attract butterflies to your garden. The vivid purple blossoms and fruity sweet fragrance of a butterfly bush will draw lots of butterflies to your garden. They'll also come to gardens with other bright purple, red, orange, and yellow flowers planted in groups rather than scattered individual plants. Big flowers, which generally aren't good sources of nectar, won't attract them. And they don't like flowers with ruffled edges or blossoms that hang upside down.

Encourage butterflies to flutter by. Get a butterfly garden started with these known butterfly "magnets" — purple coneflower, aster, cosmos, butterfly weed, dianthus, and lantana.

The latest buzz on attracting bees. Plant fragrant, colorful flowers in a sheltered, sunny part of your yard, and busy pollinators will make a beeline for your garden. Try bee balm, borage, red clover, hyssop, Joe-Pye weed, and thyme. Bees especially like purples, reds, and yellows.Leave some bare spots or a few dead branches on the ground so bees will build their nests. But remember, they do have stingers. If one gets to you, rub the sting with a comfrey, calendula, or plantain leaf.

Go wild for wildlife. If you want birds and other wildlife to enjoy your yard, leave it wild. Close-cropped grass, trimmed shrubs, and deadheaded flowers don't leave food or shelter to attract them. Not surprisingly, they feel right at home with underbrush for cover. And rotting tree trunks and branches, as well as fallen leaves, provide insects for hungry, foraging birds.

Avoid drafts in windbreaks. Some evergreens leave space between the ground and their lower branches as they grow.

Because windbreaks are most effective when they extend right down to the ground, avoid picking evergreens that will leave those open spaces for the wind to sneak through. If that can't be helped, find ways to fill in the open space.

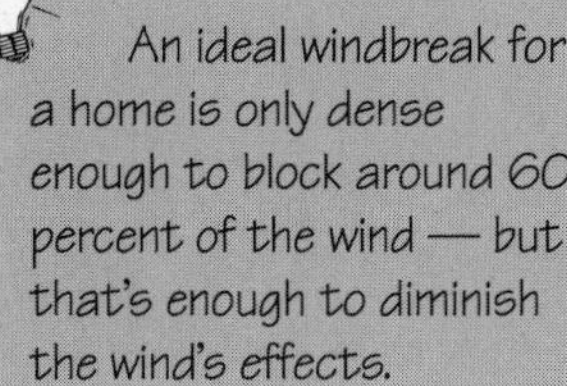
An ideal windbreak for a home is only dense enough to block around 60 percent of the wind — but that's enough to diminish the wind's effects.

Throw howling winds a curve.
Do your winter winds come from more than one direction? Instead of a straight-line windbreak, consider planting one that is curved or L-shaped.

Stagger windbreak rows. Do you have room for more than one row of trees in your windbreak? Plant staggered rows for the best results.

Whip winds with a windbreak. Subdivision yards may not have enough acreage to allow for standard windbreaks, so try this instead. Notice which side of your house the winter winds blow against. Plant a dense screen of evergreens on that side. Place them at least 4 feet away from your house, and space them so winds won't get through after the trees are mature. Instead of icy winds that suck heat out of your house, you'll have calm air — and maybe less-alarming power bills, too.

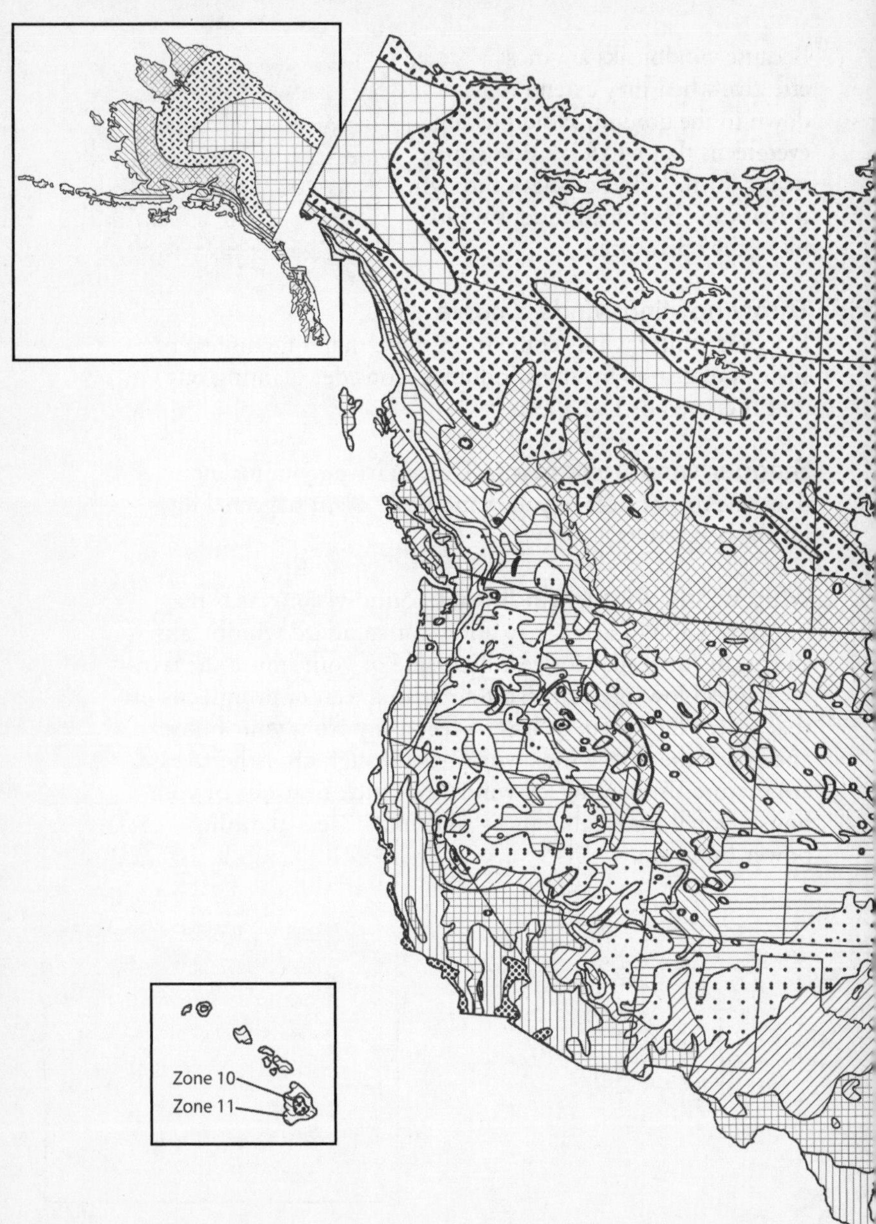

Zone 10
Zone 11

Plant hardiness zone map

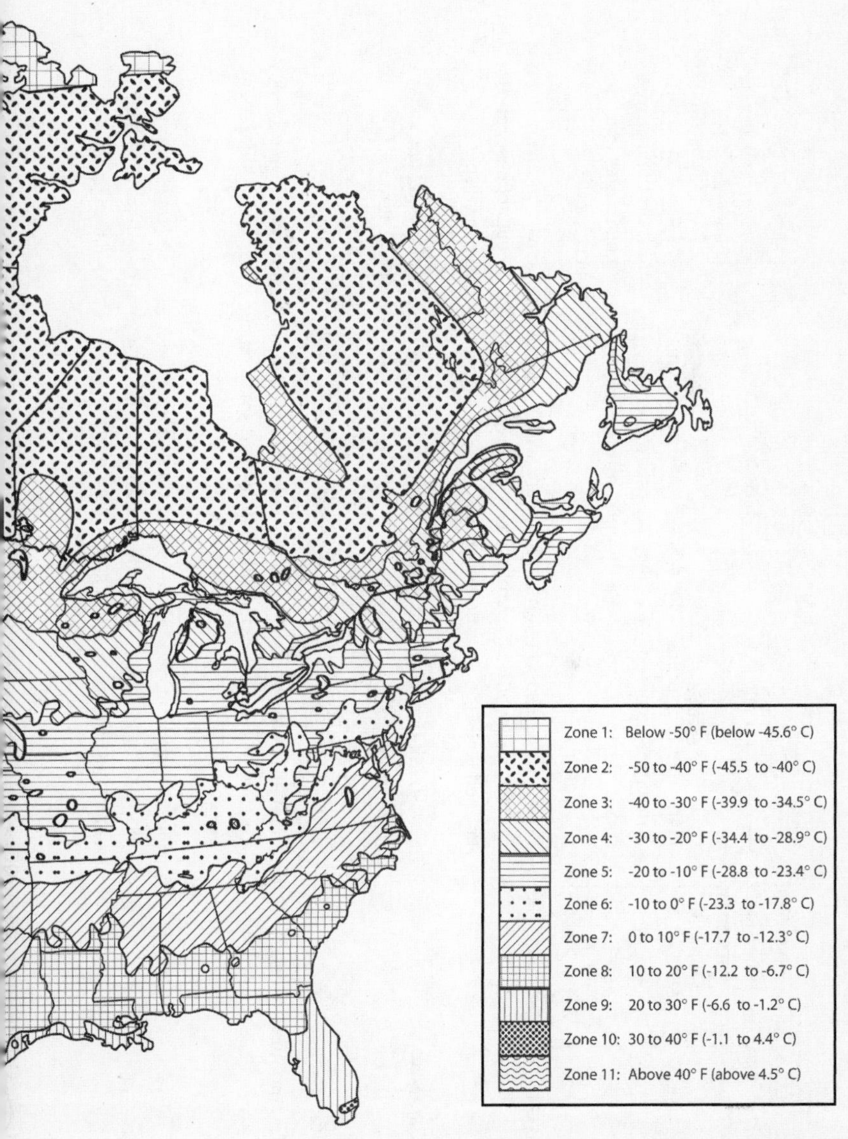

Gardener's guide to herbs

Herb	Perennial, biennial, or annual	Growing conditions	Description	Uses
Anise	Annual	Plant after last spring frost in well-drained soil.	Weed-like plant that has green feathery leaves with serrated edges topped by clusters of white flowers.	Add seeds to confections and other sweet treats. Tastes like licorice.
Basil	Annual	Plant after last spring frost in rich, well-drained soil.	Knee-high plant with green or purple leaves and white or purple flower spikes.	Leaves add a spicy taste to egg, cheese, and tomato dishes.
Caraway	Biennial	Sow in fall or spring in well-drained soil.	Knee-high plant that sprouts feathery foliage the first year and clusters of white flowers grow high in the second year.	Add seeds to pickles or meat stews.
Chamomile	Annual	Plant after last spring frost.	May be as tall as waist high with fern-like foliage and small daisy-like flowers.	Brew as tea and enjoy fresh apple-like scent.
Chervil	Annual	Plant in spring in moist, rich soil; not highly heat-tolerant.	Knee-high plant with feathery green leaves and, possibly, clusters of small white flowers.	Use leaves in omelettes or salads. Use like parsley.

Herb	Perennial, biennial or annual	Growing conditions	Description	Uses
Chives	Perennial	Plant in moist soil in spring.	Resembles clumps of tall grass and may sport clover-like pink or purple flowers.	Add grass-like leaves for light onion flavor in soups and cheese and egg dishes.
Coriander and Cilantro	Annual	Plant in spring in moist, well-drained soil.	May be as tall as waist-high with lace-like light green leaves and, possibly, small white flowers. The coriander plant produces both coriander seed and the leaf called cilantro.	Crushed coriander seeds do well in cookies and sweets, while cilantro leaf is at home in Mexican dishes.
Cumin	Annual	Plant after last spring frost.	Small herb.	Use seeds in chili or curry.
Dill	Annual	Plant in spring, after last frost.	May be as tall as waist high with feathery green leaves and clusters of small yellow flowers.	Add dill leaves to fish and fish dishes. Dill seeds add flavor to pickles.
Fennel	Perennial	Plant in early spring.	Waist high or taller plant with light green, bronze, or purple lacy leaves. May sport yellow flower clusters.	Licorice-like flavor. Fennel leaves are often used with fish. Add fennel seed to tea or breads.

Herb	Perennial, biennial or annual	Growing conditions	Description	Uses
Garlic	Bulb perennial	Where ground freezes, plant cloves in spring. Elsewhere plant in autumn. Plant in moist, well-drained soil.	Long, flat, green leaves and white flower.	Known for adding zest to Italian dishes and, of course, garlic bread.
Garlic chives	Perennial	Divide in spring or plant from seed in well-drained soil.	Knee high with long sender dark green leaves and sometimes white flowers.	Adds mild garlic flavor to salads and other dishes.
Ginger	Perennial	Find store-bought root that has bud. (Bud resembles potato eye.) Plant 2-inch slice (including bud) in pot in a sunny window.	May sport foot-long green leaves on even longer stems.	Brew as tea or include in Oriental cooking, such as stir-fry.
Lemon balm	Perennial	Plant in spring.	Knee-high plant with light green leaves and, later, white or yellow flowers.	Leaves add lemon taste or scent to drinks and salads.
Lovage	Perennial	Plant in spring after last frost in cool, well-drained, rich, moist soil.	Waist high or higher with shiny, dark green leaves and, sometimes, pale yellow flowers.	Add leaves to give celery-like accent to salads.

Herb	Perennial, biennial or annual	Growing conditions	Description	Uses
Marjoram (sweet marjoram)	Perennial grown as annual	Perennial treated as annual because it is easily killed by cold. Plant indoors and move seedlings out after last spring frost.	Knee-high or taller with small, fuzzy leaves and, later, white or pink flowers.	Add leaves to meat, poultry, and game dishes.
Oregano	Perennial	Plant in well-drained soil.	Knee-high plant with small, dark green leaves and may sport pink or purple flowers.	Leaves used in Italian and Spanish dishes.
Parsley	Biennial treated as annual	Plant in spring and summer. Seeds take six weeks to sprout. Soak before planting to get sprouts sooner.	Low-growing rosettes of bright green leaves. One variety has crinkled leaves, while another has flat leaves.	Often used as edible garnish. Parsley leaves are good with soups, salads, casseroles, vegetables, and meat.
Peppermint	Perennial	Plant cuttings in moist soil in spring. Plant in containers to keep them from spreading too much.	Up to waist-high with dark green, serrated leaves that are longer than spearmint leaves. May also have spikes of purple flowers.	Leaves make good tea and may flavor other drinks, such as lemonade. Flavors jellies and sweet treats, too.

Herb	Perennial, biennial or annual	Growing conditions	Description	Uses
Rosemary	Perennial, may be grown as annual in colder climates	Plant from cuttings for best results. Plant in spring.	Waist-high or higher with gray-green needle-shaped leaves. May also have blue flowers.	Leaves are good in meat and poultry dishes.
Sage	Perennial	Plant in dry soil in spring.	Knee-high or taller with grayish-green leaves and, sometimes, white or blue flower spikes.	Leaves are good in sausage dishes, stuffings, and salads.
Spearmint	Perennial	Plant cuttings in moist soil in spring. Plant in containers to keep them from spreading too much.	Knee high with green serrated, crinkly leaves that are smaller than peppermint leaves. May have spikes of white or purple flowers.	Leaves make good tea and may flavor other drinks, such as lemonade. Good in fruit salads or with lamb dishes.
Summer savory	Annual	Sow seed in spring in well-drained soil.	Up to 18-inches high with grayish-green leaves and, later, small white flowers.	Summer savory leaves go well with beans, egg dishes, meats, and soups.

Herb	Perennial, biennial or annual	Growing conditions	Description	Uses
Tarragon (French tarragon)	Perennial	Plant cuttings in warm weather. May need protection in winter.	Knee-high with narrow green leaves.	Add leaves to give licorice-scented accent to salads, egg dishes, and vinegar.
Thyme	Perennial	Sow in spring in light, sandy soil.	Low-growing, woody-stemmed plant with gray-green leaves and, sometimes, lilac-tinted flowers.	Add thyme to poultry, egg dishes, stuffings, and clam chowder.
Winter savory	Perennial	Sow in spring in well-drained soil.	Low-growing with glossy, dark-green leaves and, sometimes, white flowers.	Add leaves to stuffings; not as sweet as summer savory.

Diagnose houseplant woes

Symptom	Problem	Solution
Yellow leaves	Too much or too little water, nitrogen deficiency	Water when soil dries out. Improve drainage. Add fertilizer.
Brown tips	Salt burn from too many minerals in the soil or from hard water	In the bathtub, flush the soil until the water runs clear.
Stunted growth, small, brittle leaves	Too little water	Water right away, then again as soon as the topsoil dries out.
No growth, dull leaves	Too much water	Wait for topsoil to dry before you add water. Improve drainage.
Tan or brown splotches	Sunburn, too cold	Move to a sheltered spot.
Curling leaves	Too hot	Water and move to a sheltered spot.
Leaf drop	Too much water or too much fertilizer	Water sparingly and fertilize only during the growth period.
White crust on the soil	Salt buildup from too much fertilizer	Flush until water runs clear. Reduce fertilizer.
No blooms	Too much or too little light, high temperatures	Move to a dark spot during the rest period. Bring out into light when ready to bloom.
Bud drop	Too little light, humidity, or food; room too hot or too cold	Fertilize and move to sunnier spot. Mist. Stabilize temperature.
Flies appear when you water	White flies	Hang sticky traps and vacuum the plants.
Speckled, yellowing leaves	Spider mites	Wash off the leaves in the shower.

Index

C

D

E

H

I

J

K

L

M

N

O

P

R

S

T

U

V

Z